THE SWASTIKA
AND THE EAGLE

THE SWASTIKA
AND THE EAGLE

Hitler, the United States,
and the Origins of World War II

BY JAMES V. COMPTON

Illustrated with Photographs

19 67

HOUGHTON MIFFLIN COMPANY

Boston

*This book is dedicated to my mother and
to the memory of my father, Lewis Compton,
Assistant Secretary and acting Secretary
of the Navy, 1939 to 1941,
who saw the ultimate danger
and acted*

Acknowledgments

IT IS A PLEASURE to acknowledge my indebtedness to various people and institutions without whose assistance this book could not have been written. I am grateful to the staffs of the following libraries in London: The London Library of Economics and Political Science, the Royal Institute of International Affairs, the Public Record Office, the Cabinet Office, the Historical Section of the Admiralty, and especially the Wiener Library and the Foreign Office Library. Mr. Hiscock at the latter depository was particularly obliging.

Through the cooperation of the Institut fuer Zeitgeschichte in Munich I was able to contact a number of former German diplomats who assisted me with my inquiries. Dr. Erich Kordt, former Chief of the Foreign Office Secretariat; Mr. Fritz Wiedemann, former Consul General in San Francisco; and General Friedrich von Boetticher, former Military Attaché in Washington, all were helpful. I would like to make special mention of Dr. Hans Thomsen, former Chargé d'Affaires and only surviving Chief of Mission at the German Embassy in Washington. Dr. Thomsen took time out from a busy retirement to correspond with me at great length on many aspects of German-American relations in the 1930's and to talk with me during a very informative afternoon in Hamburg.

At various stages, Mr. Gaspar Otalora and Miss Bridget Smeall assisted in the proofreading. I tried out many of my ideas at the London School of Economics in the Seminar on the Origins of the Second World War presided over by Professor W. N. Medlicott. Professor Medlicott has been unfailingly courteous and encouraging throughout. I am grateful to Mr. Craig Wylie of Houghton Mifflin Company for various suggestions.

Finally, I owe a special debt to two fellow historians. Mr. D. C. Watt of the London School of Economics and the Royal Institute of International Affairs supervised much of the research and placed his great knowledge of the inter-war years and of the documentary sources at my disposal. My Edinburgh colleague, Mr. Esmond Robertson, was most generous of his time in applying to the manuscript in full measure his historical insights and Irish wit.

J. V. C.

Contents

Contents

Illustrations

Introduction

ADOLF HITLER and Franklin Roosevelt achieved power at roughly the same time, each promising radical reform to relieve the political and economic distress of his country. In both cases, a preoccupation with domestic reform seemed almost to preclude a military encounter between Germany and America in the near future. Tension did mount, however, especially after the outbreak of the European war in 1939. On December 11, 1941, Hitler translated the German-American cold war into open hostilities which were to last until the unconditional surrender of Germany in 1945, a few weeks after the death of both leaders. This declaration, this fateful extension of the war, has never been satisfactorily explained. It was indeed contrary to everything which Hitler had practiced and preached about German foreign policy in general and the United States in particular from the early days in Munich to the final hours in Berlin.

The purpose of this book is not to discuss German-American relations as such, but rather to explore the way in which the United States affected Hitler's foreign policy and the part this influence played in the expansion of the European war into World War II. For such a study we must have an idea of Hitler's personal disposition toward America as well as the attitude of the German foreign ministry. We must trace the influence of the United States upon German diplomatic and military policy in Europe and in the Atlantic and Pacific where contact between German and American interests seemed most likely. Finally, we must look at the possibility of a German attack on the United States itself.

At the outset, the reader should be cautioned that this subject has its fair share of paradox. We see a different picture of America proposed by the professional diplomats than that which was entertained by Hitler and his coterie. We observe Hitler's oft-repeated contempt for this country and yet his need to take some account of it as a factor in his calculations. We can distinguish his boldness on land and his trepidation on the sea; his certainties about Europe and his indecisiveness about areas beyond. We note his extreme caution regarding submarine warfare in the Atlantic and contrast it with his recklessness regarding the policies of his Japanese ally in the Pacific. And, finally, there is his unconcealed joy in declaring a war upon America which he had previously held to be impossible and later insisted was without logic. All of this contradiction lends a certain elusiveness, even irony, to the discussion of America and German foreign policy as the European conflict becomes a struggle of worldwide dimensions.

We are also necessarily brought into contact with broader aspects of the whole Hitler conundrum: the reliability of his statements as historical sources, the alternative views of Hitler as a crafty planner or impulsive opportunist, the place of Nazi ideology in the actions of the Reich and the actual role of the Fuehrer in German foreign and military policy. The hope and purpose of this book is that, by examining one aspect of German policy, the element of paradox may be somewhat reduced and that new light may also be thrown on the broader questions of the origins of the Second World War.

PART I

*Hitler and
the United States*

CHAPTER I

Hitler and the Americans

IN DISCUSSING Hitler's view of the United States, we must draw upon two sources: his own words and the testimony of contemporary witnesses. Both sources have their limitations. Hitler's words from *Mein Kampf* to the final *Testament* span a period from beer hall rabblerousing through supreme political power and military triumph to the final squalid days in the Berlin bunker. He spoke and wrote, therefore, in a vast variety of circumstances and, able politician that he was, he often obviously spoke and wrote for the effect his words would have upon his audience, whether the masses in the Nuremberg stadium or a small group of military advisors around the map table. Of the second source, we must bear in mind that the memory of witnesses is often shaky, especially when tinctured with self-justification. Yet from these diverse sources and the firmer supporting evidence of his actual plans and policies, which will be discussed in a later chapter, there emerges a quite consistent picture of America as seen through the eyes of the Fuehrer.

Hitler's attitude toward America was bound to be influenced by his general political outlook. His emphasis on the power of will to achieve domination (perhaps as an end in itself), his seething public and private resentments, his suspicion of traditional sources of information (generals, diplomats and economists never found much favor), all tended to make his judgments erratic and subjective, and his undoubted successes at home and abroad heightened this tendency. There is no agreement among his contemporaries or later historians regarding his attitude toward planning. The gambling Hitler and the calculating Hitler seem to merge and it is doubtful if the Fuehrer himself saw any real conflict between general goals and the opportunistic manipulation of pretexts and priorities according to immediate need. Clearly fundamental was his brutally Darwinian view of international relations ("War is life").[1]

In addition to these general conditioning factors, there were aspects of his politics which naturally had a special influence upon his attitude toward the United States: his view of the basis of national power, his particular solution to the German question and his Central European orientation.

Hitler saw nationhood in terms of social and racial dynamics rather than of objective economic and military factors. National existence was grounded in "the racial cohesion of the people, its response to leadership and its will to power."[2] He was, therefore, not sympathetic to those systems which engendered egalitarian attitudes and racial mixing and which relied upon institutions hampering the emergence of "the world historical leader." Thus for Hitler, parliamentary democracy was a hopeless system. Majority rule was "anti-racial cowardice," civil liberty a fraud, the free press a menace (sometimes capitalist, sometimes communist) and the whole liberal illusion tied up with economic injustice and "Jewish internationalism."[3] American democracy

[1] For historical discussion of Hitler's planning see: E. Faul, "Hitlers Uebermachievellismus," *Vierteljahreshefte fuer Zeitgeschichte* (hereafter *VfZG*), 1954, no. 4. A. J. P. Taylor, *Origins of the Second World War*, discounts Hitler's planning. A. Bullock, *Adolf Hitler, A Study in Tyranny*, and William Shirer, *The Rise and Fall of the Third Reich*, take the opposite view, while E. Robertson, *Hitler's Pre-War Plans and Policy*, takes a middle ground. Hitler's own comments on the problem in: N. Baynes, *Hitler's Speeches*, speeches of 15/3/36, 8/11/38, pp. 1303, 1511. See also memoranda of 23/11/39 in *Documents of German Foreign Policy* (hereafter *DGFP*), ser. D, vol. VIII, p. 441, and 12/11/40 in *ibid.*, vol. XI, p. 541. *Hitlers Zweites Buch*, chap. I. Memorandum, 23/11/39, *DGFP/D/VIII*, p. 440. Speech, Nov. 1939, *ibid.*, p. 443.

[2] *Zweites Buch*, p. 68. *Mein Kampf*, p. 555. Hitler sometimes stressed racism in the sense of racial purity and other times in the sense of racial superiority. He inevitably found the United States deficient on both counts.

[3] *Mein Kampf*, p. 81. Speeches 18/7/30, 5/2/38 in G. Prange, *Hitler's Words*, p. 42. *Zweites Buch*, p. 68. Article 13/4/23 in *Hitlers Reden*, p. 445. Speech 22/9/39 in *Documents in International Affairs* (hereafter *DIA*), 1939–1946, vol. I, p. 443.

was to be specifically included in these condemnations.

Secondly, Hitler's view of America was affected by his geo-political perspectives on the solution of the German question. The Reichschancellor saw his age as one in which land power had substantially eclipsed seapower, in which the overseas empire of the nineteenth century had yielded as the prime expression of national greatness to the acquisition of contiguous land mass; an age in which roads and armies had replaced ships and trade as the symbols of grandeur. Great Britain might still enjoy a naval role but for Hitler the older German navalist dictum *unsere Zukunft liegt auf dem Wasser* (our future lies on the sea) was strategic heresy.[4] This land-mindedness, which will be developed in a later chapter on naval policy, was ever a barrier to any realistic comprehension by the Fuehrer of America's world role.

Rejecting overseas and colonial solutions to Germany's problems ("I would not sacrifice the life of a single German soldier to get any colony in the world"),[5] Hitler also poured scorn on other remedies such as the reconstitution of the pre-1914 boundaries of the Reich or any form of internal economic readjustment ("dilettantish babbling"). He decided at an early date that only the acquisition of land in Eastern Europe could provide a realistic solution to the problems of *Lebensraum*. "The sword must be drawn for the plow . . . If a people disclaims soil, it disclaims life."[6] This obsession, endlessly repeated, suggests that every-

[4] Hitler, *Table Talk*, p. 708. *Zweites Buch*, chap. VII. *Mein Kampf*, p. 128. Doenitz testimony, *International Military Tribunal, Trial of Major War Criminals* (hereafter *IMT*), vol. XIV, p. 90. Halder, *Diaries*, vol. VI, p. 41.

[5] On colonies, see for example: *Table Talk*, p. 72. *Mein Kampf*, pp. 128, 533. Hossbach memorandum, *DGFP/C/I*, pp. 29-39. E. Kordt, *Wahn und Wirklichkeit*, pp. 87, 88. He was, however, always prepared to use the colonial issue to attack the Versailles settlement. Baynes, *op. cit.*, p. 1359.

[6] *Mein Kampf*, pp. 939, 941. Speech 21/5/30, Baynes, *op. cit.* p. 992. *Voelkischer Beobachter* 18/3/28, 7/5/28. *Zweites Buch*, pp. 62, 70. In his final order to the *Wehrmacht*, he was still not done with his *Drang nach Osten*. "The task is and remains the winning of space in the East for the German People." *Testament of Adolf Hitler*, F. Genoud, ed., p. 133.

thing else was for Hitler a tiresome distraction, an unnatural diversion from the course of German destiny. His subordination of everything to Operation Barbarossa, the invasion of Russia, and his repeated conviction that all else (the capitulation of England, the removal of the United States) would follow automatically from this eastern conquest are the most continuous features of his foreign policy in the years just prior to American entry into the war.

This brings us naturally to the third factor in Hitler's politics of special relevance to his consideration of the United States: the actual extent of Hitler's strategic and political world. The center of this world was clearly Europe, but was this an end in itself or was it to be merely the basis for a more universal domination? We cannot view the answer to this with any certainty. Like Marx's view of the final stage of communism, Hitler's vision of the post-war world is nowhere systematically developed. We do have a number of vague and contradictory statements by him, but these unwholesome reveries are so imprecise that, beyond a consistent stress on the need for German influence in the Ukraine, there is not much useful evidence to be found here.[7] He never exhibited any great or sustained interest in areas beyond Europe. He continuously expressed indifference to Africa (except as a raw material source) and to Asia as fields for conquest and, as we shall see, only intermittent interest in the Western hemisphere.[8] This dearth of personal interest appears substantiated by the relative lack of diplomatic or military planning for

[7] H. Rauschning, *Hitler Speaks*, pp. 128, 220, 230. Speech 26/9/38, Baynes, *op. cit.*, p. 1510. Conference 16/7/41, *DIA* (Hitler's Europe), vol. II, p. 279. *Table Talk*, pp. 314, 424 425, 447. Woermann testimony, *Nuremberg Military Tribunal: Trial of Former German Diplomats* (hereafter *Case 11*), vol. XXIII, p. 11256. P. Kluke, "Nationalsozialistische Europaideologie," in *VfZG*, July 1955.

[8] Interview 23/5/51, *DGFP/D/XII*, p. 857. *Table Talk*, pp. 38, 40. E. Hanfstaengl, *Hitler, The Missing Years*, p. 175. *Voelkischer Beobachter* 21/2/38. Hitler conversation with Japanese diplomats, *DGFP/D/VIII*, p. 333, and XII, pp. 101, 389. Ribbentrop spoke grandly from time to time of an Axis-Soviet division of the world, but even here certain modest possessions in Africa in support of a German-dominated Europe were given as the limit of German ambition. Ribbentrop to Stalin 13/10/40, *DGFP/D/XI*, p. 291.

non-European contingencies. We are referring here only to the
years involved in this study and all of this is certainly not meant
to preclude the possibility that the Fuehrer, if history had granted
him his European base, might have become interested in other
areas. This possibility will be raised in the final chapter.

His criteria for national power which led him to a rejection of
democracy, his obsession with Eastern *Lebensraum* rather than
maritime or economic solutions to the German question and his
strategic concentration on Europe and relative indifference to
other areas constituted the principle mental blocks to any realistic attitude by Hitler toward America.

As for his actual knowledge of the United States, we know
that Hitler drew upon a number of sources. Some of this information appears to have been, to say the least, sketchy and of
dubious origin. It can be assumed that his earlier impressions,
to the extent that he really had any, stemmed from the political
gossip of the dross houses and cafés of Vienna and Munich and
from his incessant reading of newspapers.[9] He also admitted to
his party comrade Kurt Ludecke that even after becoming
Chancellor of the Third Reich he enjoyed reading the Western
novels of Karl May.[10] He of course spoke no English and had
met few Americans prior to his accession to power. Yet he did
have in the 1920's two personal contacts who were well informed
on the subject, both of whom enjoyed Hitler's confidence in the
earlier years, both of whom fell from grace later in the 1930's,
and both of whom went into exile in the United States during
the war. One was Kurt Ludecke, a somewhat mysterious figure
on the fringes of the party who had traveled and lived in the
United States off and on as an informal fund raiser and publicity
agent for the Nazis in America. Of him, Hitler remarked to
Hermann Rauschning, the former Nazi leader in Danzig, "He

---

[9] These sources of information are described in Bullock, *op. cit.*, chaps. I and
VII.

[10] K. Ludecke, *I Knew Hitler*, p. 469.

knows more about America than the whole Foreign Ministry put together."[11] The second was a better known personality who was an intimate of Hitler's from the very early days. This was the Harvard-educated art dealer, historian, pianist, bon vivant and sometime court jester of the Hitler circle: Dr. Ernest "Putzi" Hanfstaengl, who ultimately became Hitler's special consultant on Anglo-American press relations.[12] In keeping with the spirit of interpersonal relationships among the Nazi elite, Ludecke and Hanfstaengl cordially disliked each other, but each took as his special function in the party to educate the Fuehrer about the United States and to impress upon him his view of a proper relationship between Germany and that country.

Kurt Ludecke's experiences as a fund raiser in America can hardly have been encouraging from the point of view of Nazi prospects there. His attempts to influence Henry Ford came to naught and he found the German-Americans and the Ku Klux Klan equally unresponsive. Yet in spite of this "unprofitable American begging tour," as he called it, he wrote that Hitler shared with him a considerable optimism about Nazi possibilities there.[13] He concluded on the basis of these travels (and presumably passed these conclusions on to Hitler) that because of social, historical and psychological peculiarities in America, special tactics would have to be adopted. There was little cultural tradition, he affirmed; Americans had never suffered military defeat; and there was a strong Jewish influence. Ludecke saw the United States before the Civil War as essentially Nordic. Then came an influx of Alpine, Latin and Jewish blood and the Americans became "children of the sun as well as the mist."

He forecast an ultimate struggle between the two Americas, but at the moment the German group was at a disadvantage,

---

[11] Ludecke, *op. cit.*, p. 653.

[12] *New York Times* (hereafter *NYT*) 5/7/35. W. L. Shirer, correspondent in Berlin for the Columbia Broadcasting System, was not impressed with Hanfstaengl, whom he called a "high strung, incoherent clown." Shirer, *Berlin Diary*, p. 23.

[13] Ludecke's experiences in America are described in Ludecke, *op. cit.*, pp. 180–222.

since the immigration before 1870 was now Americanized and the group after 1870 were not of the best German stock. He then admitted that no racial movement was possible at the moment, and when it came it would require American and not German leadership. In response to a question by Hitler, Ludecke told him that revolution in the United States was not unthinkable if the New Deal failed and that, in any event, a foreign policy of isolation was assured. He stressed, finally, the importance to Germany of gaining American good will.[14] We shall notice many of these observations repeated in Hitler's own comments on America in the 1930's.

Hanfstaengl, who had more continuous access to Hitler, was especially well connected in the United States. He was a guest of the Theodore Roosevelts and in 1910 he became acquainted with New York State Senator F. D. Roosevelt. He remained in New York during the first war, returning to Germany in 1921.[15] Hanfstaengl has recorded in his memoirs that he regarded it as virtually a sacred mission to impress upon Hitler the importance of agreement with the maritime powers, especially the United States. An enthusiast for the naval geo-politics of Admiral Mahan, he was convinced that one "cannot settle land questions if the maritime powers are opposed."[16] Hanfstaengl found the future Fuehrer's mind hopelessly mired in the land-based dicta of Frederick the Great and General von Clausewitz. "Neither Hitler nor any of his entourage acquired any conception of the strength of the salt water powers."

With Hitler, Hanfstaengl continued, "international power politics was based on the limitations inherent in land warfare and I never really succeeded in bringing home the importance of America as an integral factor in European politics." But he certainly tried. In 1922 he asked Hitler the question: "Why did we lose?" To which Hitler replied: "Because America came in." "If you recognize that," Hanfstaengl responded, "we are agreed

---

[14] *Ibid.*, pp. 297–299, 424, 510.
[15] Hanfstaengl, *op. cit.*, pp. 26–29.
[16] *Ibid.*, p. 15.

and that is all you need to know. If there is another war it must inevitably be won by the side which America joins. The only program for you to advocate must be friendship with the United States." "Yes, yes," Hitler reportedly agreed, "you must be right." "But," Hanfstaengl concluded, "the idea was so new to him that he never digested it."[17] In this battle for Hitler's strategic mind, Hanfstaengl felt his nemesis to be Rudolf Hess, and later, the windy racial mystic Alfred Rosenberg. Hess he especially resented as a pipe line to the anti-navalist geo-politics of General Karl Haushofer. "As often," Hanfstaengl complained, "as I tried to pump some salt water into Hitler's veins, the others blinded him with the dust of the infantry." He ascribed to Hitler a physical terror of the water.[18] He was obsessed, Hanfstaengl repeated, "by all those ridiculous prejudices of little infantry minds incapable of appreciating the balance of world forces and concentrating instead on the internecine conflicts of purely continental war and politics."

After the Landsberg imprisonment with Hess, Hitler saw Japan as the only possible non-European ally. "America," Hanfstaengl now noted,

> has simply been banished from his mind. He was not really anti-American. He regarded America as part of the Jewish problem. Wall Street was controlled by Jews. America was run by Jews and therefore he really could not take it into account. It was out of reach and not an immediate problem.[19]

Thus in the 1920's and early 1930's Hitler was exposed to certain impressions of America, aspects of which he evidently absorbed. But equally important is Hanfstaengl's opinion that America was for the future Chancellor no immediate problem requiring separate consideration. This too would be borne out in later developments.

[17] *Ibid.*, pp. 40, 41.
[18] *Ibid.*, pp. 76, 79.
[19] *Ibid.*, pp. 120, 121.

Later in the 1930's a third source of information regarding America in whom Hitler evidently reposed some confidence was the German travel writer, Colin Ross. Ross, on the basis of his considerable journeys, published two books on the United States: *Unser Amerika* (Our America) (1936), and *Amerikas Schicksalsstunde* (America's Hour of Destiny) (1937). In addition, at least one article appeared on the subject under his name, "Amerika Greift nach der Weltmacht" (America Reaches for World Power) (1939). In these writings, Ross developed an image of America, the essentials of which he explained to Hitler at an interview in 1940. It may also be that Hitler read the writings themselves. In his books Ross described an economically powerful and politically ambitious America which was nonetheless outwardly tired and old; a country in which "one no longer has the sense of being in a new world." Having passed through a political revolution (1776) and an economic revolution (1861), the Americans were now ready for a social-racial revolution. "The national world revolution could affect her like dynamite," he wrote and saw in Roosevelt's great powers the foundations of American dictatorship.[20]

The picture here was relatively optimistic from the national socialist point of view. More sober was the article for the *Zeitschrift fuer Geopolitik* in 1939. In this, Ross found America obsessed by the German menace and gripped by a war psychosis in which Germany was public enemy number one. American ambition, he wrote, is geared to nothing less than domination of an area from north to south pole and from Guam to the Cape Verdes. The United States was in his view potentially the strongest world power and Europe had to unite against this.[21] We find further commentary by Ross on America in a series of letters he wrote to the Foreign Ministry in 1938. He declared in one of these that economic insecurity had driven Jew and Anglo-

[20] C. Ross, *Amerikas Schicksalsstunde*, pp. 298, 302–311.
[21] C. Ross, "Amerika Greift nach der Weltmacht," *Zeitschrift fuer Geopolitik*, June 1939, pp. 416–418, 420, 421.

Saxon in America into a united front against the Germans. The solution to this was to arouse the German-American element with a sense of unity and mission, though he confessed that this would be unimaginably difficult.[22]

In the interview in March 1940, Ross began by telling Hitler that there had been much American enthusiasm for a European war at the time of the Czech crisis but that "a feeling of disgust for old Europe" had come over the country when the Western powers yielded at Munich and as a result of this there was now a general disinterest in European affairs.[23] Instead Ross described an imperialistic desire to widen the American sphere of influence as the leading mood in foreign affairs. (Hitler inquired at this point if this meant an *Anschluss* with Canada. Ross replied that Canada was so Americanized that this would not be necessary.) He then went on to analyze for the Fuehrer the basis for current anti-German feeling in America. There were, he reported, four reasons for this regrettable sentiment: first, the superiority complex of the Anglo-Saxon aristocracy; second, the "monstrous power" of Jewry which was waging by defamation and boycott an incredibly clever campaign against everything German; third, the lack of American civil courage which caused pro-German elements to cower in the face of economic and social pressure; finally, the greater knowledge of and attraction to England.

Turning to Roosevelt, Ross found him to be a frustrated Nazi whose consuming hatred of Hitler was in fact pure personal jealousy and lust for power. Ross then went on to describe the great role played in American history by those of German blood and declared himself encouraged by the existence of a massive anti-Semitism among the American people. These were factors which could be exploited but Ross warned that German propaganda must also and above all stress the idea that Germany

[22] Letters, C. Ross to the Foreign Office, 14/4/38, 4/5/38. The Foreign Office evidently took a cautious view of Ross's conclusions. Auswaertiges Amt, Politische Abteilung, *Akten betreffend Politischer und Kultureller Propaganda in den USA*, vol. III/291687, 291696, 291752.

[23] The transcript of this meeting can be found in *Buero des Reichsaussenministers* (hereafter *RAM*), USA/F12327. Also in *DGFP*/D/VIII, p. 910.

constituted no danger to the Western hemisphere, that on the contrary, England was the only threat. With all of this Hitler indicated assent and after his guest had left he declared the journalist to be "a very smart man who surely had many good ideas." As usual, Hitler filtered the ideas of Ludecke, Hanfstaengl and Ross, removing anything which did not substantiate his conceptions. However, as we shall see, there was much here which would prove useful. There were of course other books and articles on America published in the Third Reich, although we have no specific evidence as to which of these, if any, Hitler read. In any event with the exception of reasonable and moderate treatment of some specific aspects of American policy in the more specialized journals, most of the books on the subject tended to be sensationalist or pretentiously academic distortions along national socialist lines.[24]

There is also no reference to any extensive conversations with Hitler about America by even those members of his entourage who had some knowledge of the subject, such as Reichsbank President Hjalmar Schacht or Hitler-Youth leader Baldur von Schirach.[25] Nor did Hitler seek out those diplomats with special experience in American affairs to tap this knowledge when they were available in Berlin. The German Ambassador in Washington during the first months of the Hitler regime, Dr. Friedrich von Prittwitz und Gaffron, has recorded that Hitler asked him a few perfunctory questions about American society on his return to Berlin. His successor Dr. Hans Luther proclaimed in the *New York Times* that Hitler was "extremely interested" in the United States and had invited the Ambassador to give him a full report of his impressions. There is no evidence at all that this was any-

---

[24] For relatively objective treatment, see U. Haupt, "Eindruecke der USA," *Zeitschrift fuer Geopolitik*, June 1939, and articles by Silvanus and F. Berber in *Monatshefte fuer Auswaertige Politik*, 1940, 1941. More ideological viewpoints are found in the works of H. Kloss, *Deutschtum in Ausland* (1938), and *Um die Einigung des Deutschamerikanertums* (1937). See also Schadewaldt, *Was Will Roosevelt?*

[25] Schacht suggested to Hitler that he (Schacht) go to America on a fact-finding tour. Hitler agreed vaguely and then let it drop. Schacht testimony, *IMT*/XII, pp. 467–468. Schacht, *My First Seventy-six Years*, pp. 408, 412.

thing other than diplomatic flattery by Luther of American public opinion.[26] Fritz Wiedemann, whom Hitler knew from the world war and whom he appointed Consul General in San Francisco, found Hitler quite unwilling to discuss America at all during leave in Germany. Dr. Hans Thomsen, recalled specifically by Hitler from his position at the Washington Embassy to serve as interpreter on the Fuehrer's trip to Italy in 1937, has told the author that neither Hitler nor Ribbentrop once asked about the United States.[27]

Regarding the regular diplomatic reports from Washington, more will be said in another chapter. It is fair to assume here, however, that in general the dispatches from Washington fell under Hitler's distrust of such sources. As a final possible German source there is the press. However, a scanning of the important journals of the Reich reveals the expected Nazi distortion and caricature. P. K. Schmidt of the Foreign Ministry summed it up:

> Hitler wanted to see an America unable to wage war, in the control of the Jews, facing social catastrophe, and D.N.B. [the German news agency] brought reports that made America appear this way.[28]

Turning now to possible American sources of information, one is probably justified in ruling out any real influence by the two American Ambassadors of the period, William Dodd and Hugh Wilson, as sources of enlightenment for Hitler on American affairs. Not only were they as diplomats unlikely to find ready reception, but the Fuehrer entertained a special dislike of Dodd, whom he referred to as "an unsatisfactory representative of small mind." He remarked to Hanfstaengl that Dodd "could hardly speak German and made no sense at all." Later in the

[26] Prittwitz und Gaffron, *Zwischen Washington und St. Petersburg*, p. 228. *NYT* 10/8/34.

[27] Letter of Wiedemann to the author 9/7/63. According to Wiedemann, Hitler was, however, willing to believe the bizarre tale told in the Consul General's presence that national socialist sentiment was so rife in New York that taxi drivers, on recognizing a German fare, inevitably said Heil Hitler! Letter of Thomsen to the author 14/7/63.

[28] Quoted in O. Rogge, *Axis America*, p. 49.

Table Talk he referred to him as an imbecile.[29] Although Wilson
was more highly regarded in Berlin, there is no record of any
very extensive examination of the American scene by him in
Hitler's presence during his short embassy.

Hitler gave a number of interviews to prominent American
journalists such as William Randolph Hearst and Anne O'Hare
McCormick, but these were sessions in which Hitler did most of
the talking and in which he confined himself to vague generalities
about German-American relations, mingled with a certain surprise that the topic should be raised at all.[30] Other Americans
whom Hitler met in this period included T. J. Watson of International Business Machines in 1937, former President Herbert
Hoover in 1938, W. R. Davis, an oil millionaire, in 1939, J. D.
Mooney of General Motors and Undersecretary of State Sumner
Welles in 1940, and former U.S. Ambassador to Brussels Cudahy
in 1941.[31] He also met various German-American leaders such
as Jacob Schurmann and persons associated with fascist causes in
America such as Grant Stoddard and Fritz Kuhn. Goering and
Hess also evidently produced a few other Americans of dubious
credentials for the benefit of the Fuehrer in the late 1930's.[32]
There is no evidence that Hitler was much interested in the substance of these interviews nor was he apparently overly impressed
by the Americans themselves. As usual, Hitler did most of the
talking although he may have picked up scraps of information to
reinforce his ideas. Mooney tried to tell him that Roosevelt was
actually a moderate. Cudahy had him know that he (Cudahy)

[29] Hanfstaengl, *op. cit.*, p. 203. *Table Talk*, p. 102.
[30] See for example interview with Hearst, *NYT* 17/9/34, with McCormick
10/7/33, Baynes, *op. cit.*, pp. 428, 528. Other interviews in *ibid.*, pp. 984, 1009,
1143.
[31] For the interview with Watson: *NYT* 30/6/37; Hoover: *NYT* 9/3/38;
Davis: *DGFP*/D/VIII, p. 270; Stoddard: *RAM* 14/12/39, F-19027; Mooney:
RAM 4/3/40, F-17426. See also comment in Dieckhoff to Weizsaeker 2/3/38,
in Auswaertiges Amt, *Akten betreffend Allgemeiner Auswaertiger Politik der
Vereinigten Staaten von Amerika* (hereafter *AAP*), File: Besuch des Expraesi-
denten Hoovers, D514135–D514146.
[32] Schurmann interview in Auswaertiges Amt, Pol IX: *Akten betreffend
Politischer Beziehungen der Vereinigten Staaten von Amerika zu Deutschland*
(hereafter *Pol Bez*), I/511335. Thomsen letter to author 9/7/63.

viewed Roosevelt's policy as "wrong, utterly wrong," that England was through, and that although there was widespread fear of German tactics and even of a German invasion of the Western hemisphere he hoped to convince the American people that a German victory was no threat to America. Of the Welles interview, Hitler wrote Mussolini that it contained no new element and he declared himself at a loss to know why the American had come at all.[33] As Ulrich von Hassell, the former German Ambassador at Rome, recorded in his diary in February 1940, "Hitler and the Americans speak such an entirely different language that an understanding is almost unthinkable." Even Stoddard, who presented a rosy picture of Nazi prospects, was discouraged, while Hitler's reaction to Hoover was succinct: *"Ach, ein ganz kleiner Mann; Niveau wie ein Kreisleiter bei uns.* [A small piece of work — suitable in our country for a local Party hack]."[34]

Against this background of spotty information and meager interest, what was the actual picture which Hitler formed of America as a nation and world power? As a capitalist democracy, a non-European maritime power and a racial conglomeration with an influential Jewish element, we might easily assume that the United States faced insuperable barriers of prejudice in even gaining admission to Hitler's political world. Hanfstaengl was probably quite accurate when he designated the Americans as out of reach for Hitler. In a letter to the author, Dr. Hans Thomsen, later Acting Chief of the German Mission in Washington, who sat in on all of the cabinet meetings down to 1936, has written: "I do not recall that in these days America came up at all as a topic of special political interest." Former Consul General Wiedemann has concluded that America for Hitler was

---

[33] Hitler-Cudahy conference 23/5/41, *DGFP*/D/XII, p. 854. Memorandum (Dieckhoff) 28/3/41, Auswaertiges Amt, Buereo des Staatssekretaers, *Akten Betreffend USA* (hereafter *Sts/USA*), V/244320. Hitler to Mussolini 8/3/30, *Documenti Diplomatici Italiani* (hereafter *DDI*), ser. 9/III, p. 422. See also Hitler's memorandum 29/2/40, *DGFP*/D/VIII, p. 817.

[34] Von Hassell, *Diary*, p. 106. *RAM* Stoddard interview 19/12/39 F19027. Wiedemann to the author 9/7/63.

not even "an important concept." Except for a few references
by Dodd to some interest in American public opinion, there is no
indication that America represented for Hitler a separate factor
at all, at least prior to the outbreak of the war in Europe.[35]
Where America is mentioned it seems to have been as an illustration of some more general consideration.

Nor if we recall Hitler's criteria for national greatness can
this be surprising. He could have noted little in the United States
of the racial, cultural and spiritual values which were for him
the crucial factors in a healthy nationality. "What is America,"
he asked Hanfstaengl, "but millionaires, beauty queens, stupid
records, and Hollywood?"[36] In 1942, he saw no future for the
Americans,

> a decayed country, with problems of race and social inequality,
> of no ideas, I prefer the English a thousand times. My feelings
> against America are those of hatred and repugnance; half Ju-
> daized half negrified with everything built on the dollar.

"Americans," he said, "have the brains of a hen. The country
is a house of cards with an uneven material level. Americans
live like sows, though," he admitted, "in a most luxurious sty."[37]
When asked about German-American friendship, the Fuehrer
replied to Rauschning: "Whose friendship? The friendship of
the Jewish robbers and moneybags or that of the American
people?"[38] Hitler seemed genuinely convinced that Americans
were quite literally in the hands of the Jews. The "Jewish
clique" dominating the government and alleged Jewish control
of press, radio and cinema were special targets of Hitler's scorn.
In 1938 he referred to the country as "a Jewish rubbish heap"

[35] Thomsen to the author 14/7/63. Wiedemann to the author 9/7/63. Wiedemann did try to interest Hitler in the broader aspects of America by means of
American architecture. He does not feel that he succeeded. Dodd to the State
Department 17/10/33, *Foreign Relations of the United States* (hereafter *FRUS*),
1933/II, p. 396. *NYT*, 18/10/33.

[36] Hanfstaengl, *op. cit.*, p. 222.

[37] *Table Talk*, p. 188. Thomsen feels that Hitler took the Americans and
British to be equally degenerate. Letter to the author 14/7/63. *Table Talk*, 605.

[38] Rauschning, *op. cit.*, p. 76.

and these sentiments were repeated frequently.[39] The United
States government, he told Rauschning, was "the last disgusting
death rattle of a corrupt and outworn system which is a blot on
the history of this people." He then treated his listeners to an
analysis of American history. "Since the civil war," he began,

> in which the South was conquered against all historic logic and
> common sense, the Americans have been in a condition of poli-
> tical and popular decay. In the spurious blossoming of economic
> progress and power politics, America has ever since been drawn
> deeper into the mire of progressive self-destruction.[40]

Here we have an example then of a country faltering, due to its
racial deterioration, in its determination to maintain itself, which
Hitler regarded as the primary drive of a healthy national society.
In his use of the Civil War we may also observe Hitler's tendency
to lace his political monologues with historical items; his habit of
raiding history to justify his interpretation of a contemporary
event.

The analysis continued: "A monied clique rules the country
under the fiction of democracy . . . a mass of corruption and
legal venality." Returning to the Civil War, he mourned the
fact that the beginnings of "a great new social order based on
slavery and inequality were destroyed by that war." Was there
no hope then? "In certain sections of the American middle class
and farmers the sound fighting spirit of colonial days has not yet
been extinguished. We must awaken that spirit. It has not yet
been destroyed." He found hope in the alleged aversion in these
classes to Negroes and Jews, and concluded that "national socialism alone is destined to liberate the American people from their
ruling clique and give them back the means of becoming a great
nation."[41] Whether this rejuvenation was to be implemented by

---

[39] Speeches 13/4/23, 30/1/39, Baynes, *op. cit.*, pp. 48, 742. Hitler-Mussolini
conference 25/4/41, Ciano, *Diplomatic Papers*, p. 451. See also Ribbentrop's
comment after the war in *Nazi Conspiracy and Aggression*, sup. B, p. 1194
(hereafter *NCA*).

[40] Rauschning, *op. cit.*, p. 76.

[41] *Ibid.*, p. 77.

the same violent techniques as were to be employed in establishing the new order in Europe, Hitler did not say.

The only general aspects of American life which seem to have impressed Hitler were industrial achievement, scientific discoveries and architecture. Regarding the last, Hitler required the Washington Embassy to keep him supplied with pictures of American architecture, particularly in Washington. His well-known interest in motor cars led him naturally into admiration of the American automobile industry and its living symbol, Henry Ford. "He has," he wrote in an interview in the *New York Times* in 1933, "produced for the masses. He has done more than anyone else to destroy class differences." The Volkswagen was to be specifically the means of duplicating Ford's work in Germany.[42] In the *Table Talk* he admitted that in the economic field, Germany had much to learn from the United States and again found mass production and reduction of costs in the auto industry especially impressive.[43] Even here, however, Hitler's admiration faltered when he contemplated what he thought was the economic instability of American life. Indeed, he was convinced in 1932 that the United States was on the brink of revolution and stated that it would be a simple matter to produce unrest and revolution in America. The so-called wealth of America, he explained in 1940, was enjoyed only by the capitalists. The lot of the workers was that of misery and unemployment. Apparently Hitler's admiration did not extend in any event to American agriculture. Basing his judgment on the film "Grapes of Wrath," he informed his generals in 1943 that in America "the farmers are terribly run down, a completely up-rooted mob, wandering all over the place."[44]

Aside from American mass production and architecture, Hitler seemed only to approve of the separation of church and state,

[42] Letter, Thomsen to the author, 14/7/63. *NYT* 10/7/33. Admiration for American technology had been expressed in *Mein Kampf*, p. 399. P. Kluke, "Hitler und das Volkswagenprojekt," *Vierteljahresheft fuer Zeitgeschichte*, Oct. 1960.

[43] *Table Talk*, p. 415.

[44] Rauschning, *op. cit.*, p. 75; speech 10/12/40, quoted in Bullock, *op. cit.*, p. 580. Conference of 5/3/43, quoted in Gilbert, *Hitler Directs His War*, p. 24.

the immigration restrictions of 1924 (which he saw as an attempt
to preserve Nordic purity), the low vote enlisted by the American communist party,[45] and the sheer physical size of the country
which he designated as an outstanding example of the necessity
of possession of large contiguous land mass as a prerequisite to
national greatness. America, East Asia and Russia, he complained
in 1943, had whole continents. America's great strength, he told
his generals, "lies not only in the size of the population, but
simply in the magnitude of the national territory."[46] However,
neither mass production, architecture nor vast territory could
outweigh in Hitler's mind the appalling drawbacks to this land.
As he told the Duce in 1941:

> I could not for anything in the world live in a country like the
> United States, whose concepts of life are inspired by the most
> grasping materialism and which does not love any of the loftiest
> expressions of the human spirit such as music.[47]

Hitler's view of America was no doubt strongly influenced by
his attitude toward President Roosevelt, an attitude which
changed from a certain approving interest to the bitterest hatred.
In an interview published in the *New York Times* in July 1933,
Hitler remarked: "I have sympathy for Mr. Roosevelt because
he marches straight toward his objectives over congress, lobbies,
and the bureaucracy." He designated himself as "the one official
voice in Europe that expresses understanding of the methods and
motives of President Roosevelt." The President appeared to the
Fuehrer to be acting purely in the interests of the American
people and that, he concluded, "is as it should be."[48]

It is quite possible that Hitler actually saw in the early New

---

[45] *Table Talk*, pp. 552–553 (church and state). Baynes, *op. cit.*, p. 728; *Mein
Kampf*, p. 658 (immigration). He told Dodd: "Happy country! Your people
seem so sensible in this respect." *Ambassador Dodd's Diary*, p. 101 (low communist vote).

[46] Baynes, *op. cit.*, p. 1255 (interview with United Press 25/11/25). *Mein
Kampf*, p. 419. Quoted in Gilbert, *op. cit.*, pp. 75, 25 (meeting of 5/3/43).

[47] Ciano, *Diaries*, 1939–1943, p. 436 (meeting of 20/4/41).

[48] *NYT* 10/7/33.

Deal some national socialist parallels. He sent a message to the President in 1934, in which he

> sincerely congratulated President Roosevelt for his heroic efforts in the interests of the American people. The successful battle against economic distress is being followed by the entire German people with interest. . . . The Chancellor is in accordance with the President in the view that the virtues of duty, readiness to sacrifice, and discipline should dominate the entire people . . . the quintessence of the German state philosophy.[49]

He told Ambassador Wilson in 1938 that he watched with interest the progress of the New Deal. As late as 1940 he expressed to J. D. Mooney of General Motors firm admiration for the President even to the point of insisting that he really favored Roosevelt's re-election that year because the President was the only man who could deal with America's problem. He was certain that Roosevelt was the kind of man with whom he could come to an agreement ultimately.[50]

Such words, however, scarcely coincided with the press conference remarks in 1939 that FDR was a "Second Wilson . . . the number one warmonger . . . [who] wants to make the world happy after he has produced an unparalleled war psychosis." By 1941, Hitler had evidently accepted Colin Ross's line that Roosevelt's actions sprang from envy of the dictators of Europe who had solved their problems while the President had accomplished nothing. He was, Hitler told Mussolini, "undoubtedly acting from jealousy."[51] In his speech declaring war on December 11, 1941, Hitler gave expression to years of pent-up rage against the President, "this limited intellect," "this man who while soldiers

---

[49] Message, Hitler to Roosevelt, 28/3/34, *FRUS*/1934/II, p. 419. This embarrassing addition to the ranks of the New Dealers aroused no enthusiasm in Mr. Hull, who noted that "no publicity is being given here."

[50] Wilson to Roosevelt 3/3/38, in H. Wilson, *Career Diplomat*, p. 19. Mooney-Hitler interview 4/3/40, *RAM*/F 17426.

[51] Press conference 15/4/39, in W. Hofer, *Der Nationalsozialismus*, p. 93. Hitler-Mussolini conference 3/6/41. *DGFP*/D/XII, p. 949.

fight in the snow, likes to make chats from the fireside."[52] Hitler invited his listeners to compare his career with that of the President.

> Roosevelt was rich, I was poor; Roosevelt did business in the world war, I bled; Roosevelt speculated and made millions, I lay in a hospital; Roosevelt relied on the power of a capitalist party, I led a popular movement.

Only one thing was seen in common: "We both took over a country in poor condition, thanks to capitalist democracy." Roosevelt's criticisms of national socialism were brushed aside. "That he calls me a gangster is uninteresting. I cannot be insulted by Roosevelt, for I consider him mad, just as Wilson was."

Not surprisingly, American entry into the war was purely a matter of Roosevelt's manipulation. The President, in Hitler's view, needed the war to cover up the New Deal, "the biggest failure ever experienced by man." The only solution for Roosevelt lay in "directing public attention from home to foreign policy." In this effort, "the full diabolic meanness of Jewry rallied around this man and he stretched out his hands." How had it all come about? "He began to create complaints. His desire was that conflict should break out somewhere, preferably in Europe where the economic interests in one belligerent would bring the United States closer to war." Hitler then proceeded to an attack on each stage of Roosevelt's implementation of these objectives. The Quarantine Speech in 1937 he found "particularly mean." Economic threats and "measures short of war" were denounced. Roosevelt's various efforts at mediation were held to be "a clumsy combination of geographical and political ignorance." The revision of American neutrality and recognition of exile governments were part of Roosevelt's "methodical incitement to war." Thus American involvement was a demonstration of racial decay, the failures of democracy, Jewish intrigue and an anti-German conspiracy led by Franklin Roosevelt.

---

[52] Excerpts from the speech of 11/12/41, in Prange, *op. cit.*, pp. 368–375.

"He incites wars, falsifies the causes, odiously wraps himself in the cloak of Christian hypocrisy, and slowly but surely leads mankind to war . . . Roosevelt's policy," he concluded, "is one of world domination and dictatorship."

With American entry into the war, Hitler's invective became even shriller. Roosevelt was now exclusively to blame for the whole unfortunate world situation. In the *Table Talk*, the President became "a torturous pettifogging Jew," "a sick brain given to mouthing Hebraic noises at press conferences."[53] He told Goebbels that he considered Roosevelt to be one of the worst enemies of modern civilization. The Fuehrer considered the Pearl Harbor attack ("which fills all decent people with satisfaction") to be a suitable reply to "the insolent provocations of that lunatic." "There is," he wrote in the *Voelkischer Beobachter* later in 1942, "no need to waste a word to reply to the lying phrases of that old cheat. He is without doubt the chief gangster in the whole coterie which opposes us."[54] Finally, Hitler predicted a dismal fate for the President. He would probably lose the next election, Hitler told his generals in 1943, and then "he will be tried by an American court six months later . . . his successor will have to indict him." This would surely happen because "they will look for someone to blame and he is to blame." Hitler's ecstatic reaction to Roosevelt's death and his conviction that this was a divine stroke which would enable him even in April 1945 to liquidate the war successfully ("Now that fate has removed from the earth the greatest war criminal of all time . . .") are a final morbid commentary on Hitler's disposition toward the president.[55]

---

[53] *Table Talk*, pp. 434, 179. Nor was Mrs. Roosevelt ("a completely negrified appearance") spared Hitler's abuse.

[54] Goebbels, *Diaries*, entry for 11/3/42, p. 79. *Voelkischer Beobachter* 26/4/42, 8/11/42.

[55] Quoted in Gilbert, *op. cit.*, p. 79. Meeting 22/12/43. H. Trevor-Roper, *The Last Days of Hitler*, pp. 141–143. W. Hubatsch, ed., *Hitlers Weisungen fuer die Kriegsfuehrung*, Directive of April 15, 1945.

CHAPTER 2

Hitler and America as a World Power

WITH THIS dreary picture of the American scene in mind, what role could Hitler have expected the United States to play in world affairs? His statements on America certainly suggest that he was prepared to write the country off internationally. Although not entirely consistent, his comments on American foreign policy reflect his contempt. This does much to explain his confusion and rage when, contrary to his expectations, the United States emerged as a factor of importance in the years before the war.

America's role as a world power began for Hitler with the First World War. Hitler's judgment of this participation changed with the years from a ready acknowledgment of American influence to a dismissal of it out of hand. We have him writing in a letter in 1919 that "the United States, as the land of money, was bound to enter the war" and crediting that country with the lion's share of winning the war. In the *Zweites Buch*, he concluded in fact that the war had made America a great power.[1] He never of course accepted any notion of rectitude or idealism in the American entry, even while conceding the important military consequences. Such idealistic pretensions, he wrote in 1923, were "a farrago of lies and forgeries." The fact was that "the great peace-loving American people" had been forced into the war by the munitions makers and the press, both controlled, needless to say, by the Jews. This had all been

---

[1] Deuerlein, "Hitlers Eintritt in die Politik," *Vierteljahreshefte fuer Zeitgeschichte*, April 1959. *Zweites Buch*, p. 140. The so-called "Second Book" was written by Hitler probably about 1928 but never published in his lifetime. It was discovered after the war.

proved, he announced in 1939, by the investigations of Senator Nye in Washington.[2]

In the 1930's he came to ridicule America's military role in the war. He told Rauschning in 1932 that the United States had been no danger at all.

The Americans behaved like clumsy boys; they ran into the line of fire like young rabbits. The American is no soldier. The inferiority and decadence of this allegedly new world is evident in its military inefficiency.[3]

This sentiment is repeated in the *Table Talk*. Based on his war experience, he assured his listeners of his total disbelief that the American soldier could "fight like a hero." He explained to Japanese Ambassador Oshima in 1941 that American fighting power in 1918 was low. "How could troops whose God is the dollar, hold firm to the last?"[4]

With mounting bitterness Hitler turned his fire on Wilson as Roosevelt's predecessor in infamous deeds. In 1935 he denounced the Fourteen Points as a fraud. "Where are Wilson's Fourteen Points today?" he asked. "Like a breath of spring" he recalled in 1936, "the ideas of the President of the United States had reached the ears of mankind; they bespoke new times and a better world." But all had been betrayed and by a country, he pointed out in his Reichstag speech of January 1937, which had attacked Germany although Germany had aided in the War for Independence.[5] In 1939, the lost colonies were laid at Wilson's door. "The greatest breach of faith of all time was committed against Germany . . . equal rights, peace without vengeance, open diplomacy, equal consideration of colonial claims became blackmail, robbery and extortion."[6] In the *Voelkischer Beobachter* he

[2] Speech of 13/4/23, Baynes, *op. cit.*, p. 49. *Hitler's Reden*, speech of 17/4/23, pp. 47, 48. Speech of 30/1/39, Baynes, *op. cit.*, p. 737.

[3] Rauschning, *op. cit.*, p. 79

[4] *Table Talk*, p. 181. *International Military Tribunal in the Far East* (hereafter *IMTFE*), XVI, p. 6673.

[5] Speeches of 22/5/35 and 12/9/35 in Prange, *op. cit.*, pp. 233, 235. Speech of 8/3/36, *ibid.*, p. 235. Speech of 31/1/37, Baynes, *op. cit.*, p. 737.

[6] Speech of 31/1/39, Prange, *op. cit.*, p. 243. Speech of 3/4/39, *ibid.*, p. 244.

recalled: "For four years our enemies tried to defeat us and they finally came up with an American medicine man who found the formula that deceived the German people." "History," he said a month before the German declaration of war on America, "has already passed its verdict on Wilson; his name stands for one of the basest breaches of the given word."[7] This condemnation was clearly directed as well against the policies of the Roosevelt administration during the years before Pearl Harbor. "It would," he told the Reichstag in April 1939, "be a noble act if President Franklin Roosevelt were to redeem the promises made by President Woodrow Wilson." Finally, in 1943, he concluded that from 1918, "the word of an American president counts for no more to the German people than in the United States, that is: precisely nothing."[8] Here, of course, the American role in both wars was fused together in one continuous malevolent conspiracy.

This was Hitler's evaluation of that earlier American intervention. But what were his views of America's world role in the years down to 1941? There is only one lengthy theoretical examination of America as an international factor in Hitler's writings, and this is found in the *Zweites Buch*.[9] In the course of this extensive treatment of American power and its implications for Europe Hitler assigned to America an international significance which he never again explicitly repeated. The passage is, however, less a radical departure from Hitler's general disinterest in the United States, since it is actually part of a broader treatment of European problems and their possible solution ("Neither Border Policy, Economic Policy, nor Pan-Europe").

Hitler prefaced his discussion with this assertion: "With the

[7] *Voelkischer Beobachter* 8/11/40. Prange, *op. cit.*, speech of 11/11/41, p. 231.
[8] Speech of 28/4/39, Baynes, *op. cit.*, p. 1453. Speech of 1/1/43, Prange, *op. cit.*, p. 247.
[9] *Zweites Buch*, pp. 110–132. This treatment of America is the only really new addition in the book to the generally known lines of Hitler's foreign policy thought. The rest of the volume is largely a rehash of certain themes in *Mein Kampf*, especially in regard to the necessity of an Italian alliance and the inevitability of war with Russia.

American union there has emerged a power which threatens to throw the entire previous order of power and precedence into the discard." In the course of a rejection either of reliance on trade or a return to the 1914 borders as a solution to the German problem, he held that no merely economic program could compete with America. The quest for markets upon which a trade policy depended would only lead to collision with the United States; a contest which Germany would lose because (again alluding especially to the car industry) the unique combination of raw materials, productive technique and an insatiable domestic market permitted low prices impossible in Europe and placed the United States at the pinnacle of the market arrangements of the world.

But if America had attained this growth and power, it had to have, in the Hitlerian scheme of things, a racial foundation. How could this be squared with the mixture of races constituting the American people? This contradiction is resolved ingeniously by distinguishing between types of racial mixture. "The United States," Hitler advised,

> is not by accident the state in which the almost unbelievably clever inventions are made. Compared to old Europe which through war and emigration has lost its best blood, America emerges as a young racially select people.

Only a racial policy in Europe could redress the balance. Thus it was not to be an economic, political or armaments competition between Europe and America, but a competition for blood purification. This had to be won by Germany or she must forswear her claim to greatness and degenerate to a point where even the memory of past grandeur would be forgotten and where the most that could be hoped for was the present status of Switzerland or Holland.

And what was to prevent this catastrophe? A European federation to preclude American hegemony is rejected by Hitler since it placed numbers ahead of values.

United States greatness lies in a rich land and a racially select people. If this greatness were due simply to land or resources or even to the people-land ratio, Russia would be as much a danger as America. The missing element [in Russia] is race. Thus the only danger from Russia is bacteria.

European union was, to Hitler, therefore, "a denial of values" and no solution to the American threat. Not in federation, but in a Europe dominated by Germany lay the hope. Otherwise the result would be

> racial pollution and no one can build a state racially defective which can stand against America. Only a state which understands the importance of racial elements can put up a bold front to the United States.

Unlike the situation in Europe, the racial strains of the United States were essentially related in that they consisted of the most talented and virtuous elements of Europe: "the Nordic elements which exist in all countries." Immigration restrictions were, for Hitler, an indication of "America's conception of itself as a Nordic-Germanic state and not an international brew." Therefore, he continued, "to put a Europe of Magyar, Slav, German and Latin up as a counterweight against this racially dominant Nordic state is utopian." Proclaiming a Europe led by Germany as the only hope, Hitler ended his discourse with these words:

> In the distant future, a new organization of nations can be imagined which, consisting of states of high racial value, could meet the then threatening conquest of the world by the American union. For it seems to me that the existence of English world domination poses less threat than the rise of American domination.[10]

In the development of these ideas we have a classic example of the virtuosity which Hitler could display in manipulating concepts in the interests of momentary argument. It should also be

[10] *Zweites Buch*, p. 218.

noticed that even in this relatively extensive discourse on America as a factor in international affairs, the treatment of that country is less as a problem in itself than as a rhetorical device to validate the solution to European problems.

Three years later, Hitler had reversed himself completely. America was no longer a threat. He apparently no longer needed this concept. Indeed, he suggested to Hermann Rauschning that America now needed Germany to revive her and gave the assurance: "I shall undertake this task." He saw the revival of Germanic influence as the basis for a political and material reconstruction. "The American people," he went on, utterly contradicting the *Zweites Buch*, "are not a nation. It is a composite of disparate elements. The Yankee is too materialistic to accomplish national unity." He spoke of the organization of American storm troops and youth groups which would "continue the great statesmanlike mission of George Washington."[11] So far from a threat, Hitler expressed hope in an interview with the Hearst Press in 1931 that "America will also be sympathetic to National Socialism and that America will help in removing some of the causes of Bolshevism." In responding to Roosevelt's appeal for world peace in May 1933, Hitler "welcomed the proposal of bringing the United States into Europe as a guarantor of peace" and called the proposal "a ray of light."[12] He expressed the conviction to his associates that "at the right moment, a new America will exist as our strongest supporter."

The position of 1928 came full circle when Hitler expressed the desire for an American alliance to Otto Strasser.

The interest of Germany demands co-operation with England since it is a question of establishing a Nordic-German supremacy over Europe and in conjunction with Nordic-Germanic America over the whole world.[13]

[11] Rauschning, *op. cit.*, pp. 77, 78.
[12] Speech of 13/12/31, Prange, *op. cit.*, p. 345. Speech of 18/5/33, Baynes, *op. cit.*, pp. 1055–1056.
[13] *Ibid*, p. 989.

This sentiment was reiterated in an interview with the *Daily Mail* in 1937. He spoke now of an Anglo-German alliance containing 120,000,000 of the most valuable people of the world. He predicted a union of the unique colonial aptitudes and naval power of Great Britain with one of the first military powers of the world.

> If still further enlarged by the adherence of the American nation, it is impossible to see who in the world could disturb a combination for peace which would never neglect the interest of the white people.[14]

Notwithstanding these extravagant notions, when it came to the specifics of American foreign policy, Hitler clearly counted on American isolationism. Mussolini was informed that isolationism was an insuperable factor to an active foreign policy for the United States.[15] Hitler told Italian Foreign Minister Count Ciano that in his view, the more serious the crisis, the more likely was America to remain isolationist. He assured Molotov that the United States had nothing to seek in Europe or Africa or Asia.[16] General Ott, the German Ambassador in Tokyo, testified to a conversation with Hitler before the outbreak of the European war in which Hitler affirmed his faith in American non-intervention and dismissed all remarks regarding the decisive importance of the United States. The assurance regarding American isolation flowed quite naturally from his disparaging concept of America as a nation. As the former Chief of the Foreign Ministry Secretariat has explained:

> As a political factor, Hitler evaluated the United States from the day of his seizure of power as nil. His National Socialist

----

[14] *Ibid.*, p. 1354.

[15] Hitler-Mussolini conference 4/10/40, Ciano, *Diplomatic Papers*, p. 395; *Les Lettres Secrètes enchangées par Hitler et Mussolini*. Mussolini to Hitler 27/8/40, p. 79. Mussolini was not so certain of this.

[16] Quoted in M. Toscano, *Le Origini Diplomatiche del Patto d'Acciaio*, p. 52. Schmidt, *Statist auf Diplomatischer Buehne*, p. 532; DGFP/D/XI, p. 549.

advisers strengthened his idea that the United States was in an incurable inner crisis and incapable of pursuing a strong foreign policy.[17]

This enabled Hitler to push America into a limbo of wishful thinking.

More specifically Hitler seemed impressed with the Neutrality Acts of 1935 to 1937 as a confirmation of his convictions. He thought these acts to exemplify the weakness and confusion rampant in American political life. In a conference of November 23, 1939, he assured his colleagues that "America is still not a danger to us because of her neutrality laws." These acts seemed to Hitler to be of a pattern with America's previous performance in international affairs. Here was a country which had decided the last war, without seizing advantages at the peace conference, had proposed the League of Nations and let it fail, and now was making grandiose gestures while keeping its hands tied with neutrality legislation.[18] Having thus concluded that internal contradictions had compelled America to take an isolationist line, Hitler then rejected any evidence to the contrary as propaganda.

A leading example of this was Hitler's dismissal of American rearmament. Basing his judgment largely on the optimistic reports of the German Military Attaché in Washington, Hitler told Mussolini that American armament claims were "lies pure and simple."[19] The diaries of General Halder contain several of Hitler's comments in the fall of 1940 to the effect that United States rearmament could not reach a peak before 1945 and that American rearmament in general was a "big bluff." According to Admiral Doenitz, Hitler told Japanese Ambassador Oshima

[17] Ott testimony, *Case 11*/XXI/10,175. See also the statement of Kurusu that Hitler was "quite unimpressed" with the idea of American intervention. *DGFP*/D/XII, p. 9. Conference of 3/2/41. *Wahn und Wirklichkeit*, p. 140.

[18] *IMT*/XXXVI, document 7989-PS. *Wahn und Wirklichkeit*, p. 139. In a letter to the author, Kordt has suggested that it was "inconceivable" to Hitler that a nation which had played such a previous role could now withdraw and concluded from this that "internal politics precluded another American intervention unless actually attacked." Kordt to author 9/7/63.

[19] Hitler-Mussolini conference 4/10/40, *DGFP*/D/XI, p. 248.

not to worry about the American navy because "the United States will run out of sailors." At the Montoire conference with Marshal Pétain in October 1940, he scoffed at American aircraft production. In June 1941 he described American aircraft and shipbuilding goals to Mussolini as a "gigantic exaggeration" and insisted that the United States had neither the manpower nor the resources for such a program.[20]

This contemptuous view of American armament materially colored Hitler's appraisal of American aid to Germany's enemies. Hitler no doubt assumed American overtures on behalf of the Western powers in the event of war. In the discussion and directive for "Extended Case Green" (the possibility of war with Britain following an attack on Czechoslovakia) in 1937, there is the assertion that the United States "will immediately support the fight of the Western powers with strong ideological and economic means."[21] "The Fuehrer," Ciano recorded in his diary in October 1939, "is fully aware of the fact that America may be considered completely won over to the cause of the democracies." In 1941, Hitler wrote Mussolini that "behind the two great nations [Great Britain and the Soviet Union] hidden but nonetheless involved, there is the United States."[22] Hitler was apparently convinced that American aid to England was actually a disguise for American imperial ambition. Spanish Foreign Minister Ramon Serrano-Suñer found Hitler somewhat obsessed with this notion. The Fuehrer told Molotov in November 1940 that the United States planned to take over the British Empire. Roosevelt, he wanted the Soviet diplomat to know, "is doing nothing but picking out of this bankrupt estate a few items particularly suitable to the United States."[23]

[20] Halder, *Diaries*, vol. III, entries for 14/9/40, 15/10/40. Doenitz testimony, *IMT*/XIII, p. 373. *DGFP*/D/XI, p. 391, dated 24/10/40 (Pétain conference). *DGFP*/D/XII, p. 945, dated 3/6/41.

[21] *NCA*/III, p. 280, dated 25/3/38. Later, however, this is tempered with the note that American aircraft industry is "at the moment fully occupied," p. 289.

[22] Hitler-Ciano meeting 1/10/39, Ciano, *Diplomatic Papers*, p. 315. *Les Lettres Secrètes*, p. 322, dated 2/6/41. Ciano, *Diaries*, p. 436, entry for 20/4/41.

[23] Serrano-Suñer, *Entre Hendaye y Gibraltar*, p. 175. Hitler-Molotov meetings 12, 13/11/40, *DGFP*/D/XI, pp. 546, 558.

But if Hitler was aware of the possibility and reality of American aid, he never considered it to be decisive. He told Ciano shortly after the outbreak of the war that his submarines would prevent any real support from reaching Britain. The next month at a conference Hitler announced that the strengthening of Germany's opponents by America was still not important. He assured Japanese Foreign Minister Matsuoka in 1941 that the two American goals of arming herself and aiding England were contradictory, and that Germany had long taken American assistance to Britain into account. He predicted that only at the end of 1942 could such aid materialize in substantial quantities and by that time German production would have advanced even faster and canceled out the effect.[24] American claims to the contrary, Hitler told Mussolini, were "childish." Even in December 1943, he told his generals that America could not make up for Britain's deficiencies and in any event American supplies were diminishing.[25]

What, finally, was Hitler's estimation of the chances of an actual entry of America into the war? This problem can be more fully dealt with in later chapters in connection with various aspects of German policy. However, regarding Hitler's personal viewpoint the answer is to a certain extent already clear from the discussion above. From his own statements, it emerges that Hitler did not at first think of American entry as any real possibility because of her weakness and isolation. Later he apparently came to accept the possibility as undesirable, but not of great importance even if it occurred. In the spring of 1938 when asked about the chances of an American military intervention in the event of a European war, he replied by ruling it out on the ground that "the United States was incapable of conducting war."

In 1940, he predicted that the United States would not dare enter the war for the foreseeable future and later assured Molotov

---

[24] Meeting of Ciano and Hitler 1/10/39. *DDI*, ser. 9/1, p. 431. Conference 23/11/39. *IMT/XXVI*, p. 327. *DGFP/D/XII*, p. 789, dated 1/4/41. Also, Hitler-Mussolini conference 28/10/40, Ciano, *Diplomatic Papers*, p. 401.

[25] Hitler-Mussolini conference 3/6/41, *DGFP/D/XII*, p. 940. Quoted in Gilbert, *op. cit.*, p. 77, meeting of 20/12/43.

that the Americans could not "endanger the freedom of other nations before 1970 or 1980."[26] In January 1941 he allowed that a simultaneous war with the United States and the Soviet Union would be "very complicated," and used this as a reason for eliminating such a danger by attacking the U.S.S.R. Later in the month however, he stated that he did not see a great danger from America even if she did enter. He boasted to Matsuoka in April 1941 that German preparations were such that no American could land in Europe and that in the event of a German-American war, Germany would wage it with submarines and *Luftwaffe*, while the German soldier was "obviously superior" to the American.[27]

Even after the formal opening of hostilities between the two countries, Hitler seemed to have little appreciation of what it meant. When Chargé Hans Thomsen returned from Washington he was received by Hitler and expressed his concern about the introduction of American power into the anti-Axis coalition. "But as usual," Thomsen has written to the author, "Hitler talked incessantly and knew everything better." [28] Such indifference did not, of course, prevent Hitler from expressing rancorous judgments about what had happened. Hitler now felt confirmed in the view that the United States was simply waiting to pick up the pieces of the British Empire. Reviving an idea expressed in *Mein Kampf*, he foresaw a great enmity between England and the United States. "England and America will some day have a war with one another, waged with the greatest hatred imaginable. One of the two countries will have to disappear." He even saw the possibility in 1942 of "England and Germany marching to-

[26] *Wahn und Wirklichkeit*, pp. 140, 257. Hitler-Molotov meeting 12/11/40. *Nazi-Soviet Relations* (hereafter *NSR*), p. 217.

[27] *Fuehrer Conferences on Naval Affairs* (hereafter *FCNA*) 1941, 8–9/1/41. *IMT*/XXXIV, p. 462. Conference of 20/1/41. Hitler-Matsuoka meeting 4/4/41, *DGFP*/D/XII, p. 455. Hitler-Mussolini meeting 21/6/41, *NSR*, p. 349. *NCA*, supl. B, p. 1199.

[28] Thomsen to the author, 14/7/63. Thomsen feels that Hitler may have believed that the United States could have been "blitzed" by cutting off the armaments industry from its oil supply by naval and submarine action.

gether against America," though he admitted he would probably not live to see it.[29]

At the close of his life, Hitler did not neglect the United States. In the *Testament* we have Hitler's final American reflections. After consigning the British "to die of hunger and tuberculosis on their accursed island," he turned his final wrath on America.

> At a time when the whole of Europe — their own mother — is fighting to ward off the Bolshevik peril, the United States guided by the Jew-ridden Roosevelt can think of nothing better to do than to place their fabulous resources at the disposal of these Asiatic barbarians who are determined to strangle her.

His hopes of a Germanic revival in America were gone and he regretted the millions of Germans who had emigrated to the United States and who were now the backbone of the country. This "hemorrhage of German blood" had all been a ghastly error.

> It is eastwards and eastwards only that the views of our race must expand; nature itself has decreed this direction. Only in a vigorous climate can there be virility. Transfer a German to Kiev, and he remains a perfect German. Transfer him to Miami and you make a degenerate of him — in other words — an American.[30]

In the later pages of the *Testament*, he recapitulated many of his earlier ideas. The oft-accused scapegoats are invoked for the last time: the Jews, the press, the failure of the New Deal, the machinations of the infamous Roosevelt ("Pearl Harbor was balm to his soul"). Finally, after declaring himself free of prejudice and assuring posterity that he was Europe's "last hope," he predicted war between America and Russia; a war in which there was little for the European to choose as between "Bolshevism or Jew-ridden America, this giant with feet of clay."[31] These

---

[29] *Table Talk*, pp. 14, 26, 93, 202; *Mein Kampf*, p. 896. W. Warlimont, *Inside Hitler's Headquarters*, p. 488.

[30] *Testament*, pp. 34, 45, 46.

[31] *Ibid.*, pp. 57, 76, 87–90, 101, 107–108.

are Hitler's last recorded words about the United States.

Notwithstanding the fact that Hitler was undoubtedly speaking for effect in many of his remarks on America, we may observe an obvious pattern of contempt. This makes it most unlikely that he held to any clear or realistic conception of the United States as a nation and world power. It is obvious that this country was, in his personal outlook, no immediate problem, no really vital factor. This attitude flows naturally from two sources. In the first place, there was the absence in America of those political and racial elements and conditions required for national greatness. In the second place, the geo-politics of America was such as to almost physically remove the country from Hitler's political and strategic world, a world, it will be recalled, which involved: a fundamental concern with land mass and the acquisition of *Lebensraum* in the East; a disinterest in maritime affairs and overseas colonization; a Central European orientation and lack of direct concern with areas beyond Europe. Hitler's words, then, do not suggest any disposition to incorporate the United States into his planning and strategic thought as a goal or project in itself. This is not to say, as we shall see in subsequent chapters, that the United States had no effect on German policy. But it does mean that any American influence on German destiny was bound to seem an unnatural thing to Hitler. Any realistic adjustment to American power would thus be difficult.

The essentially negative disposition of Hitler toward America may also serve to illuminate certain aspects of Hitler's political mind of a more general nature. It may be useful to understand the Fuehrer's political thinking on three levels. At the first level there unquestionably existed a hard core of ideas on such topics as race, power, *Lebensraum* and Bolshevism to which he clung with unswerving conviction. On the second level, there was the application of these doctrines to the European world. Here there is greater variation and tactical expediency but still a degree of consistency as reflected in his attitudes toward Russia, France,

England and Italy. On the third level, moving out into the non-European world, we get the least consistency, the minimum coherence, an element of discomfort.

Thus, though he lacked a systematic attitude toward the United States, one cannot necessarily conclude from this that he had no definite foreign policy program at all.[32] He had in fact a roughly coherent system of ideas about world affairs, but only in regard to his own world, and his world was Central Europe. It simply did not include in any immediate or fundamental way the non-European areas. As can be seen from his thoughts on America, of these areas there is scant knowledge and fleeting reference. It is especially in his view of these non-European lands that one finds what Professor Trevor-Roper has called "the festering litter and old lumber of his rancorous, seedy past."[33] Here was a jumble of ideas upon which Hitler could draw to support or refute policies pertaining to more immediate problems, and then disregard. Even with America in the war, there seems to have been no great expansion of Hitler's strategic horizon; no attempt to move from level two to level three. Here was an unexpected and unnatural intruder which seemed to surprise Hitler by its very presence in international affairs.

When Louis P. Lochner, the Berlin correspondent of the Associated Press, called upon Hitler in 1934 to direct his attention to the importance of German-American relations, he reported Hitler's reaction in this way: "For a moment he blushed like a schoolboy, hemmed and hawed, then stammered an embarrassed something about having so many other problems to ponder that he had not yet had time to take up America."[34]

It is evident that he never found that time. And yet, in this respect as in others, time was to catch up with Adolf Hitler. He eventually found himself faced with a world conflict extending well beyond the confines of *Mitteleuropa* into areas where he

[32] The Nuremberg Prosecutor spoke of "many separate plans rather than a single conspiracy." *IMT/I*, p. 225.
[33] *Testament*, p. 1.
[34] Lochner, *What About Germany?*, p. 47.

could not be at ease. By plunging Europe into war in 1939, he unleashed a train of events which brought American power into play against Germany, indirectly and then in full confrontation. This had been predicted by German diplomats in Berlin and Washington who sought, unsuccessfully, to impress this disagreeable fact on the Fuehrer. He could not adjust himself to it in any realistic way. Hitler's unwillingness to take full account of the impact of the United States on German foreign policy, understandable in the light of his political attitudes, must nevertheless be counted as one of his most disastrous errors.

PART II

*America and
the Wilhelmstrasse*

CHAPTER 3

America and German Diplomacy

HITLER'S OPINIONS about the United States and its world role were a product not so much of the diplomatic reports about America sent to Berlin but rather of his general political biases and assumptions. The German Embassy in Washington and the professional diplomats in Berlin did not for the most part share the Fuehrer's contempt and indifference but held to quite another picture of America upon which they based their recommendations for dealing with American influence. But did all of this make any difference in the totalitarian conditions of Nazi Germany? Could the viewpoint of the diplomats have had any effect on policies in which the Dictator's opinions were so predominant? Hitler might speak of his Foreign Ministry as "an intellectual garbage dump" and of the diplomats as "gentlemen who spend the day cutting out newspaper articles and pasting them back together again," but the plain fact of the matter is that, in spite of his immense powers, he could not entirely dispense with his diplomats nor attend to every aspect of foreign policy personally.[1]

Moreover, it may well be argued that in areas, such as the United States, where Hitler had little natural interest, the role of the traditional diplomat was bound to be greater. Furthermore, although we cannot be sure which dispatches were shown to Hitler by his Foreign Minister, the diplomats had other channels of influence such as the General Staff.[2] The considerable testi-

[1] Rauschning, *op. cit.*, p. 268. *Table Talk*, pp. 101, 102, 104.
[2] For diplomatic connections with the General Staff see for example H. Foerster, *Ein General Kaempft gegen den Krieg* and *The Halder Diaries*. State

mony to the effect that the *Wilhelmstrasse* was reduced to impotence has probably been exaggerated.[3] There is little real evidence of Nazification of the personnel although there was a considerable intrusion into the conduct of foreign affairs by various party agencies and individuals. This was especially true in matters involving the *Volksdeutsche* (racial Germans) living abroad. The establishment of alternative foreign ministries (*Buero Ribbentrop, Buero des Reichsaussenministers* and, after the outbreak of war, the Foreign Minister's special railway car) must have caused confusion, and the nomination of the calamitous Ribbentrop as Foreign Minister in 1938 was not welcomed either by German or foreign diplomats. (Undersecretary of State Sumner Welles found him "pompous and absurd" and allowed that he had "never met a man I disliked more.")[4]

Yet, for all of this, the basic apparatus of diplomacy remained intact, the embassies continued to perform their normal functions, the *Wilhelmstrasse* carried on the usual tasks of a foreign ministry. The dispatches, recommendations and instructions flowed to and from Berlin. Confusion, duplication and ideological interference certainly added to the burdens of German diplomats but this should not persuade us that the role of these men had been extinguished, nor should our attention be distracted from that day-by-day routine without which no state can conduct its re-

---

Secretaries von Buelow and Weizsaeker are especially important here. On Ribbentrop's blocking of dispatches from Hitler, see Lammers testimony, *Case 11/XXX*, p. 19783. *Nicht aus den Akten*, p. 435. Letter, E. Kordt to the author, 9/7/63.

[3] Von Hassell, *Diary*, p. 26. F. von Papen, *Memoirs*, p. 340. *Nicht aus den Akten*, pp. 122–124. Weizsaeker testimony, *Case 11/XVII*, p. 8274. For discussion see P. Seabury, *The Wilhelmstrasse;* G. Craig, *The Diplomats*, chap. 13; D. Watt, "German Diplomats and the Nazi Leaders," in *Journal of Central European Affairs*, July 1955.

[4] On problems with the party see Bohle testimony, *Case 11/XXVIII*, p. 13510; Kordt testimony, *ibid.*, XV, pp. 7337, 7341; Papen testimony *IMT/XVI*, p. 316. H. Dirksen, *Moskau, London, Tokio*, p. 183. Duplication is treated in Seabury, *op. cit.*, pp. 32–39. Papen, *op. cit.*, p. 335. Craig, *op. cit.*, p. 428. Ribbentrop is harshly treated in *Nicht aus den Akten*, p. 61. Papen, *op. cit.*, p. 373; Schmidt, *op. cit.*, p. 571. Woermann testimony, *Case 11/XXII*, p. 10869. S. Welles, *Time for Decision*, p. 75.

lations with the international system. And it is clear that the confusion of the German response to the United States stemmed in part from the chasm which developed between the America of the diplomats and the America Hitler chose to see.

We can perceive this divergence at the highest level within the *Wilhelmstrasse*. Ribbentrop's predecessor as Foreign Minister was Konstantin Freiherr von Neurath. Of Neurath's attitude toward the United States we have no direct evidence. A cautious professional diplomat, his disposition toward America was probably close to that of the German ambassadors in Washington. The same may be said of Ernst von Weizsaeker, the State Secretary in the Foreign Ministry from 1938 to 1943, whose general agreement with the appraisals and suggestions of the Washington Embassy we shall observe in examining the dispatches.

Of Joachim von Ribbentrop's attitude on America we know much more, partly because he held office at a time when America loomed as a factor in German policy, partly because he was much given to lengthy and pretentious disquisitions on the world situation in which America was bound to figure. Ribbentrop, arrogant and opinionated, clearly shared many of Hitler's attitudes toward diplomacy in general and probably derived his knowledge of foreign countries from the same dilettantish sources (Goering remarked that Ribbentrop's knowledge of foreign countries was limited to French champagne and English whisky), supplemented by his personal travels as a young man in Europe and North America. His distinction between "small foreign policy" and "large foreign policy" (the latter described by a former colleague as "so abstract and fantastic" as to be incomprehensible) sounds much like Hitler's tendency to shade off into romanticism when considering the larger world arena in which there was no immediate problem for Germany.[5]

Although Ribbentrop had spent three years in North America

---

[5] Weizsaeker testimony, *Case II*/XVI, p. 7702.

(mostly in Canada) prior to the First World War and claimed on the basis of this experience an understanding of the New World, the attitudes on the United States he expressed while Reich Foreign Minister have a familiar Hitlerian ring to them. Indeed, French Ambassador François-Poncet found him in general *"plus Hitlerien que Hitler."*[6] Roosevelt was seen as the one really responsible for the war, which was useful to him in distracting attention from his domestic failures. He told Mussolini in September 1940 and Japanese Ambassador Oshima in February 1941 that Roosevelt was the bitterest enemy of the Axis. With Ambassador Wilson he drew the familiar distinction between the American people (who enjoyed "the respect and sympathy of Germany") on the one hand and the incomprehensible attitude of the American press on the other. He was certain that German propaganda activities had helped keep American public opinion isolationist and that he had been able to expose Roosevelt's foreign policy as the "biggest bluff in world history."[7]

He assured Matsuoka, the Japanese Foreign Minister, in March 1941 that although aid to England had given that country new hope, it would be a long time before this aid would be effective. Besides this, he insisted, American munitions were "junk." Ribbentrop warned American Diplomat Cudahy in May 1941 that an American invasion of Europe was hopeless ("an American Dunkirk") and that the position of the American navy and air force was such as to rule out even the attempt. Regarding American military involvement, Ribbentrop on several occasions professed himself uncertain about American intentions but also indifferent to American action. He told Japanese Ambassador Oshima that although the American people were anti-Nazi, they were un-

---

[6] A. François-Poncet, *Souvenirs d'une Ambassade à Berline*, p. 291. Ciano wrote that "If Hitler wants anything—and God knows he wants enough—Ribbentrop always goes him one better." Ciano, *Diary* 2/10/39, p. 192.

[7] Ribbentrop, *op. cit.*, chap. 1. Conversation with Mussolini 22/9/40, *DGFP/D/XI*, p. 151. Ribbentrop memo 29/4/38, *DGFP/D/I*, p. 704. Oshima-Ribbentrop conversation 23/2/41, *DGFP/D/XII*, p. 147. Ciano, *Diplomatic Papers* 11/8/39, p. 298.

willing to sacrifice for a war effort to stop Germany. Even if they were, Germany was more than prepared to deal with any American military intervention.[8]

Ribbentrop's longest exposition of American policy took place during a meeting with Admiral Darlan in April 1941. Again admitting uncertainty regarding American plans ("does she delude herself that she would be able to wage war in Europe?"), he went on to explain to the Frenchman that "in politics, the Americans are like children and in military matters something worse." However, there was nothing to fear in any event since German economic and political power was unassailable. Besides, he pointed out, Japan would enter if the United States did and under those circumstances American intrusion into the European war would be "sheer insanity." Actually, he confided to the Admiral, American policy was "the biggest and stupidest imperialism in world history" and consisted essentially of Roosevelt's "sticking his nose into all sorts of places where he has no business to be."[9] Obviously, in these various conversations Ribbentrop was trying for effects which would influence his hearers in a direction he thought desirable. Yet his attitude toward America and American policy is fairly consistent and there is no evidence of any outstanding difference between Hitler and his Foreign Minister on this subject.

As for the organization of German relations with the United States, the American section at the Foreign Ministry occupied an organizational position commensurate with the importance of the country, and the personnel of this section (Pol IX) evidently performed their duties in a routine way with occasional interruptions, as we shall see later, from party sources.[10] In Washing-

[8] See conversation with Matsuoka 31/3/41, *DGFP*/D/XII, p. 381. Conversation 13/2/41, *NCA*/IV, pp. 470–471.

[9] Ribbentrop-Darlan conference 11/5/41, *DGFP*/D/XII, p. 758.

[10] For details see *DGFP*/1933–1941/appendix A. The head of Pol IX was a career diplomat and former consul in St. Louis named Freytag. Woermann testimony, *Case 11*/XXIII, pp. 11039–50. Letter, Dr. Hans Thomsen to author 14/10/63.

ton, the staff consisted of the usual officers until the recall of the Ambassador in 1938. Thereafter, the mission was increasingly reduced in its activity by a hostile public opinion and governmental restrictions.[11] Four men were responsible, as chiefs of the Washington mission, for reporting to Berlin on American affairs. Since these reports are to be discussed in some detail in the following chapters, a brief sketch of each of these figures may be useful.

At the time of the Nazi assumption of power the Embassy was in the hands of Dr. Friedrich Wilhelm von Prittwitz und Gaffron. A career diplomat who had seen previous service in Washington from 1908 to 1910, Prittwitz was an aristocrat of deep liberal convictions and an ardent supporter of the Weimar Republic. He had become increasingly pessimistic about political events in Germany and the possible effects of these on German-American relations. As he wrote later in his memoirs: "I had not the remotest interest in putting my name at the service of something which was bound to bring unspeakable sorrow to Germany." On March 11, 1933, Prittwitz submitted his resignation from his post and from the foreign service.[12]

Prittwitz's successor was Dr. Hans Luther, the only one of the four chiefs of mission who was without prior diplomatic experience. Luther, an economist, former Chancellor during the Weimar Republic and President of the Reichsbank, was a surprise appointment. It is not entirely clear why Hitler made this particular selection. One writer who was in Berlin at that time claims that he was "packed off to Washington" to make room for Hjalmar Schacht at the bank. On the other hand, it is possible, as the *New York Times* suggested, that by appointing a Weimar figure and a solid conservative Hitler was trying to show that

---

[11] Thomsen to Foreign Ministry 9/2/41, *StS/USA/V/*244056. *NYT* 13/4/41. *FRUS/*1941/II, p. 268. Letters, Thomsen to author, 14/7/63, 14/10/63.

[12] Prittwitz, *op. cit.*, pp. 217–219, 222. Prittwitz-Castle conversation 2/2/33. *FRUS/*1933/II, p. 187. Prittwitz to Neurath 11/3/33. *DGFP/C/I*, p. 148; see *NYT* comment 20/3/33, 13/4/33. He tried to get the German envoys in London and Paris to resign with him. Prittwitz, *op. cit.*, p. 278.

there would be "nothing startling or wild in German foreign policy" at least vis-à-vis the United States.[13]

In any event, Luther's appointment was well received by the press, although his elaborate public defenses of the Nazi regime were not appreciated.[14] Secretary of State Cordell Hull found him "a very agreeable man personally," though Roosevelt discovered a "rigidity of mind which will not add to his effectiveness here." Jay P. Moffatt of the European Section of the State Department pictured him as given to "Teutonic blasts."[15] Messersmith, consul-general in Berlin, warned the State Department that "Dr. Luther may talk bravely and fairly about Germany and the United States, but he cannot tell you what he knows and even if he could, there is a great deal he does not know." This detachment from political affairs was noted by Dr. Hans Thomsen, who served as Counsellor under Luther. The Ambassador left political reporting largely to his colleagues, "not feeling much at ease in foreign policy." In spite of these deficiencies and a notable lack of humor (French Foreign Minister Briand was reported to be the only man who ever made him laugh in public), Luther was praised on his recall to Berlin and retirement from the diplomatic corps for having represented his country with dignity.[16]

The last Ambassador was Dr. Hans Heinrich Dieckhoff, a man whose activities both before and after his brief ambassadorship were considerably involved with German-American relations. A career diplomat of wide experience, Dieckhoff had served in Tangier, Constantinople, Santiago, Lima and Prague prior to the World War, during which he was a cavalry officer. He was Counsellor of Embassy in Washington from 1922 to 1927, and in London from 1927 to 1930. He held various positions at the Ministry until 1937. He was the German Ambassador in Washington from March 1937 until December 1938. Thereafter, he was Ambassador on Special Assignment until 1943, when he was

13 Shirer, *Third Reich*, p. 204. *NYT* 19/3/33, 20/3/33.
14 *NYT* 19/3/33, 15/4/33, 29/4/33, 10/8/35, 7/10/35.
15 Hull, *op. cit.*, p. 230. J. Moffat, *The Moffat Papers* 9/10/33, p. 101.
16 Hull, *op. cit.*, p. 235. Letter, Thomsen to author, 14/7/63. *NYT* 25/3/37.

assigned to Madrid, where he remained until the end of the war.[17] He was Joachim Ribbentrop's brother-in-law and his advice on America may have carried more than usual weight. A man of undoubted ability and charm, Dieckhoff enjoyed a liberal reputation. He was never a member of the Nazi party and Ribbentrop once accused him of having "no conception of the dynamics of national socialism." He had impressed Dodd as "a liberal German" and "perhaps the most conciliatory high official with whom the Embassy has to deal."[18] That he did not resign for his liberal principles may have been due to a desire to exercise a restraining influence or to timidity.[19]

Dieckhoff's general diplomatic attitude, as we shall notice in his dispatches, was moderate and traditional rather than adventurous or ideological. His appointment was very well received in the United States. He was described as a man of engaging personality, "well known and popular here" and as "one of the ablest German diplomats." It was emphasized that he was in the close confidence of Hitler and that this might be the sign of a genuine interest by the Nazi regime in improving German-American relations. There was nothing in the subsequent months to indicate any such thing.[20]

Dieckhoff was no doubt a far abler diplomat than Luther and more suited personally to the American climate. But German-American relations continued to deteriorate steadily to such an extent that he told Sumner Welles on November 1, 1938, of his fear that a major contention between the two countries was inevitable and that he regarded his mission as "a complete failure."

[17] Details of Dieckhoff's early career can be found in the various issues of *NYT* on his arrival and also in the obituaries, *NYT* 22/3/52 and *Frankfurter Allgemeine Zeitung* 26/3/52.

[18] *NYT* 12/3/37. Ribbentrop comment quoted in Bullock, *op. cit.*, p. 450. Dodd to State Department 8/8/33, *FRUS*/1933/II, p. 389. Dodd, *Diary* 24/5/34, pp. 112, 113; 30/3/37, p. 399.

[19] Hassell, *op. cit.*, p. 270. Shirer, *Third Reich*, p. 400. Shirer has this comment to make on Dieckhoff's anti-Nazi reputation: "My own feeling was that he lacked the guts to be." *Ibid.*, p. 897.

[20] *NYT* 24/3/37, 25/3/37.

Following Roosevelt's denunciation of the anti-Semitic outbursts that month and the recall of Ambassador Wilson for consultations, Dieckhoff was ordered to Berlin to explain Roosevelt's "singular attitude" toward Germany. On his departure in December, he expressed his doubts about returning and after the outbreak of the European war nine months later, it was announced that he would not return.[21]

Dieckhoff's connection with German-American relations was maintained from Berlin through a series of lengthy memoranda on American affairs which he submitted for the guidance of the Foreign Ministry as head of an advisory "America Committee." The contents of these reports will be examined in the following chapters, but it may be said here that the general tone was restrained, non-ideological and sober regarding the possibility of American intervention.

In addition, Dieckhoff wrote a series of articles in 1941 which appeared in the *Monatshefte fuer Auswaertige Politik* under the pen name "Silvanus." These articles were collected and expanded into a book entitled *Zur Vorgeschichte des Rooseveltkriegs* (On the Background of the Roosevelt War), published in 1942.[22] Under the circumstances of censorship and pressure in Nazi Germany during the war it cannot be said that this volume represented Dieckhoff's considered judgment freely expressed. Nevertheless, the book is interesting because it is the most extensive writing of a man who was probably the leading figure in German-American relations at that time and also because the book necessarily had to reflect to some extent official thinking on the subject. It may be said in general that although the book was unexceptionable from the German standpoint it was relatively free of ideological posturing, party clichés and turgid social analysis. The search for conspiracy, the denigration of American

[21] Welles memo 1/11/38, *FRUS*/1938/II, p. 446. *NYT* 19/11/38, 23/12/38, 28/9/39.

[22] Dieckhoff, *Zur Vorgeschichte des Rooseveltkriegs*, published by the Institut fuer Aussenpolitische Forschung. On the "Amerika Ausschuss" Weizsaeker Memo 28/5/41, *DGFP*/D/XII, p. 906. Thomsen to author 14/10/63.

power and the reveries about Nordic elements are absent.[23]

The essence of the book was expressed in the first chapter: America has since the late nineteenth century "trod the road of imperialist expansion" under the influence of England and Anglophile Americans. This tendency had caused the United States to take the path of obstruction regarding any move to unify Europe or Asia. In the 1930's the role of Roosevelt had been decisive and grounded in his "overriding enmity to Japan and his old deeply rooted hatred of Germany." Thus, he bore the main responsibility for the war. Roosevelt's motives were, Dieckhoff admitted, difficult to disentangle. But starting in 1937 a three-fold program was put into operation: unity in the Western hemisphere, intimidation of the Axis and encouragement of the Western Allies. Cleverly manipulating congressional and public opinion, Roosevelt left no diplomatic stone unturned to impede the Axis.[24]

In a chapter on German-American relations he described the intrusion of the English into what had been a cordial relationship. American hostility toward Germany beginning in the last years of the nineteenth century was instigated by the English: "The key to German-American relations lies in London." In order to clear the decks for the coming struggle with Germany, the English together with an Anglophile elite had succeeded in foisting upon American opinion a distorted image of Germany. Roosevelt had endorsed these efforts and they had reached a climax just before the war.[25]

Roosevelt, Dieckhoff continued, had sought to block German moves in France,[26] and similar obstructionist tendencies were

[23] The Jews for example are only mentioned twice and then merely as being anti-German and pro-English.

[24] Dieckhoff, *op. cit.*, forward, pp. 13, 14. The alteration of the Neutrality Acts, the destroyer deal and Lend-Lease were given as the major symbols of this policy. *Ibid.*, pp. 19–26.

[25] *Ibid.*, pp. 57, 59–62. Dieckhoff mentioned Carnegie and Rhodes, the Episcopal church, the English Speaking Union, the *New York Times*, the National Broadcasting Company, the Boy Scouts and the Y.M.C.A. as leading agencies of this offensive.

[26] *Ibid.*, pp. 69, 92–100.

revealed in American policy to Japan. Through military intimidation and economic pressure, the Roosevelt administration had sought to forestall Japanese expansion. The negotiations of 1941 had been doomed by American insistence on fraudulent issues such as Japanese abandonment of the Axis. Thus did America keep up pressure in an area in which she had no "historical, racial or economic claims." When Japan "cut the noose with a sword" at Pearl Harbor, Washington had only itself to blame.[27]

Roosevelt had also sought to use the U.S.S.R. to prevent European unity. Roosevelt's desire was "a torn, disunited, weak Europe" to serve as "a pawn of Anglo-Saxon politics and finance." "With unique frivolity," Dieckhoff charged, Roosevelt unleashed the war.

What does he care if Europe is a bloodbath?
What does he care if European culture is threatened?
What does he understand of the European soul? Hand in hand
　　with Bolshevism, the America of Roosevelt seeks to bring
　　Europe to her knees.[28]

One-sidedly pro-German and oversimplified, the book nevertheless reveals a trained and informed mind in the service of a national cause. A comparison with his secret memoranda uncovers the considerable amount of padding in both style and content which he evidently felt compelled to put into this public writing.[29]

Dieckhoff retired from the foreign service in 1945 and died in 1952. At his death, the *Frankfurter Allgemeine Zeitung* eulogized him as a proven liberal and a man with an "incorruptible sense of justice" (*unbestechlichem Rechtsinn*), while the *New*

---

[27] Recognition of the U.S.S.R., build up of the U.S. navy, delay of Philippine independence, the quarantine speech, abrogation of the commercial treaty in 1939, support for China and the oil and scrap embargo were all part of this policy. *Ibid.*, pp. 117–135, 138–139.

[28] *Ibid.*, p. 190

[29] That Dieckhoff much preferred the confidential letter to public writing has been affirmed by a letter from his former colleague Dr. Thomsen to the author dated 14/7/63.

York Times less generously pictured him as "a heel clicking representative of the German junker class."[30] As he was certainly the most complex of the major figures involved in German-American relations, a final judgment of him remains difficult. In the view of the author, Dieckhoff was an able and realistic diplomat and a political moderate who for diverse personal reasons as well as his sense of professional obligation was able to accommodate himself to public service in the Third Reich.

While Dieckhoff was seeking to influence the course of German-American relations from Berlin, the Washington Embassy during the tense three years from December 1938 to December 1941 was in the care of the Counsellor, Dr. Hans Thomsen, who now served as Chargé d'Affaires. Thomsen, of partial Norwegian descent and member of a distinguished Hamburg banking family, was also a career diplomat who had seen service in Italy and at the Ministry in Berlin. In 1932, he left the *Wilhelmstrasse* to enter the Reichschancellery under Franz von Papen and to act as liaison man between the two offices. In charge of protocol at the early cabinet meetings under Hitler, he also served as one of the Fuehrer's interpreters. In 1936 he was assigned to Washington as Counsellor, becoming Chargé on Dieckhoff's recall.[31]

Under the restricted circumstances of the relations which existed between Germany and America, especially after the outbreak of the European war, Thomsen never really had the possibility of public appearances and social contact available to the full ambassadors. There was therefore less comment on his abilities and activities. His public speeches were relatively few in number and were largely confined to routine explanations of the German position. He was favorably regarded by Sumner Welles, who spoke of his work to Weizsaeker during the trip in 1940.[32] In general his reports were factual, restrained and concerned

---

[30] *Frankfurter Allgemeine Zeitung* 26/3/52. *NYT* 22/3/52.

[31] This information was given to the author by Dr. Thomsen in two letters dated 14/7/63, 27/7/63.

[32] *NYT* 13/9/39, 17/11/40. "The calm sure eye of Thomsen" was praised in this discussion, both by Welles and by Weizsaeker. *DGFP/D/VIII*, p. 831.

about American involvement against Germany. He was mentioned favorably by Hitler in the *Table Talk*.[33] However, it is possible that this recognition was based on the reports of the Military Attaché which Thomsen had to countersign rather than his own which, as discussed elsewhere, Hitler probably never saw.

Thomsen's final acts were of course to deliver the German declaration of war to the State Department and to close the Embassy. He was repatriated some weeks later via Portugal and was decorated with the knight's cross of the war service cross.[34] He made two subsequent public statements on the United States. On May 1, 1942, he expressed the view that American production figures were exaggerated, but some weeks later he made some rather unusual comments for a German official at that time. In an interview outside Germany, Thomsen warned strongly against underrating American power. He then went on to praise Roosevelt as a "super-intelligent leader of great energy," while Mrs. Roosevelt was described as having "great charm and presence of mind" and as being a credit to her country. Asked by foreign journalists why he presented a picture at variance with that of the German government he defended his view as the accurate one. Thomsen was sent to Stockholm as Minister, where he remained until his retirement in 1945.[35]

Finally, among the important figures in German relations with the United States must be counted the Military and Air Attaché, General Friedrich von Boetticher. Von Boetticher, who was appointed in April 1933, was the first German military attaché assigned to Washington since 1917. An artillery officer in the first war, he had risen from Captain to General and served on the General Staff. During the 1920's he had been superintendent of the artillery school and had visited the United States briefly as chief of the foreign armies section of the German Ministry of Defense. On his arrival in New York in 1933 he had stoutly

[33] *NYT* 12/28/40. *Table Talk*, p. 216.
[34] *NYT* 27/5/42.
[35] *NYT* 18/5/42, 18/6/42, 3/1/43.

denied that the army had played any role in the Nazi take-over or indeed in politics at all.[36] As will be seen in a later chapter, his own politically tinged reporting from Washington was scarcely an illustration of this point. During his term of office the General was in close contact with American military leaders and according to one report in 1941, had the "professional respect" of these circles. (Thomsen commented on the fact that in the final years, the attachés had more freedom of access and contact with American officials than had the diplomats.) On his return to Germany in 1942, Boetticher was received by Hitler and served as advisor on American affairs to the *Oberkommando der Wehrmacht* (Military High Command). He was captured by the American 7th Army in April 1945 and retired.[37]

[36] *NYT* 15/4/33.
[37] *NYT* 13/4/41, 2/5/41. Thomsen to Woermann 21/10/39. *Pol Bez*/XIII/ 511820. Thomsen has also suggested that American officers were one source of Boetticher's confidence in a quick German victory. Letters, Thomsen to author, 14/7/63, 22/10/63.

CHAPTER 4

The German Diplomats and America Before the War

As the Third Reich and the New Deal took shape in the 1930's we have observed that Hitler's attitude toward Roosevelt and his works became increasingly hostile and contemptuous. What, however, did the German Embassy in Washington find regarding American opinion of Nazi Germany and its domestic and foreign policies? What was the state of the American nation as reported back to Berlin and what was to be the course of Roosevelt's foreign policy regarding Europe in the years before the outbreak of the European war? In general it may be said that the picture of America transmitted through the Washington Embassy and accepted at the *Wilhelmstrasse* was anything but cheerful from the German point of view. The diplomats were not apparently concerned to flatter Hitler's comfortable notions about the United States. They saw instead an America of ever increasing hostility to the Third Reich. They reported a public opinion offended by the internal policies of the Nazi regime and made anxious by external aggression. The diplomats were at pains to warn that economic power and determined political leadership would not be restrained indefinitely by isolationist sentiment and laws of neutrality. They insisted that here, in short, was a force to be reckoned in German calculations.

American reaction to national socialism was adverse from the start, according to reports reaching Berlin. Ambassador Prittwitz reported as early as March 1933 that Nazism had met with a wave of disfavor in the United States.[1] That same month the

[1] Prittwitz to Foreign Ministry 16/3/33, *DGFP*/C/I, p. 175. Prittwitz to Foreign Ministry 29/3/33, Documents of the Former German Embassy in Wash-

American Embassy in Berlin informed the Foreign Ministry of the concern felt in the United States at anti-Semitic tendencies in Germany, and in May Hull made "full and emphatic representations" to Ambassador Luther on this question. These formal approaches were regularly supplemented by reports of protest demonstrations, petitions, public denunciations and congressional resolutions, all presenting a picture of a public opinion considerably aroused.[2]

In March of 1934, Ambassador Luther reported further anti-Nazi manifestations in New York City including a mock trial of Hitler for murder ("this impossible insult") and later gave an itemized account of the points of friction with the United States.[3] The real problem was, he suggested, the prospect of national socialism in America, rather than in Germany, and American fears of Nazi subversion financed from Berlin were stressed. Luther had to admit a year later that anti-German propaganda had become so intense that the United States had become one of the main centers of anti-German agitation.[4] As the summer of 1935 progressed, the reports grew even more pessimistic. Leitner, the German Chargé d'Affaires, cabled in July that American reaction to anti-Semitic outbursts in Berlin that month had damaged the whole point of view regarding Germany, even in normally pro-German quarters.[5]

By 1938, a strong pessimism marked Ambassador Dieckhoff's reports, and Hull's representations on a wide range of disagree-

---

ington selected by American Historical Association, committee for the study of war documents, serial AHAI (hereafter *AHAI*) (*Po3 Deutsche Innere Politik*).

[2] Seckett to State Department 16/3/33, *FRUS*/1933/II, p. 322. Interview with Luther 3/5/33, *FRUS*/1933/II, p. 353. Washington Embassy to Foreign Ministry 25/6/33, *AHAI* (*Po3 Deutsche Innere Politik*).

[3] Ambassador (U.S.) to Foreign Ministry 3/3/34, *DGFP*/C/II, p. 552. Department III to Washington Embassy 20/3/34, *DGFP*/C/II, p. 641. Luther to Foreign Ministry 22/3/34, *DGFP*/C/II, p. 653.

[4] Luther to Foreign Ministry 18/6/35, *DGFP*/C/IV, p. 316. Memo (State Secretary) 18/6/34, *DGFP*/C/III, p. 36.

[5] Leitner to Foreign Ministry 24/7/35, *Akten betreffend politischer Beziehungen USA zu Deutschland* (hereafter *AHAI/Pol Bez*), IV. Leitner to Foreign Ministry 31/7/35, *DGFP*/C/IV, p. 515. La Guardia became a veritable *bête noir* in the German press. See for example *Voelkischer Beobachter* 5/3/37, 6/3/37, 17/3/37.

ments were vigorous.[6] The Washington Embassy left little doubt that German anti-Semitism, which Hull had denounced as "outrageous" and "frightful," underlay the most deeply seated prejudices of American public opinion about the Third Reich.[7] In November there occurred the appalling attacks on Jewish life and property allegedly in revenge for the assassination of a German diplomat in Paris. These "crystal night pogroms" which had so shocked the President ("I myself could scarcely believe that such things could occur in a twentieth century civilization"), and which led to the recall of the American Ambassador from Berlin, caused as well a profound indignation in public opinion, according to the Washington Embassy. Dieckhoff wrote of a "storm of anti-German feeling sweeping America."[8] Ambassador Wilson, who had cabled a description of the rioting from Berlin with the comment that "these pogroms dispel any hope of moderation in German-American relations," now confirmed from Washington Dieckhoff's description of American popular reaction to these events. "The blaze of hatred has to be seen to be believed," he cabled the American Chargé d'Affaires in Berlin.[9]

The storm that Dieckhoff spoke of swept him back to Berlin, not to return. His successor as chief of mission, Hans Thomsen, found that a full month later public opinion was still so incensed that he considered relations between the two countries to have reached "a decisive stage" over the Jewish issue. Freytag of the American Department, writing a summary of the situation based on these and other reports, concluded that "the rage against Germany has now reached proportions which could not have been observed in the World War."[10] However, this burst of

---

[6] Dieckhoff to Foreign Ministry 25/6/38, *DGFP*/D/I, p. 720. Memo (Dieckhoff) 28/7/38, *DGFP*/D/I, p. 724.

[7] Hull memo 15/8/35, *FRUS*/1935/II, pp. 404, 405.

[8] Roosevelt statement, *NYT* 16/11/38. Dieckhoff to Foreign Ministry 14/11/38, *DGFP*/D/IV, p. 639.

[9] Wilson to Hull 10/11/38, *FRUS*/1938/II, p. 395. Wilson to Hull 16/11/38, Wilson, *op. cit.*, p. 60. Wilson to Gilbert 1/12/38, *ibid.*, p. 87.

[10] Thomsen to Foreign Ministry 17/12/38, Auswaertiges Amt, *Buero des Unterstaatssekretaers, USA* (hereafter *UStS/USA*), vol. I/26297. Memo (Frey-

indignation marks the end of the period in which reaction to German domestic affairs dominated the Washington dispatches. By this time commentary was already focused increasingly on external policy.

The United States, its isolationist longings and its suspicions of the World War and the Versailles settlement much deepened by the persistent economic crisis, was in no mood to embrace collective security against a reviving Germany. German departure from the League of Nations and her rearmament and remilitarization of the Rhineland did not seem so terribly alarming across the Atlantic. The Spanish Civil War, the absorption of Austria, the dismemberment of Czechoslovakia and the march into Poland probably intensified isolationist determination even while arousing anxiety. Indeed, the Washington Embassy made little mention of American reactions to German foreign policy prior to 1937. Until that year the occasional foreign policy item often revealed a certain element of sympathy for German diplomatic goals as then understood. In May 1933, Hjalmar Schacht called Hitler's attention to this from Washington. There was, he wrote, a certain sentiment in America for more equitable treatment for Germany internationally. He pointed to sympathy in some congressional circles for the recovery of German colonies as well as understanding for German rearmament.[11] Luther confirmed this view in April 1935 when he cabled that in spite of the press slanders against the Nazi regime internally, German requests for equality of treatment internationally were held by many to be "just." There was some sympathy for German hostility to the League and in 1936 "considerable understanding" for the occupation of the Rhineland. Luther urged that this understanding would be sustained if Germany could present its foreign policy as one of national fulfillment to counteract the impression of aggression.[12]

---

tag) 9/12/38. *Pol Bez*/VIII/511581.

[11] Schacht to Foreign Ministry (for Hitler) 15/5/33, *DGFP*/C/I, p. 424.

[12] Luther to Neurath 8/4/35, *DGFP*/C/IV, pp. 24, 25. Luther to Propaganda Ministry 16/6/36, *AHAI, Pol Bez*/V.

If German activities in Europe were not unduly disturbing to American opinion prior to the absorption of Austria, however, German cooperation with Japan raised more comment. Luther pointed to these American suspicions in April 1935, and Ambassador Dodd raised the question with Foreign Minister von Neurath in November 1936 after the signing of the Anti-Comintern Pact with Japan.[13] In June Luther had informed Berlin that close German-Japanese relations constituted "a shadow from the Far East falling across German-American relations." This shadow deepened as Italy adhered to the Pact and appeared to give some substance to the American propaganda picture of the world-wide fascist conspiracy.[14]

Moreover, by the spring of 1937 American concern was reported to have increased regarding German policy in general. The problem was, the Embassy explained, that everything Germany did was becoming automatically attributed by American public opinion to *Angriffslust* (thirst for aggression).[15] In December Dieckhoff expounded on this at length in the course of a report on the first nine months of his mission. As the Rome-Berlin Axis began to take shape, Americans conjured up a vision of international conspiracy. This was accompanied, according to the Ambassador, by a shift in emphasis toward an ideological interpretation of world developments which involved a contest between democracy and totalitarianism, freedom and despotism, Christianity and paganism. He warned of the growing conviction that the export of Nazism had become the prime objective of German foreign policy. This conception of a "Nazintern" had been strengthened, Dieckhoff explained, by a number of expressions both in Germany and America in recent months of the international solidarity of people of German blood and the obligations which these *Volksdeutsche* had to the Third Reich.[16]

[13] Luther to Neurath 8/4/35, *DGFP/C/IV*, pp. 24, 25. Dodd, *Diary* 25/11/36, p. 371. Luther to Foreign Ministry 15/2/37, *AHAI, AAP/V*.

[14] Luther to Foreign Ministry 6/4/37, *AHAI, AAP/V*. Thomsen to Foreign Ministry 12/8/38, *AHAI (P03 Tschechoslovakei)*.

[15] Washington Embassy to Foreign Ministry 26/4/37, *AHAI, AAP/V*.

[16] Dieckhoff to Weizsaeker 20/12/37, *DGFP/D/I*, p. 659.

Thus, prior to 1938, American comment on German foreign policy as reported to the *Wilhelmstrasse* tended to be general, sketchy and marked by vague anxieties rather than specific criticism. With the *Anschluss* of Austria in March 1938, however, the tone changed to one of continuous and hostile examination of German aggression. Dieckhoff reported that the State Department was filled "with powerless rage" over the Austrian affair. By March 22, he cabled that the *Anschluss* had provoked "a fantastic press reaction," that the American people had been presented with a picture of "the Prussian wolf raging among the Austrian sheep."[17]

As Hitler turned his attention to Czechoslovakia in May and June, Dieckhoff reported on growing concern about German aggressive designs in that country and the strength of Anglo-French propaganda to this effect.[18] By this time, according to reports from the Consulate in Chicago, the growing Czech crisis had stirred even the isolationist Midwest to the conviction that a break with Germany was inevitable.[19] The Munich settlement in September was reported to have been well received at first, although by November Dieckhoff told Ambassador Dirksen in London that disillusionment was again setting in. He reported to Berlin later in the month that Munich was now reckoned by the Americans to have been a decisive setback for England.[20]

American uneasiness turned to renewed hostility with the occupation of Prague by the Germans in March 1939.[21] Thomsen, now apparently thoroughly alarmed at the extreme anti-

[17] Dieckhoff to Foreign Ministry 14/3/38 and 15/3/38, *Pol Bez*/VI/511516, 511518. Dieckhoff to Weizsaeker 22/3/38, *DGFP*/D/I, p. 696.

[18] Dieckhoff to Weizsaeker 31/5/38, *DGFP*/D/II, p. 370. Dieckhoff to Foreign Office 15/6/38, *AHAI* (*Po3 Tschechoslovakei*).

[19] Isolationist sentiment, the Consul added, could not block administration policy. Reports of Chicago Consulate 2/8/38, 7/8/38, *AHAI* (*Po3 Tschechoslovakei*).

[20] Dieckhoff to Foreign Ministry 30/8/38, *DGFP*/D/IV, p. 633. Thomsen to Foreign Ministry 1/9/38, *DGFP*/D/II, p. 680.

[21] According to Jay P. Moffatt of the European Division at the State Department, the occupation of Prague ended all discussion at the State Department about returning Ambassador Wilson to Berlin. Moffatt, *op. cit.*, p. 232.

German tendency in the United States, wrote at length later in March of a "psychosis" transcending that of 1917. He warned that the "incredulous and easily led majority of the mentally dull American people has completely succumbed to the insidious view that Germany is America's public enemy number one." German colonial desires and activities in Latin America were now pictured as the foundations for the establishment of German bases to attack the Panama Canal and the United States itself. Certain circles, he warned, had a vested interest in sustaining this hostile mood for their own purposes.[22] In addition, Hitler's disdain for Roosevelt's mediation attempt that month had resulted in a growing conviction in America of the inevitability of a European war. Opinion was now, Thomsen reported, "unfailingly pessimistic and spiteful."[23]

The final month of peace was marked in America by both resignation to a European war and belief in the unique guilt of Germany for that war. On August 8, the Embassy was able to report that in the event of conflict, American public opinion was already quite convinced in advance of Germany's responsibility.[24] This view was substantially sharpened by the signing of the Nazi-Soviet Pact of August 21. The Pact, Thomsen wrote, had caused consternation in the State Department. The feeling in Washington was that the balance had now shifted to the Axis. However, Thomsen warned that this had made the threat to the United States seem even more stark and it had in fact strengthened Roosevelt's resolve to support the democracies.[25] On September 2, the final remarks regarding American opinion of German pre-war policy were sent to Berlin. Germany was held to have been insincere regarding the final proposals to Poland; German ex-

---

[22] Thomsen to Foreign Ministry 18/3/39, *DGFP/D/VI*, p. 35. Hull, *op. cit.*, p. 615. Thomsen to Foreign Ministry 27/7/39, *DGFP/D/VI*, p. 131.

[23] Thomsen to Foreign Ministry 28/4/39 and 29/4/39, *DGFP/D/VI*, pp. 357, 363.

[24] Thomsen to Foreign Ministry 10/8/39, *DGFP/D/VI*, p. 8.

[25] Thomsen to Foreign Ministry 22/8/39, *DGFP/D/VII*, pp. 180, 181. Thomsen to Foreign Ministry 24/8/39, *DGFP/D/VII*, p. 281.

planations about the cause of the war were "totally rejected"; Germany was considered exclusively responsible; and the Germans were held to be an incurably war-like race. He concluded with the statement made by a State Department official to a German journalist to the effect that unlike 1917, "there is no division of opinion. Your government already stands convicted."[26]

✓This was the discomforting picture of Germany in America as reported back to Berlin. But what of America itself as seen through German diplomatic eyes? Although unemployment, labor strife and Mr. Roosevelt's picture of "one third of a nation ill-clothed, ill-housed, and ill-fed" could have formed the basis for reports of a weakened, divided and demoralized country, in fact exactly the opposite tone was adopted regarding the American political, economic and social scene in the dispatches to Berlin. There were to be sure occasional reports of economic distress, social tension, anti-Semitism and labor unrest which were sent to Germany.[27] But in general, the picture was rather that of great economic power and social cohesion and of a force in international affairs that Germany dare not have arraigned against her.[28] It is of some interest to note at this point by way of contrast that the German press painted a far more dismal picture than that conveyed by the diplomats. Social strife, unemployment, poverty and an appalling Jewish influence were some of the features of the American way of life to which newspaper readers in the Reich were treated during the 1930's.[29]

The general tone of the Washington dispatches, on the other hand, was set by Luther in 1935 when he warned that one could

[26] Thomsen to Foreign Ministry 2/9/39, *DGFP/D/VII*, p. 520.

[27] Schacht to Foreign Ministry 6/5/33, *DGFP/C/I*, p. 392. Sallett to Propaganda Ministry 3/8/34, *DGFP/C/III*, p. 1151. Luther to Foreign Ministry 6/4/37, *AHAI, AAP/V*.

[28] Washington Embassy to Foreign Ministry 14/7/37, *AHAI, AAP/V* ("Just what we are trying to accomplish with national socialism in Germany"). See *NYT* 14/8/34 for additional reports along this line.

[29] See for example: *Voelkischer Beobachter* 19/9/33, 19/5/36, 15/3/37, 29/12/38. *Angriff* 15/8/35, 7/1/38. *Frankfurter Zeitung* 9/1/38. Neurath told Dodd he was "extremely embarrassed" by German press excesses. Dodd, *Diary* 12/3/37, p. 397.

not overlook the possibility of the "immense economic forces of this country" acting against Germany. In June of that year Luther described the Americans as a skillful people in possession of vast natural and technical resources. He warned that neither geographical distance nor poor government offered any escape from the conclusion that Americans would be "through the sheer weight of their own momentum a decisive factor in world affairs." He urged his superiors to remember that Germany's doom in the World War had been finally sealed by American power and that it was, therefore, of critical importance to prevent this power from becoming anti-German. This two-fold emphasis on American power and its relevance for Germany is a theme from which neither Luther nor his successors, Dieckhoff and Thomsen, ever deviated.[30]

Much of the discussion of the American domestic scene was focused on the German-Americans and how they might be manipulated to advance the cause of the Third Reich. More optimistic about German cultural prospects than his successor, Luther in June 1935 advocated extensive educational activities among German elements to balance the obvious cultural advantages of Britain in America. Specifically, he suggested a cultural offensive which would reawaken the German-American community and advance German culture into the American vacuum. Luther's discussion revealed a fatal misunderstanding of the assimilation process which had affected the German-Americans along with the other immigration groups by this time. There was a tendency in some Berlin circles to see the German-Americans as a kind of irredendist problem. Dieckhoff did not fall into this error, as he made quite clear in a report in January 1938.[31]

The Ambassador began by examining the possibility of strengthening the political role of the German-Americans. He admitted that the question was significant due to the accelerating

[30] Luther to Neurath 8/4/35, *DGFP*/C/IV, p. 27. Luther to Propaganda Ministry 28/6/35, *DGFP*/C/IV, p. 384. See for example Dieckhoff to Weizsaeker 20/12/37, *DGFP*/D/I, p. 660.

[31] Luther to Propaganda Ministry 28/6/35, *DGFP*/C/IV, p. 385. Dieckhoff to Foreign Ministry 7/1/38, *DGFP*/D/I, p. 669.

drift from isolationism. Yet, unlike Luther, he found the prospects of such an attempt completely negative. In the first place,
he pointed out that the German element was numerically weak
and thoroughly assimilated. Therefore, they could not be compared with the German communities in Transylvania or the
Sudetenland or even in Brazil. Those speaking German and
having a real consciousness of being German numbered only
four to five million.[32] In response to the notion that the Nazi
party in Germany had also been small and still had come to
power, Dieckhoff was firm: "In the United States this is not
possible."

In America, he continued, the Germans have had little political influence.[33] Furthermore, the German-Americans were never
more divided than now into a small group of Nazis, a small group
of anti-Nazis and the great indifferent mass. Therefore, he insisted, folk unity among the Germans in America must simply be
written off as hopeless. To the suggestion of establishing even a
small band of American S.S. of ten to twenty thousand young
men "ready for any sacrifice," Dieckhoff was contemptuous
and sarcastic: "I cannot express my warning against this viewpoint with sufficient emphasis." Such cloak and dagger notions
were perhaps all right for the Balkans but most certainly not in
the United States. "I know that scarcely anyone sincerely be-
lieves in anything so nonsensical, but I repeat that such ideas are
not merely childish, they are dangerous." To seek to reverse the
melting pot or to attempt to establish a totalitarian regime in
America would, Dieckhoff warned, arouse the most violent hostility, receive the closest attention of the government, and be
repressed. He urged a severance of all connections with the
German-Americans. "We must," he concluded, "make a clean
sweep of it."

[32] This was also the figure given to Goering by Ambassador Bullitt, who
added that there were in America "enough trees to hang the five million German
speaking Americans if that were necessary," quoted in Craig, *op. cit.*, p. 657.

[33] Prittwitz made the same point in his memoirs. He believed that the German-Americans had contributed to "bourgeois attitudes of law and order," but
had not provided any political leadership. Prittwitz, *op. cit.*, p. 214.

It is to be noted, then, that the observations of the German diplomats in Washington as well as the recommendations based on these observations concerning the German-Americans were restrained and for the most part exhibited caution and realism, two traits for which the more ideologically minded circles in Berlin were not conspicuous. As a result, the image of America thus compounded had constantly to be defended against the efforts of Nazi groups in both countries who sought to distort it along ideological lines.

In Berlin there was, for example, the affair of the Rechenberg pamphlet. This booklet, produced in 1937 by a former German immigrant to the United States, was entitled *Roosevelt — Amerika — Eine Gefahr* (Roosevelt — America — A Danger) and presented the picture of an America totally in the clutches of Jewish interests and of Roosevelt as a front man for communism. A copy of this was sent by the Chief of the Chancellory to the Propaganda and Foreign Ministries with the note that Hitler had read it with "great interest." Davidsen of the American desk at the *Wilhelmstrasse* responded that the book had no claim to reliability and no factual basis whatever; that the charge regarding communism in America "has not been proved and cannot be proved"; that the general impression was completely distorted and could only create confusion and "gravely imperil German-American relations." His colleague, Freytag, added to this critique that the pamphlet was one-sided, especially in discussing the Jewish problem in America. Roosevelt, he pointed out, citing one example of distortion, could not possibly be held responsible for the speeches of someone like Mayor La Guardia.[34]

The Embassy in Washington had also to resist various projects for the manipulation of public opinion and the German-Americans suggested to them from Berlin. A proposal which originated with Goering in 1938 that efforts be made to repatriate *Volksdeutsche* (persons of German blood) as well as *Reichsdeutsche*

---

[34] Chief of Chancellory to Foreign and Propaganda Ministries 15/10/37, *DGFP/D/I*, p. 642. Memo (Davidsen) 28/10/37, *DGFP/D/I*, p. 642. Memo (Freytag) 15/11/37, *DGFP/D/I*, pp. 643, 646.

(persons of German nationality) from America was rebuffed by Dieckhoff as hopelessly unrealistic and potentially dangerous.[35] In general Dieckhoff opposed tours and special missions sent out to America from Berlin to gather information and influence American affairs. He was unreceptive to Ribbentrop's suggestion in a "Dear Hans" letter in 1938 to a series of American lecture tours to be undertaken by prominent Germans such as Schacht in order to sway American opinion. In a "Dear Joachim" reply, Dieckhoff rebuffed the idea. "The ground," he wrote, "is so hard at present that no seed can sprout."[36]

If the Ambassador was unenthusiastic about lecture tours, he was positively appalled by a notion late in 1938 to send a former Consul General in New York to the United States to meet German officials and American friends of Germany in order to explore "the possibilities of collaborating with Roosevelt's opponents." Dieckhoff's reaction was vigorously negative and the mere suggestion of such a project apparently convinced him that his reports had not cleared the fog of misconceptions in Berlin about America. He had previously inquired if there was any use in sending American press clippings revealing the state of American opinion ("who reads them?") and he now complained: "My opinion has not been sought. Please trust my judgment. I do have some knowledge of this country and people."[37]

Without doubt the most continuous and obnoxious nuisance in this area was the pro-Nazi Friends of the New Germany, later called the German-American Bund, and its connections with Berlin.[38] This small but noisy group of German-Americans was proud of its high contacts in the Third Reich and evidently succeeded in conveying to party circles in Berlin a grossly exag-

[35] Memo (Weizsaeker) 16/12/38, *DGFP/D/IV*, p. 651. Memo (Dieckhoff) 16/12/38, *DGFP/D/IV*, p. 653.

[36] Ribbentrop to Dieckhoff 29/3/38, *DGFP/D/I*, p. 698. Dieckhoff to Ribbentrop 14/4/38, *DGFP/D/I*, p. 703.

[37] Memoranda (Weizsaeker) 24/12/38, 30/12/38, *DGFP/D/IV*, pp. 665, 667. Dieckhoff to Weizsaeker 12/1/39, *DGFP/D/IV*, pp. 671–672.

[38] For the early background and formation of the Bund, see Rogge, *op. cit.*, p. 17. Also, Remak, *The Bund and German American Relations*.

gerated picture of its own power and influence as well as a distorted image of the United States quite at variance with the diplomatic reports. As a result, the Embassy pressed continuously for dissociation between the Bund and anything or anyone official in Germany. Special concern was felt regarding connections with the party *Auslandsorganisation*, whose leader issued bombastic proclamations ("A German day in Buenos Aires or Chicago concerns us just as deeply as the struggle of our brethren near our frontiers"), which were, however, more propaganda than substance.[39] Hitler, who had told Ambassador Dodd that any allegation that German-Americans owed allegiance to Germany was "a Jewish lie" and that he would personally "throw any official into the North Sea who sent Nazi propaganda to the United States," became involved in the problem in 1934 when he was warned about the Bund by the chairman of the Steuben Society, a German-American group in New York. Hitler professed complete agreement regarding the participation of *Reichsdeutsche* in such groups. He promised to see to a rigorous enforcement of directives prohibiting such participation.[40]

These assurances failed to impress the American Embassy in Berlin, which pressed on the *Wilhelmstrasse* the American concern about control from Germany of the Bund and similar groups. Emphasizing traditional American sensitivity to connections between immigration groups and the former mother countries, the American diplomats urged a total severing of ties by Germany with the German-Americans. Yet neither these pressures nor Dieckhoff's cables explaining the damage wrought by these "stupid and noisy activities" were sufficient to remove the problem.[41]

[39] Washington Embassy to Foreign Ministry 11/2/34, *DGFP/C/II*, p. 467. *Voelkischer Beobachter* 12/9/36, 14/10/38. Bohle to Hess 16/11/34, *DGFP/ C/III*, p. 1119. Bohle testimony, *Case II/XXVIII*, p. 13492.
[40] Dodd, *Diary* 7/3/34, p. 100, and 21/5/35, p. 254. Lammers to Foreign Ministry 2/11/34, *DGFP/C/III*, p. 1115.
[41] Memo (Weizsaeker) 2/10/37, *DGFP/D/I*, p. 635. Memo (Freytag) 11/10/37, *DGFP/D/I*, p. 635. Dieckhoff to Mackensen 24/11/37, *DGFP/D/I*, p. 648.

Regarding any really systematic cultural offensive during these years, there existed of course the usual agencies of propaganda at the Embassy as well as the German Library of Information and the Transocean News Service in New York. In addition, there were the sporadic efforts through the various means described above to exercise some influence in this area. However, it is clear that the efforts by the more realistically minded diplomats had a certain success in dissuading the Nazi government from some of its projects of propaganda. The directives issued restraining the contacts of German citizens and officials with American public life do not suggest any really persistent interest in or at least hope for turning American opinion in a pro-German direction. However, the Washington Embassy had to deal with a situation in which American opinion was increasingly inclined to believe in the existence of a vast program in America sponsored by the Reich government.

CHAPTER 5

The German Diplomats and American Foreign Policy Before the War

ALTHOUGH INTERESTED in the American domestic scene, the German diplomats in Washington naturally kept a very close watch on foreign policy. In their analysis of these diplomatic developments in the United States before September 1939, they were essentially describing a tension between an increasingly interventionist President on the one hand and a stubbornly isolationist public opinion and Congress on the other. The warnings sounded in the "quarantine speech" in the autumn of 1937, for example, had to be balanced against the Neutrality Act of the same year. This made prediction of American actions, involved as they were with a host of domestic considerations, especially difficult. It also obliged the Foreign Ministry to take careful note of the attitudes of Mr. Roosevelt and of his close advisors in the field of foreign affairs.

In the dispatches Secretary of State Cordell Hull, who was described by Dieckhoff as "an idealist who lives somewhat up in the clouds," was generally dissociated from the more extreme anti-German tendencies and manifestations.[1] In spite of Hull's moderation, however, Dieckhoff was convinced by 1938 that there existed in the State Department an anti-German majority led by Francis Sayre, George Messersmith, Undersecretary Welles and J. P. Moffatt, Chief of the European Department.[2]

[1] Luther to Foreign Ministry 4/6/36, *AHAl/Pol Bez/V*. Dieckhoff to Weizsaeker 20/12/37, *DGFP/D/I*, p. 458. Dieckhoff to Foreign Ministry 25/10/37, *DGFP/D/I*, p. 639.
[2] Dieckhoff to Foreign Ministry 26/1/38, *Pol Bez/V/511486*. Dieckhoff to Foreign Ministry 25/6/38, *DGFP/D/I*, p. 719. Messersmith certainly entertained

To Ambassador William E. Dodd, who served at Berlin from 1933 to 1938, there was a generally negative reaction. Foreign Minister von Neurath found Dodd's views "extremely confused" and so vague that he could not reply to them.[3] Dodd, who admitted to "a sense of horror" when he looked at Hitler, made no attempt to conceal his loathing for the Nazi regime. A distinguished historian of lofty Jeffersonian ideals but without previous diplomatic experience, he began his embassy in high hopes. His health and spirit, however, were broken by the harsh and illiberal realities of the Third Reich and his diary recorded the mounting depression and isolation ("nothing can be done," "what can I do?" "the tension is unbearable").[4] On the occasion of an anti-Nazi speech by Dodd in Washington early in 1938, Dieckhoff wired that the Ambassador had "emptied his chamber pot before our door" and protested to the State Department against "this insolent breach of the most elementary propriety." Dodd's position became untenable when, contrary to his wish, the American Chargé at Berlin joined the *Corps Diplomatique* at the 1937 Nuremberg party rally, and he resigned shortly thereafter.[5]

The point has been made by the former French Ambassador at Berlin, André François-Poncet, that the Germans might have learned something of value from their experience with Dodd. Conceding the American's temperamental unsuitability for his post, the French diplomat added: "All the same, here was an excellent man of strong character . . . a singularly honorable

the deepest suspicions about the Nazi regime. See his vigorous attack on the German leadership in 1933. Hull, *op. cit.*, p. 242. Memo 2/2/38, *Pol Bez*/VI/ 511499. See comment on this in Rothfels, "Adam zu Trott und das State Department," *Vierteljahreshefte fuer Zeitgeschichte*, July 1959.

[3] *DGFP*/C/II, p. 12. Dodd himself recorded in his diary that "it is clear that some dislike of me is arising here now in official circles." *Diary* 15/10/33, p. 41. Memo (Neurath) 6/7/35, *DGFP*/C/IV, p. 420.

[4] Dodd, *Diary* 13/7/34, 12/8/33. *NYT* 6/7/33. Dodd, *Diary* 6/2/35, 29/10/37, 3/11/37. Roosevelt found Dodd's letters "the most depressing I have ever read." Ickes, *Diary*, II, p. 494. Dieckhoff to Foreign Ministry 5/8/37. *DGFP*/D/I, p. 627.

[5] Dieckhoff to Foreign Ministry 14/1/38, *DGFP*/D/I, p. 679. For Hitler's reaction, Lammers to Neurath, 21/1/38, *DGFP*/D/I, p. 685.

example of American idealism . . . Had the Nazis studied his reactions more carefully, they would have spared themselves many a disagreeable surprise in store for them."⁶ This lesson was lost, however, and there was only considerable relief felt in German diplomatic circles with the appointment in January 1938 of the able career diplomat, Hugh Wilson. No less repelled than Dodd at the Nazi regime, he was far more adroit at concealing his personal inclinations during his ten months in Berlin. Thus Ribbentrop found him sympathetic and Weizsaeker termed him "fair and independent."⁷

Finally, there was another American diplomat who, although not directly connected with German-American relations, played some role in forming German impressions of American diplomatic policy. This was Joseph Kennedy, the American Ambassador in London. Herbert Dirksen, his German colleague, reported to Weizsaeker in June 1938 certain remarks which Kennedy allegedly made to him concerning German relations with the United States. The American was, Dirksen wrote, impressed by many of Hitler's accomplishments and was sure of American understanding for the German position on the Jewish question. He quoted Kennedy as expressing confidence in overwhelmingly pro-German sentiments in America in the event of a conflict. Dirksen apparently accepted the view of the American envoy that Roosevelt was on bad terms with the State Department and his picture of the President as "cool" and by no means a member of the extreme anti-German school. In spite of Dieckhoff's subsequent warning about Kennedy's "too optimistic" views, Dirksen thought it urgent that Kennedy go to Berlin to see Hitler. This visit never took place.⁸

⁶ François-Poncet, *op. cit.*, pp. 270-271.
⁷ According to one American diplomat, Roosevelt had by this time quite given up hope of doing anything about Germany from within. The decision was taken, therefore, to appoint a career diplomat. Davies, *Mission to Moscow*, p. 255. Memo (Ribbentrop) 29/4/38, *DGFP/D/I*, p. 704.
⁸ Dirksen to Weizsaeker 13/6/38, *DGFP/D/I*, pp. 714, 715, 717. Dirksen to Weizsaeker 20/7/38, *Pol Bez*/VIII/511563. Kennedy allegedly identified Wilson, Grew and himself as the only diplomats who had the President's ear.

But clearly it was, in the minds of the Germans, Franklin Roosevelt who dominated the American foreign policy scene in the 1930's. The dispatches refer again and again to "Roosevelt's policy," "Roosevelt's calculations," "Roosevelt's tactics." There was an increasing emphasis throughout the period on Roosevelt's obsession with foreign policy and his determination to cut for himself a role of decisive importance in world affairs.[9]

Furthermore, the dispatches as early as 1934 made clear that this role was an anti-German one motivated by a profound personal hostility to the Nazi regime. Luther cabled in February 1937 that "Roosevelt has left no doubt about which side his sympathies are on in the event of conflict." Following an interview with Gilbert of the American Embassy, Counsellor Freytag noted the distressing fact that "the President and Mrs. Roosevelt do not love Germany." At the same time the *New York Times* reported that in diplomatic circles in Berlin Roosevelt was, by the end of October 1937, already regarded as the "chief architect" of the resistance to Germany; a kind of "Wilson quicker on the trigger."[10] Asked to comment on Kennedy's statement that Roosevelt was not really anti-German but merely misinformed, Dieckhoff would have none of it. Kennedy was a politician and the assertion that he could give Roosevelt better information simply "cut no ice" because, Dieckhoff insisted, volition and not misinformation was at the base of Roosevelt's anti-German activity.[11]

However, Roosevelt was seen almost as a moderate compared

Woermann to Kordt 16/8/33, *DGFP/D/I*, p. 725. Dirksen to Weizsaeker 13/10/38, *DGFP/D/IV*, pp. 634, 636.

[9] Washington Embassy to Foreign Ministry 14/7/37, *AHAI/AAP/V*. Prittwitz to Foreign Ministry 16/3/33, *DGFP/C/I*, p. 173. Luther to Foreign Ministry 23/6/33, *AHAI, AAP/IV*.

[10] Leitner to Foreign Ministry 26/4/34, *AHAI, Pol Bez/IV*. Luther to Foreign Ministry 15/2/36, *AHAI, AAP/V*. In fact Roosevelt's suspicions of Germany, Italy and Japan were expressed at least as early as 1933. *Letters*, vol. I, p. 370. Memo (Freytag) 9/10/37, *DGFP/D/I*, p. 637. *NYT* 11/10/37.

[11] Dirksen to Weizsaeker 13/6/38, *DGFP/D/I*, p. 714. Dieckhoff to Dirksen 2/11/38, *DGFP/D/IV*, p. 637. Dirksen to Weizsaeker 20/7/38, *DGFP/D/I*, p. 723.

to certain figures in American public life, notably Treasury Secretary Henry Morgenthau and Interior Secretary Harold Ickes. Morgenthau's anti-German bias was noted by Luther ("a deep revulsion, indeed hate for us") early in 1934 while Ickes' flamboyant speeches were the source of unending protests to the State Department.[12] Indeed, Ickes slowly replaced Mayor La Guardia as the American *bête noir* of the German press (*"Ickes der Deutschfresser"*). Hitler himself was reported to be "exceedingly irritated" at Ickes and mentioned him by name in a speech early in 1939.[13]

Thus, although Thomsen could report in September 1938 that Roosevelt did nothing rashly and sought to gain time, the President's course had in fact become so alarming to the *Wilhelmstrasse* that in November Woermann of the Political Department found it necessary to compose a memorandum on the subject "Political consequences of a possible rupture of German-American diplomatic relations." This event would be, he wrote, the logical conclusion of Roosevelt's policy. The United States was being prepared by the President for war and this policy was so generally approved that "the entire country is behind him almost unanimously," hardly an accurate statement in 1938.[14] In 1939, Roosevelt's anti-German bias was seen to harden ("a pathological hatred"). In March, Thomsen warned that Roosevelt's aim had become in fact the annihilation of Nazi Germany and nullification of the New Order in Europe.[15]

---

[12] Dieckhoff noted for example Roosevelt's irritation over Ickes' refusal to sell helium to Germany. Dieckhoff to Foreign Ministry 21/5/38, *DGFP*/D/I, p. 706. Luther to Foreign Ministry 6/1/34, *AHAI, Pol Bez*/III. Thomsen to Foreign Ministry 21/12/38, *UStS/USA*/I/26308. Memo by Hull (7/7/38) and Welles (21/12/38) of German protests regarding Ickes are found in *FRUS*/1938/II, pp. 442, 451.

[13] *Voelkischer Beobachter* 22/12/38. *Frankfurter Zeitung* 22/12/38. Gilbert to State Department 27/12/38, *FRUS*/1938/II, p. 454. *NYT* 25/12/38. Ickes, *op. cit.*, p. 573 ,vol. II.

[14] Thomsen to Foreign Ministry 10/9/38, *DGFP*/D/II, p. 735. Memo (Woermann) 20/11/38, *DGFP*/D/II, p. 644.

[15] Thomsen to Foreign Ministry 17/5/39, *DGFP*/D/II, p. 533. Thomsen to Foreign Ministry 27/3/39, *DGFP*/D/VI, p. 129.

The President's doctrine of "all measures short of war" was, Thomsen insisted, merely a camouflage to cover the unleashing of economic war, rearmament and the penetration of Latin America. Roosevelt was, of course, a realist and recognized the serious problems arising from the outbreak of war. But he had become inwardly convinced that a German victory would lead to American "humiliation and ignominy." Thus Roosevelt was determined not on peace but on a trial of strength between democracy and totalitarianism. In this trial, Roosevelt regarded the European democracies as America's first line of defense. The foundations for this new world role were now being laid in the step-up of production and raw material processing, military maneuvers, renewed efforts to repeal the Neutrality Acts and Roosevelt's general plan for economic rather than military support, all to be accompanied by the most ruthless propaganda.[16] Consul General Wiedemann in San Francisco reinforced this gloomy picture of Roosevelt's direction of foreign policy by sending on to Berlin an assertion by the influential journalist Karl von Wiegand that

> Roosevelt is Hitler's most dangerous opponent. Roosevelt fights for his democratic aims with the same fanatic idealism as does the Fuehrer for national socialism. Britain and France are no longer dragging America behind them. Today, America is dragging them both before her.[17]

The Embassy found evidence of Roosevelt's new conception of his role in the various appeals made to the dictators prior to the war. Thomsen wired that the President's message in April 1939, requesting that Germany promise not to attack certain specified countries, had been widely popular with all segments of American opinion. It was, Thomsen reported, another step in Roosevelt's goal of "weakening and isolating the totalitarian states" and forcing Hitler and Mussolini to show their hand, while he appeared before domestic and foreign opinion an apostle of

---

[16] Thomsen to Foreign Ministry 2/5/39, *DGFP*/D/VI, p. 407.
[17] Wiedemann to Weizsaeker 17/4/39, *DGFP*/D/VI, p. 272.

peace. Dieckhoff back in Berlin added his own view of the matter when he warned Weizsaeker that Roosevelt would behave like Wilson, that is, a disclaimer followed by an expeditionary force.[18]

Hitler's contemptuous and slashing reply to the telegram was reported to have invoked a "pessimistic and hateful reaction" and a growing conviction of the immediacy of war. Roosevelt's final peace appeals in August were acknowledged perfunctorily and Thomsen labeled them frantic efforts to isolate Germany. The German press entered harsher judgments.[19]

Thus the picture was presented of the American President as a dedicated and determined figure of deeply felt democratic and anti-Nazi convictions, rising to a position of leadership in an anti-totalitarian front. An adroit politician, he was held to be restrained by political realities but the initiative in American foreign relations was clearly in his hands. Foreign policy, as Thomsen expressed it, was "bound up with the personality of Roosevelt."[20]

The diplomats were, of course, concerned not only with Roosevelt and his colleagues but about the tendencies of American foreign policy itself. The problem of isolationism was very prominent. It is noteworthy that in these dispatches there was never any complacency about American isolationism, nor illusion that this attitude was either total or could be assumed under all circumstances. Indeed, the diplomats probably underestimated the strength of isolationist sentiment. In any event, little en-

---

[18] Roosevelt to Hitler 15/4/39, *DGFP*/D/VI, p. 243. See circular to German missions in the designated countries 17/4/39, *DGFP*/D/VI, p. 264. Thomsen to Foreign Ministry 17/4/39, *UStS/USA*/Roosevelt Telegram/38985. Thomsen to Foreign Ministry 20/4/39, *DGFP*/D/VI, p. 297. Dieckhoff to Weizsaeker 25/4/39, *DGFP*/D/VI, p. 331.

[19] Thomsen to Foreign Ministry 28/4/39, 29/4/39, *UStS/USA*/Roosevelt Tel/38985. Mussolini, who was fond of ridiculing Roosevelt's disability, declared the gesture to be "the result of polio." Ciano, *Diary* 1939–1943, entry for 15/4/39, p. 70. *NYT* 26/8/39. *Voelkischer Beobachter* 20/8/38, 6/1/39, 2/2/39; *Frankfurter Zeitung* 6/1/39, 2/2/39.

[20] Thomsen to Foreign Ministry 17/5/39, *DGFP*/D/VI, p. 527.

couragement was given to the comfortable notion, widely circulated in the German press, that American isolationism was an insuperable barrier to intervention in a European war.[21]

Isolationist feeling was deeply colored by the memories of the World War, according to the analysis of the Washington Embassy, and these memories had been kept alive by the investigations of Senator Nye into the role of the armaments industry at that time and by certain revisionist books on the background of the American entry in 1917. Although this experience tended to strengthen isolationist tendencies, Luther made clear that it also encouraged a conviction about the inevitability of European conflict and perhaps as well a certain resignation about a subsequent American involvement. Moreover, although American entanglement was termed impossible at that time (1935), yet Luther warned that this attitude "could change overnight" under certain circumstances, especially if Japan became involved.[22]

Dieckhoff contributed a lengthy discussion of isolationism in America in December 1937.[23] He began by agreeing with the estimate of the isolationists themselves that they represented at that time the majority view and he asserted that this was certainly to Germany's advantage. However, he warned against the confusion of isolationism with positive friendship toward Germany. He mentioned the considerable anti-German sentiment even among isolationists. "We must not," he said, "delude ourselves about that." And if, he concluded, the isolationists should be aroused, they would turn their activity against Germany. His basic point was put bluntly: "We must not count on American isolationism as an axiom."

The European crises in 1938 continued to erode isolationist

---

[21] This picture of a totally isolationist America was avidly peddled in the *Voelkischer Beobachter*, especially in 1939. See for example issues of 8/1/39, 22/3/39, 8/7/39, 29/11/39.

[22] Washington Embassy to Foreign Ministry 26/4/39, 9/5/35, 1/8/36, *AHAI, AAP*/IV, V. Luther to Neurath 8/4/35, *DGFP/C/IV*, pp. 23, 26.

[23] Dieckhoff to Foreign Ministry 7/12/37, *DGFP/D/I*, p. 653. Dieckhoff to Foreign Ministry 21/12/37, *AAP*/III/514064.

influence as the conviction grew that neutrality was aiding the aggressor.[24] After the Austrian *Anschluss*, Dieckhoff warned that "Some motive will be found to get America in." Thomsen felt it necessary to report that the isolationists were in fact rapidly losing ground everywhere except in the Midwest, where interventionism was still considered a sacrilege.[25] Furthermore, he continued, propaganda shrewdly managed by the administration in terms of a "spiritual mobilization" was having its effect. Concerned with a massive shift in the balance of power and possible disruption of world trade, Thomsen was sure that the Americans could never voluntarily concede the rights of the totalitarian powers. Concluding with a comment upon the chances of an active American intervention in the event of war, the Chargé suggested that it depended on whether the totalitarian powers appeared to be winning. Against intervention were admittedly the fear of the U.S.S.R., high taxes, and finally the cautioning influence of the armed forces.[26] However, Dieckhoff warned in August that if Germany chose force to resolve the Czech crisis, the United States would be with the Western Allies. "I consider it my duty to emphasize this very strongly," he added.[27]

This cautious appraisal of American isolationism was reflected in the analysis offered of American neutrality legislation. These acts, passed during 1935 to 1937 and often regarded in both Europe and America as firm barriers against any American international entanglement, were never so regarded in the Washington reports. From the outset, the view was taken that these acts were signed by a reluctant President pressured by public opinion. But, as we have seen, American public opinion was a changeable

[24] Dieckhoff to Foreign Ministry 2/2/36, *AAP*/IV/514076. Dieckhoff to Weizsaeker 22/3/38, *DGFP*/D/I, p. 697. Thomsen to Foreign Ministry 12/8/38. *DGFP*/D/I, p. 726.

[25] See also statement on Midwestern opinion from Chicago Consulate 7/8/38 *AHAI* (*Po3 Tschechoslovakei*). The German press often eulogized "The real Americans of the Midwest." *Voelkischer Beobachter* 1/1/39.

[26] Thomsen to Foreign Ministry 12/8/38, *DGFP*/D/I, p. 726. Thomsen to Foreign Ministry 13/4/39, *Pol Bez*/XI/511717.

[27] Dieckhoff to Foreign Ministry 27/8/38, *DGFP*/D/II, p. 981.

thing and the President a masterful politician. During the debate on the proposals, Luther reported that although they had been applauded by the public, the administration was not happy about the situation and that Roosevelt was pressing for wider presidential discretion and determined to continue to assert his freedom of action. Thomsen was sure that if war broke out Roosevelt would have his way on the issue.[28]

Of the various circumstances which might have affected American policy, none was held to be so crucial as the fate of Great Britain in the event of war. There was scarcely a dispatch from Washington which did not in some way take note of the special Anglo-American relationship. Luther professed no doubt at all in 1937 that "the United States will always be found on the side of England." He pictured Anglo-American solidarity as especially close in the Far East, and the German Embassy in London gave steady support to this picture of a growing Anglo-American entente.[29] At the *Wilhelmstrasse*, State Secretary Weizsaeker recorded his agreement in October 1937 predicting that American policy would be passive until Great Britain was involved. At that point, he wrote, "the weight of the U.S.A. will soon be thrown into the scale on the side of the British."[30]

During the Czech crisis, Anglo-American relations were described as strengthened. Ambassador Wilson told Ribbentrop in May 1938 of English support for Czechoslovakia and that "behind England would stand the mighty potential of America."[31] Thomsen in August stressed American reactions to a possible German victory over Britain and predicted the imme-

---

[28] Luther to Foreign Ministry 9/5/35, *AHAI, AAP*/IV. Roosevelt had written, "I did not want to see legislation which by telling in advance what we would not do in case of war, would prevent our exercising an influence to avoid war." Hull, *op. cit.*, p. 406. Letter to Dodd 2/12/35, *Letters*, vol. II, p. 163. Washington Embassy to Foreign Ministry 15/7/39, *UStS/USA/*I/26380.

[29] Luther to Foreign Ministry 15/2/37, *AHAI, AAP*/V. Luther to Foreign Ministry 6/4/37, *AHAI, AAP*/V.

[30] Memo (Weizsaeker) 2/10/37, *DGFP/D/*I, p. 635. Dieckhoff to Foreign Ministry 15/10/37, *AHAI, AAP*/V.

[31] Wilson to Moffatt 24/5/38, Wilson, *op. cit.*, p. 36.

diate entry of America if Britain were invaded.[32] In February, referring to Roosevelt's determination to prevent a second Munich at all costs, Thomsen warned that the "measures short of war" Roosevelt spoke of might change to something more substantial at the announcement of a German air attack on Britain and France.[33]

Two months later Thomsen submitted a report on the topic "Foreign Policy of the United States in the Event of an Anglo-German War." American entry, Thomsen insisted, must now be regarded as axiomatic. Public opinion would demand, in the event of war, the greatest possible aid to the democracies without thought of further consequences. This would mean in effect that the entire economic and financial might of the country, though probably little military aid, would be at the disposal of the allies.

Going into further details of American intentions, Thomsen predicted that Roosevelt could come to the aid of the allies with "full moral weight by creating conditions for and by a skillful timing of the entry into the war on their side." Such an early entry by the U.S., Thomsen warned, would have two main results: first, a devastating effect on Axis morale and, second, an adverse effect on neutrals who then might be tempted to join the anti-Axis coalition. There was no reason, Thomsen warned, to expect in the event of an Anglo-German conflict anything other than "America's participation in another war of annihilation against Germany." Again, Thomsen's alarm was exaggerated, perhaps deliberately.[34]

---

[32] Thomsen to Foreign Ministry 12/8/38, *DGFP*/D/I, p. 730. Thomsen to Foreign Ministry 1/9/38, 10/9/38, *DGFP*/D/II, pp. 680, 735.

[33] Thomsen to Foreign Ministry 29/12/38, *UStS/USA*/I. Thomsen to Foreign Ministry 1/2/39, *AAP*/V/514120. Thomsen to Foreign Ministry 27/3/39, *DGFP*/D/VI, p. 132. For Roosevelt's "short of war" speech (4/1/39) *Public Papers and Addresses of Franklin D. Roosevelt* (hereafter *PPA*) 1939, pp. 1–12.

[34] Thomsen to Foreign Ministry 17/5/39, *DGFP*/D/VI, pp. 527–533. The German Ambassador in London told Halifax that in his view the United States would enter an Anglo-German war not within a month but within two days. Kennedy to State Department 23/2/39, Langer and Gleason, *Challenge to Isolation*, p. 507.

If Great Britain was to be, in the German view, the trip wire of American intervention, Japan was seen as the brake. As we have noted, for Luther the Far East was the exception to an otherwise quiescent American foreign policy by 1935. He termed this a reassertion of the traditional American preoccupation with the Pacific and described the issues as raw materials, Chinese investments and the protection of the Philippines.[35] In 1939 Thomsen reported that according to information from a Japanese diplomat the American support which would be so readily forthcoming in the event of an Anglo-German war might have to be denied to England in the event of an Anglo-Japanese war.[36] Thomsen in a later report stressed the Japanese threat to the American west flank in the event of a European war. Japan was, therefore, the "incalculable factor." Since the United States could not attack Japan, American policy, he concluded, must be studiously to avoid a Japanese war.[37]

In his May report flatly predicting American entry, Thomsen saw Japan as the only substantial hope for restraint. If Japan should take advantage of a European war to expand, the entry of the United States would be prejudiced. In June, Thomsen gave the Foreign Ministry a detailed picture of American Far Eastern policy and its implications for Germany.[38] American policy in this area aimed at normalization of relations with Japan. This caution Thomsen assigned to the need for protecting the considerable American investments in the area. The United States, he concluded, would probably not fight to defend the status quo in the Pacific, providing Japan did not attack. Since nothing was more distasteful to the Americans than a German-Japanese mili-

[35] Tokyo to Foreign Ministry 30/6/33, *AHAl (Po3 Japan)* V. Washington to Foreign Ministry 16/4/34, *AHAl (Po3 Japan)* VI. Luther to Foreign Ministry 30/4/35, *AHAl, AAP*/IV. Luther to Foreign Ministry 6/4/37, *AHAl, AAP*/V.

[36] Dieckhoff to Foreign Ministry 7/10/37, *DGFP*/D/I, p. 633. Dieckhoff to Foreign Ministry 25/10/37, *DGFP*/D/I, p. 639. Thomsen to Foreign Ministry 22/3/39, *DGFP*/D/VI, p. 75.

[37] Thomsen to Foreign Ministry 27/3/39, *DGFP*/D/VI, pp. 134, 135.

[38] Thomsen to Foreign Ministry 17/5/39, *DGFP*/D/VI, p. 531. Thomsen to Foreign Ministry 22/6/39, *DGFP*/D/VI, p. 766.

tary alliance, America would avoid giving offense to the Japanese. This intimidation of America was to be the main objective of the Triangle Pact among Germany, Italy and Japan in September 1940, and Hitler often expressed his confidence in American fears of a two-ocean war. Thomsen's observations, not entirely valid in view of American fleet movements back to the Pacific in April 1939, may have had some influence on Hitler in this regard, if in no other.[39]

The third geographical area of American diplomatic interest about which there was considerable comment was Latin America. In an area where German penetration had created alarm in Washington, the reports from German missions were in fact anything but encouraging. In general, these dispatches emphasized strong anti-German sentiments continuously fanned by American propaganda, commercial pressures and control of the news services. In the event of war, American policy was working to prevent any possibility of neutrality in this area.[40] Building on Roosevelt's Good Neighbor Policy, the Americans were now determined to construct an anti-German bloc in the hemisphere. "America is already fighting against us today in Latin America," Thomsen warned. The Pan American Conferences in Buenos Aires in December 1936 and in Lima in 1938 had provided a rich opportunity to Roosevelt for asserting hemispheric leadership. Moreover, the loan to Brazil of six American destroyers was seen by the German Naval Attaché as a symbol of the "terrific pressure from the U.S.A." upon the South American states.[41] As a result of these efforts, Woermann in Berlin expressed the conviction that by late 1938 Pan America could be viewed as a

---

[39] See Hitler statements in Chapters 13–15. For fleet movements, Langer and Gleason, *op. cit.*, p. 104.

[40] See for example: Chile to Foreign Ministry 8/3/38. Brazil to Foreign Ministry 30/3/38. Mexico to Foreign Ministry 8/4/38. Uruguay to Foreign Ministry 21/4/38, 14/11/38. All in *DGFP/D/V*, pp. 821, 824, 827, 930.

[41] Thomsen to Foreign Ministry 12/8/38, *DGFP/D/I*, p. 731. Peru to Foreign Ministry 28/12/38, *DGFP/D/V*, p. 885. Rio de Janeiro (Naval Attaché) to OKM 10/8/37 (E559168); Washington (Naval Attaché) to OKM 9/8/37 (E559170); both in Oberkommando der Marine, DK 9, *Anfragen und Berichte deutscher Attachés 1936–1939.*

"growing ideological bloc," and this view was expressed to Hitler himself by the Argentine Ambassador.[42]

There remains finally the question of American military policy. Was it such as to give military significance to the predicted American involvement in a European war? More specifically, did the Washington mission believe that the United States would be willing or able to bring armed force to bear against Germany? The answer to this crucial question as conveyed from Washington lay of course to a considerable extent in the hands of the German Military Attaché, General Friedrich von Boetticher, whose reports begin to appear prominently in 1939 and figure very importantly after the outbreak of war. The essential feature of the General's viewpoint was the considerable doubt cast upon the possibility of any military implementation of American policy in the event of a European war. Boetticher based this on his personal contacts with American military leaders whom he found as early as 1937 to be cautious, influential and sympathetic to Germany.[43]

On January 12, 1939, the Military Attaché and his naval colleague, Admiral Robert Vitthoeft-Emden, submitted a report on Roosevelt's plans for rearmament which they labeled "defensive" in nature. The American air force was held to be thinly spread over the continental United States, Alaska, Hawaii, Puerto Rico and the Panama Canal. In general, the present requests were described as "toned down from the extravagant and provocative rearmament campaign of late weeks" and a victory for strategic moderation.[44] In response to a request from Berlin regarding the possibility of an American expeditionary force in the event of war, Thomsen cabled that at least seven months would be needed to train such an A.E.F.; that there was some disunity on

---

[42] Memo (Woermann) 20/11/38, *DGFP*/D/IV, p. 647. Statement by Argentine Ambassador in *DDI*, ser. 8, XII, p. 305.

[43] Dieckhoff to Foreign Ministry 2/6/37, *DGFP*/D/III, p. 304. Dieckhoff to Foreign Ministry 3/1/38, *DGFP*/D/I, p. 663. Dieckhoff, however, expressed his own anxieties regarding American naval rearmament.

[44] Washington Embassy to Foreign Ministry 12/1/39, *DGFP*/D/IV, p. 672.

these subjects in the armed forces; and that the United States Navy was incapable of Atlantic action while the role of Japan was uncertain. Thomsen added, however, that he was speaking of the immediate situation. The military posture in six months, he warned, was "anybody's guess."[45]

Boetticher, a week before the outbreak of war, reiterated that the lack of personnel and other factors simply precluded American military action outside the United States for a year. He then went on to draw a distinction (which rapidly became his stock in trade thereafter) between the politicians and press under Jewish domination on the one hand and the military on the other who were "the stronghold of all that is best in American life." Roosevelt's peace appeals, he announced, introducing political commentary never subsequently absent from his reports, were therefore to be written off as camouflage for his own weakness and a trick to gain time. Similarly, military maneuvers could be safely ignored as crude attempts to influence the Japanese and Latin Americans. It is of some interest to note that on the same day (August 25) the Naval Attaché cabled a far more pessimistic report regarding naval preparedness. He informed his superiors that the American fleet was close to war readiness and that any deficiencies could be made up in short order.[46]

Thomsen in his last dispatch before the war on this subject, dated August 28, accepted Boetticher's assertions about the impossibility of sending American troops to Europe within one year. However, he cautioned that American involvement was inevitable if England appeared bound for defeat, that Roosevelt counted on a long war of attrition to give him time to prepare, and that in any event there would no doubt be a massive economic intervention in the form of raw materials and machinery "in unlimited quantities."[47]

*

[45] Political Department to Washington Embassy 26/4/39, *DGFP*/D/VI, p. 344. Thomsen to Foreign Ministry 26/4/39, *DGFP*/D/VI, p. 335.
[46] Washington Embassy to Foreign Ministry 25/8/39, *DGFP*/D/VII, p. 275. Witthoeft to OKM 25/8/39, *OKM-Attaches*.
[47] Thomsen to Foreign Ministry 28/8/39, *DGFP*/D/VII, p. 376.

Thus, on the eve of war German policy makers had for their information a cumulative picture of America built up during the previous six years of reporting. We do not know how much of this picture reached Hitler and his colleagues. In any case, it is almost impossible to believe that he was much affected by the hostility of American public opinion and there is little evidence that the reports of American economic strength or of Roosevelt's political power and his disposition toward Germany made much impression. Hitler evidently chose to disregard the view that American isolationism was ephemeral, and he was probably not wide of the mark to do so in the years before the war. He accepted, as we already know, the probability of American economic assistance to the democracies while dismissing any military move as very unlikely. The one aspect of the pre-war dispatches which Ribbentrop may well have passed on to the Fuehrer was the Japanese factor, which became, as we shall see, highly significant in the development of German Far Eastern policy. In short, it is entirely unlikely that the American factor was a substantial one in Hitler's decision to open the European war. As the dimensions of the war expanded in the years 1939 to 1941, however, he could not so blithely disregard the picture his diplomats continued to convey to him.

The German diplomats at Washington had done their work reasonably and conscientiously. It is hardly their fault that their reports made so little impression on the political leadership of the Reich in the years before the war. The situation was acknowledged by State Secretary Weizsaeker, who wrote to Dieckhoff when the latter expressed a fear that he was boring Berlin with his repeated cautions: "Your warnings against any illusions about the American attitude in case of world conflict are only valuable. It can do no harm at all if you stress the point repeatedly."[48]

[48] Weizsaeker to Dieckhoff 30/4/38, *DGFP/D/I*, p. 706.

CHAPTER 6

The German Diplomats and American Foreign Policy
Between Poland and Pearl Harbor

As the tide of Nazi victory flooded Europe and the position of Britain became desperate, the Roosevelt administration, in spite of continuing isolationist opposition, reacted with a series of sharply anti-German moves. Specifically, the repeal of the arms embargo and the establishment of maritime combat zones in the autumn of 1939 clearly made American neutrality benevolent to the naval powers, i.e. the Allies. The German conquest of the Low Countries, France and Scandinavia and the entry of Italy into the war in the spring of 1940 brought intolerable pressure to bear upon Britain which Roosevelt sought to relieve. Verbal assurances were enforced by increasing economic and military assistance, most notably symbolized in the Anglo-American exchange of destroyers for Caribbean bases in September 1940. In 1941, Lend-Lease in March, the seizure of Axis ships and funds, the declaration of "unlimited national emergency" in May and the intensification of the Battle of the Atlantic in the months before Pearl Harbor all had clear enough implications for German-American relations.

The German Embassy, still under the Chargé, Hans Thomsen, had to report this dramatic chain of events in an atmosphere of extreme hostility ("an anxiety psychosis") and virtual ostracism.[1] Propaganda and party activity were now almost out of the question in America, although the Propaganda Ministry in Berlin did

---

[1] Thomsen to Foreign Ministry 18/6/40, *DGFP*/D/IX, p. 604. Thomsen to Foreign Ministry 23/5/40, *StS/USA*/II/12109. Thomsen to Foreign Ministry 18/8/40, *UStS/USA*/38846.

have one unpromising suggestion for a weekly broadcast to be called "The Goebbels Hour." More common and burdensome to the diplomats in these years were the military espionage and sabotage activities of the Military High Command (OKW) which were, however, blundering and ineffectual. (Thomsen called them "no work of art.")[2]

Thomsen was equally blunt about American opinion: "They want Britain to win the war and us to lose it," he said. If the Allies faced defeat, he warned, the will to intervene would gain the upper hand.[3] At the same time, Thomsen had to report that people were beginning to believe in the threat which a German victory might pose for America itself. The anti-German propaganda pictured Germany as the ideological, political and economic enemy which aimed at world domination. If England fell, the Americans were being successfully told, the United States would be compelled to establish its own Atlantic defense line while Britain continued the fight from Canada. Early in 1940 Thomsen admitted that his chances for reversing this sentiment or indeed having any influence on American opinion were limited.[4]

Germany's march across Europe all but extinguished any hope of a favorable public response. The invasion of Scandinavia had produced an immediate upsurge of opinion in favor of the Danes and Norwegians which had weakened isolationist sentiment among Scandinavian-Americans of the Midwest. The job of the interventionist agitators had now been made easier. Although this group was still restrained by Republican isolationism, the

[2] Weizsaeker's comment on the Goebbels Hour ("a massive switching off of radios") in Weizsaeker to Prop. Ministry 28/5/41, *DGFP/D/XII*, p. 906. On OKW activity, Thomsen to Foreign Ministry 21/5/40, 23/5/40, *DGFP/D/IX*, pp. 393, 411. Thomsen comment in H. Trefousse, "The Failure of German Intelligence on the United States," *Mississippi Valley Historical Review*, June 1955.

[3] Dieckhoff Memorandum 7/9/39, *DGFP/D/VIII*, p. 21. Thomsen to Foreign Ministry 24/9/39, *DGFP/D/VIII*, p. 127. Thomsen to Foreign Ministry 30/10/39, *DGFP/D/VIII*, p. 359.

[4] Thomsen to Foreign Ministry 16/5/40, *Pol Bez/XIV/511883*. Thomsen to Foreign Ministry 30/5/40, *StS/USA/II/12150*. Thomsen to Foreign Ministry 29/3/40, *DGFP/D/IX*, p. 43.

Pacific problem and the slow pace of rearmament, yet Thomsen expressed his conviction that hatred for Germany had now wiped out the disillusioned memories of 1917.[5] The attack on the Low Countries, Thomsen reported, had "so greatly narrowed down the moral and political ground on which we can operate here in America that only a tight-rope walker could keep his balance."[6] By June with France collapsing Thomsen spoke of the rapidly thinning ranks of the isolationists, of the ever widening circles joining the anti-German chorus, and, with the entrance of Italy, of a popular rage which had reached a point that "could scarcely be exaggerated." True, it was doubtful that even this heightened public feeling could be converted into an enthusiasm for an American military intervention. However, in regard to every form of assistance to England short of war, Thomsen warned, the attitude of the American people was abundantly clear.[7]

There were three aspects of German policy which had made the German threat vivid to American public opinion: the conclusion of the Tripartite Pact, German penetration into Latin America and the incidents in the Atlantic between German and American ships. The Pact, Thomsen reported, had lent substance to the picture of a world conspiracy which had been so assiduously cultivated by the administration in the public mind. Roosevelt was now able to press for a counter-alliance to block these world-wide moves. Furthermore, since the specter of a two-front war was bound to have a sobering effect on American opinion, the administration would now concentrate also on splitting the Axis.[8]

[5] Thomsen to Foreign Ministry 10/4/40, *DGFP/D/IX*, p. 118. Thomsen to Foreign Ministry 19/4/40, *DGFP/D/IX*, p. 206. This was also the gist of the report sent to Rome by Ambassador Colonna. Colonna to Rome 10/4/40, *DDI*, ser. 9, IV, p. 16.

[6] Thomsen to Foreign Ministry 11/8/40, *StS/USA/II/12240*. Thomsen to Foreign Ministry 12/6/40, *StS/USA/II/12252*.

[7] Thomsen to Foreign Ministry 14/5/40, *DGFP/D/IX*, p. 339. Thomsen to Foreign Ministry 16/5/40, *DGFP/D/IX*, p. 351.

[8] Thomsen to Foreign Ministry 1/10/40, *StS/USA/III/22927*. Thomsen to Foreign Ministry 6/10/40, *StS/USA/III/22951*. Thomsen to Foreign Ministry 19/12/40, *StS/USA/IV/62249*.

The second area of American sensitivity regarding German policy was Latin America. Here German infiltration and influence was causing considerable alarm, especially regarding the Panama Canal. The Consul General in San Francisco advised that this be counteracted by a joint declaration from Hitler and Mussolini recognizing American rights in the hemisphere in order to "take the wind out of their sails." In the summer and autumn of 1941, the issue was raised again, with every riot or disturbance in Latin America now blamed on the Germans. The climax was reached in October, when a map alleging to show German plans to take over Latin America was printed in a New York newspaper and used by Roosevelt to demonstrate his allegations about German activity in the hemisphere. Thomsen labeled the map "a fabrication."[9]

Finally, the attack on American ships in the Atlantic, Thomsen reported, had sharpened the sense of German menace. The incidents with the destroyers *Greer* and *Kearney* and the sinking of the *Reuben James* in the autumn of 1941 had been used by the administration to arouse public opinion and had, according to the Chargé, caused "great bitterness" among the people.[10]

As before the war, the diplomats saw Roosevelt's leadership as the mainspring of American policy. His anti-German attitude was now "a tremendous fury." Dieckhoff in Berlin added an analysis of the President's motives which included Anglophilia, vaulting ambition as a compensation for his physical disability, his need for the Jewish vote and a repressed admiration of Hitler. All of this had led Roosevelt into a veritable obsession with his role as the savior of the world from the "German menace."[11]

[9] Thomsen to Foreign Ministry 5/6/40, *StS/USA*/II/12200. Report of San Francisco Consulate 5/6/40, *StS/USA*/II/12206. Washington Embassy to Foreign Ministry 25/7/41, *StS/USA*/VII/37345. Thomsen to Foreign Ministry 31/10/41, *StS/USA*/IX/422268. Ribbentrop termed it "absurd" and a "fraud of the crudest type." Memo (Ribbentrop) 1/11/41, *StS/USA*/IX/422271.

[10] Thomsen to Foreign Ministry 5/9/41, 17/10/41, 22/10/41, 3/11/41, *StS/USA*/VIII/375741, IX/422171, 422214, 422889.

[11] Thomsen to Foreign Ministry 12/6/40, *DGFP*/D/IX, p. 550. Memorandum (Dieckhoff) 29/7/40, *ibid.*, X, p. 359.

Roosevelt's election victory in 1940, which Thomsen never doubted, his appointment to the war and Navy Departments of the interventionists, Henry Stimson and Frank Knox (who promptly joined Morgenthau and Ickes in the German rogues' gallery of warmongers), and especially his proclamation of the unlimited national emergency in May 1941 clearly impressed Thomsen with the President's determination.[12] Regarding the emergency proclamation, Ribbentrop was also sufficiently concerned to request further information about its effect in America. The Foreign Minister also wired Rome and Tokyo calling attention to the very real dangers of American entry and suggesting a joint reply to Roosevelt's proclamation.[13]

The open letters sent by Roosevelt to Hitler and Mussolini and the use of special envoys were not regarded as impartial attempts at mediation but rather as partisan gestures calculated to embarrass the Axis. The most notable example of these efforts was the mission of Undersecretary of State Sumner Welles in February of 1940. Thomsen described this and other initiatives as the result of Roosevelt's confusion about the causes of the war, a fear that it would spread while America was unprepared, and the needs of domestic politics. The sterile monologues in Berlin did not permit Welles to reveal much of American policy to the Germans beyond Roosevelt's general interest in a peace settlement. He did tell Weizsaeker that the United States could not remain indifferent to the destruction of civilization in a general war, but this scarcely constituted a commitment to anything very specific.[14]

---

[12] Thomsen to Foreign Ministry 28/6/40, *DGFP/D/X*, p. 49. Thomsen was horrified by open support from Berlin for Wilkie. Thomsen to Foreign Ministry 5/10/40, *StS/USA/III/22948*. On Stimson and Knox see Thomsen to Foreign Ministry 19/12/40, *DGFP/D/XI*, p. 906. Some publicists in Berlin pictured Mrs. Roosevelt as "one of the most evil warmongers . . . the embodiment of the decadent American female." K. Schadewardt, *Was Will Roosevelt?* For reaction to the emergency proclamation, Thomsen to Foreign Ministry 28/5/41, *StS/USA/VI/345247*.

[13] Circular Memo 30/5/41, *StS/USA/VI/245283*. Speech in *PPA/1941*, p. 181. Ribbentrop to Embassies in Rome and Tokyo 30/5/41, *StS/USA/VI/245284*.

[14] Thomsen to Foreign Ministry 10/2/40, *DGFP/D/VIII*, p. 757. Welles and

Of greater interest to Berlin than these gestures was the question of American aid to the Allies. The gradual destruction of the Neutrality Acts, which had been predicted prior to the war, could only be noted with resignation. The end of the arms embargo and Roosevelt's intention to evade what was left of the laws seemed inevitable to the diplomats. Neutrality had become non-belligerency and this could easily become full belligerency.[15] As the President succeeded, Thomsen warned, the United States would be able to transfer goods directly to the Allies, travel would be allowed to the war zones and on belligerent ships, and American merchant ships would be armed. Thus the effect would be to release the full resources and transportation facilities of America to supply the Allies. In addition, there would be increased chances of incidents on the high seas. When the final repeal was accomplished in November 1941 ("we will not let Hitler prescribe the waters of the world on which our ships may travel"), Thomsen wrote that Roosevelt had "Draconian powers" to conduct an undeclared war.[16]

Thomsen was convinced by the summer of 1940 that this evasion of neutrality along with other acts and statements had created a *de facto* alliance between America and England. It was in the context of this alliance that American actions should be judged. The most dramatic example of this Anglo-American solidarity was the agreement to exchange a number of old Ameri-

---

Ribbentrop 1/3/40, Welles and Hitler 2/3/40, Welles and Goering 4/3/40, Welles and Weizsaeker 1/3/40, *DGFP*/D/VIII, pp. 821, 838, 850, 830. There is also substantial evidence that the *Wilhelmstrasse* did not attach undue importance to the mission. Hassell, *op. cit.*, p. 106. Weizsaeker, *op. cit.*, p. 276. Attolico to Ciano 5/3/40, *DDI*, ser. 9, III, p. 392.

[15] Memo (Dieckhoff) 7/9/39, *DGFP*/D/VIII, p. 21. Thomsen to Foreign Ministry 9/10/39, 25/10/39, 28/11/39, *DGFP*/D/VIII, pp. 245, 321, 460. Roosevelt's request for repeal was treated in the *Deutsche Allgemeine Zeitung*, 22/9/39. Thomsen to Foreign Ministry 19/12/40, *DGFP*/D/XI, p. 906.

[16] Memo (Dieckhoff) 24/9/41, *StS/USA*/VIII/375862. Thomsen to Foreign Ministry 10/10/41, *StS/USA*/IX/422128. Thomsen to Foreign Ministry 8/11/41, *StS/USA*/IX/422320. Thomsen to Foreign Ministry 15/11/41, *StS/USA*/IX/422355.

can destroyers for certain rights in British bases in the Western hemisphere. On September 9, the day the proposals were adopted, Thomsen could only express the comment that the whole operation represented Roosevelt's ruthless determination, devious *modus vivendi* and total disregard for congressional and military advice. In October, Thomsen said he had no doubt that the deal would be implemented to the full by the use of the President's power as commander in chief of the American forces.[17]

In 1941, Lend-Lease was viewed as another link in the chain of American commitment to Britain. In addition, Thomsen saw the measure as an attempt to paper over New Deal domestic failures and a symbol of Roosevelt's determination to make his claim to world leadership prevail. Dieckhoff followed this up with a description of the act as a complete victory for Roosevelt which would be implemented to the fullest.[18]

The dispatches as well as the commentary at the *Wilhelm-strasse* throughout 1941 testified to ever closer Anglo-American relations. The missions of Harry Hopkins in January and July, the use of American shipyards to repair British ships, the arming of merchantmen and the whole question of American convoys were taken seriously by the German diplomats. Notwithstanding the inability of the American navy to cover the entire Atlantic and the vacillation of the administration on the convoy issue, Thomsen felt that these moves coupled with the assumption by American forces of responsibility for the defense of Iceland showed American readiness "to put every available ship at the

[17] Thomsen to Foreign Ministry 3/9/40, *DGFP*/D/XI, pp. 12, 13. Thomsen to Foreign Ministry 18/10/40, *DGFP*/D/X, p. 508. Although one report had the press in Berlin making light of the arrangement (*NYT* 4/8/40), there is some evidence that it made a considerable impression on Hitler. Ribbentrop examination, *NCA*, sup. B, p. 1196.

[18] Thomsen to Foreign Ministry 9/31/41, *DGFP*/D/XIII, p. 251. As an example of implementation, Thomsen warned the OKW that British ships had repair priority in American shipyards. 18/4/41, StS/USA/V/244428. Memo (Dieckhoff) 10/3/41, *DGFP*/D/XII, p. 258. For a German critique of Lend-Lease from the legal viewpoint, see Grewe "Das Englandhilfgesetz der USA," *Monatsschrift fuer Auswaertige Politik*, March 1941.

disposal of England."[19] The Anglo-American entente was sealed, Thomsen felt, by the meeting of Roosevelt and Churchill and the signing of the Atlantic Charter in September. Churchill was now pictured as trying to persuade Roosevelt to enter the war outright or accept the consequences for an English collapse.[20] Thomsen described the Charter as the kind of thing that appealed to the American people and labeled it an "international New Deal." It represented, however, something more substantial than this and Thomsen warned of a growing American military commitment involved here. The Japanese Ambassador told Weizsaeker that the effect of the Charter was to bring the United States into the war without a declaration.[21] Final expressions of the Anglo-American alliance involved, according to reports in October and November 1941, American supplies to English positions in Africa and the Middle East and a "master plan" in which extensive involvement in British military planning and operations would be agreed to in exchange for Lend-Lease.[22]

Nor was England the only European country in which American interest was noticed. According to the German reports, the removal of France from the actual fighting had by no means lessened American concern with that country in the anti-Axis struggle. From Washington Thomsen wrote that the administration was determined to do everything to make difficulties for Germany and provide support for England through its French policy. The attempt by diplomatic pressure to keep France from

[19] Hopkins Missions in Thomsen to Foreign Minister 6/1/41, *StS/USA/IV/* 62322. Thomsen to Foreign Minister 24/7/41, *StS/USA/VII/*373718. Use of American shipyards in Thomsen to Foreign Ministry 6/4/41, *StS/USA/V/* 244354. Armed merchantmen in Thomsen to Foreign Ministry 18/10/41, *StS/USA/IX/*422199. On the convoy question see: Thomsen to Foreign Ministry 10/4/41, *StS/USA/V/*244379.

[20] Thomsen to Foreign Ministry 8/9/41, *StS/USA/VIII/*375589. Thomsen felt sure that Roosevelt was too familiar with bluffing tactics to be taken in by this. See also Moltmann, "Die fruehe Amerikanische Deutschlandplanung," *Vierteljahreshefte fuer Zeitgeschichte,* July 1957.

[21] Thomsen to Foreign Ministry 19/9/41, *StS/USA/VIII/*375639. Memo (Weizsaeker) 4/9/41, *StS/USA/VIII/*375737.

[22] Washington Embassy to Foreign Ministry 31/10/41, *StS/USA/IX/*422265. Thomsen to Foreign Ministry 20/11/41, *StS/USA/X/*44619.

allowing her fleet and colonial possessions from falling into German hands was a matter of some anxiety. Dieckhoff late in 1940 described the appointment of Admiral Leahy as American Ambassador in Vichy as proof that Roosevelt was determined to play an active hand in Europe by obstructing Franco-German cooperation.[23] In 1941, Abetz, the German representative in France, felt the American role in Franco-German relations to be so substantial that ultimately France would be compelled to choose between America and Europe.[24]

American policy in Spain was reported to have taken the form of pressure to ensure Spanish neutrality. Warning that Spain in its present weakened condition was easily subject to Allied pressure, the German Ambassador at Madrid described in December 1940 American efforts to exchange food deliveries for Spanish abstention from the Axis. It was reported in March that General William Donovan of the United States Office of Strategic Services had conferred with the Spanish Foreign Minister to try to persuade him of the ultimate defeat of the Axis and in April further efforts along these lines by American Ambassador Weddell were noted.[25]

In other parts of Europe, Thomsen reported American aid to the Soviet Union following the German attack in June 1941 to be of no great importance. On the other hand, American activity in the Balkans did not go unnoticed by German diplomats.[26] Thus American policy in Europe was reported to Berlin as one of commitment to the anti-German cause by means of massive

[23] Thomsen to Foreign Ministry 2/8/40, *StS/USA*/II/12534. Thomsen to Foreign Ministry 10/1/41, *StS/USA*/IV/62354. Paris Embassy to Foreign Ministry 1/11/40, *StS/USA*/III/23091.

[24] Paris Embassy to Foreign Ministry 1/2/41, 24/4/41, *DGFP*/D/XII, pp. 3, 627.

[25] Madrid Embassy to Foreign Ministry 29/12/40, *DGFP*/D/XI, p. 975. See Hull, *op. cit.*, pp. 874–882. Madrid Embassy to Foreign Ministry 6/3/41, *StS/USA*/V/244188. Madrid Embassy to Foreign Ministry 20/4/41, *DGFP*/D/III, p. 590.

[26] Thomsen to Foreign Ministry 19/8/41, 17/9/41, *StS/USA*/VIII/375639, 379833. Belgrade Embassy to Foreign Ministry 6/2/41, *StS/USA*/V/244043. Ankara Embassy to Foreign Ministry 28/4/41, *StS/USA*/V/244489.

aid to Great Britain and a consistent checking of German purposes on the continent through a variety of diplomatic and economic pressures.

United States' policy in Africa was also pictured as an effort
to contain German expansion. Here an American role was seen
in the French possessions, especially Morocco and Dakar and in
the Spanish and Portuguese islands. Thomsen pointed to the
opening of American consulates in the Azores and to American
fears that Germany would use Dakar to attack Latin America
and the British colonies in Africa.[27] In July 1941, there was a
flurry of reports concerning American policy in this area. Thomsen reported that Roosevelt intended to occupy Dakar and the
Cape Verdes within weeks. This project along with the move
in Iceland Thomsen interpreted not only as constituting support
for England, but also as preparation of a forward position should
England fall.[28] A dispatch from Lisbon described an American
plan for securing positions in the Atlantic, Latin America, and in
West and North Africa in preparation for the outbreak of hostilities. This involved a bomber base in Brazil, a supply station for
North Africa in the Azores, Mediterranean influence from Dakar
and Morocco, and occupation of Greenland and Iceland to bolster England. Ribbentrop's concern with this report is suggested
by his urgent cable to Lisbon requesting further details. In September Dieckhoff warned of American moves in French equa-
torial Africa and labeled American policy "perfidious" since it
dealt with Pétain in France and De Gaulle in North Africa.[29]

[27] Thomsen to Foreign Ministry 19/8/40, *UStS/USA/ — /38849*. American
interest in Dakar was also reported by the German missions in Madrid and
Paris. Military Attaché (Madrid) (undated) and Military Attaché (Paris)
30/12/40, *StS/USA/IV/62278*. Watkins, *op. cit.*, pp. 327–328.

[28] Boetticher to Foreign Ministry 5/1/41, *StS/USA/IV/6237*. Thomsen to
Foreign Ministry 10/7/41, *StS/USA/VIII/373638*. Roosevelt had written of a
possible American "protective defense force" in the Portuguese islands. See
Roosevelt, *Letters*, III, p. 372.

[29] Informationsstelle III 12/7/41, *StS/USA/VII/373663*. Ribbentrop to Lisbon
13/7/41, *StS/USA/VII/373669*. Churchill informed the British Foreign Office
that Roosevelt would move if the islands were endangered and was "holding

In the Western hemisphere, the diplomats found no cause for satisfaction. The pre-war initiatives were now discovered to be much accelerated with the goal of welding America's northern and southern neighbors into an economic and military bloc. The proclamation of a Pan American Security Zone in September 1939 and the Roosevelt-Mackenzie King declaration of American-Canadian military cooperation issued at Ogdensburg a year later were seen as stepping stones to this goal.[30] From the fall of 1940 the emphasis in American policy was on the implementation of joint military arrangements. In March 1941 Washington and South American embassies reported American determination to weld the area "from Alaska to Panama into a unified military bloc" with states to the south under United States military control.[31]

Not only was Roosevelt tightening the unity of the hemisphere, he was also expanding its limits. In the fall of 1940 Thomsen sent reports of American interest in Greenland and Iceland and predicted an attack upon them as part of the American-Canadian defense agreement, possibly supported by the British fleet. When the Americans took over the defense of Greenland through an agreement with the Danish Minister at Washington, Thomsen described the action as a diplomatic counterstroke to Axis successes in the Balkans, a bolstering of British morale and a reply to the German blockade of Iceland.[32]

When the Americans took over Iceland as well in the name of the Monroe Doctrine ("an icy hand to snatch hope from every

strong forces available for this purpose." Churchill, *op. cit.*, III, p. 389. Memo dated 11/8/41. Langer and Gleason, *Undeclared War*, p. 519. Memo (Dieckhoff) 9/9/41, *StS/USA/*VIII/375756.

[30] Montevideo Embassy to Foreign Ministry 12/8/40, *StS/USA/*III/22672. Thomsen to Foreign Ministry 17/8/40, 20/8/40, *ibid.*, 22706, 22722. Memorandum (dept. IX) 17/9/39, *DGFP/D/*VIII, p. 86.

[31] Boetticher to OKW 7/11/40, *StS/USA/*III/23127. See Langer and Gleason, *Undeclared War*, pp. 588–601, for American military negotiations with Brazil. Boetticher to OKW 26/11/41, *StS/USA/*X/44672. Rio de Janeiro to Foreign Ministry 18/6/41, *StS/USA/*VII/373563.

[32] Thomsen to Foreign Ministry 18/10/40, *DGFP/D/*X, p. 508. Thomsen to Foreign Ministry 11/4/41, *DGFP/D/*XII, p. 510.

soldier in Hitler's line"), Thomsen was alarmed. He presented this action as a proof of Roosevelt's vigorous and adroit leadership by which he had gradually been able to bring public opinion around to his view by words and acts. The motives here, he said, were to release British troops, to put the sea routes to Iceland under American protection, to strengthen the British will to resist, to intimidate Japan and to provoke Germany. It was this last point that seemed to concern Thomsen especially. Public opinion he felt had now been brought to the point where it was prepared for an incident which was "now practically a certainty."

Three days later, Thomsen took an even more serious view. He warned that according to reliable sources, the sinking of American ships en route to Iceland would cause a rupture of diplomatic relations. Furthermore, he now saw a wider implication of the action. Citing statements by Republican leader Wendell Wilkie and Navy Secretary Frank Knox, Thomsen now viewed Iceland as a possible staging area for a later invasion of Norway. Indeed, as noted above, Iceland in the context of American interest in Africa and the Portuguese islands might be part of a plan to prepare "forward positions in the event of England's defeat." The announcement in September by Knox that ships of all flags carrying Lend-Lease supplies would enjoy United States naval protection as far as Iceland underscored in Thomsen's view American determination to implement its Atlantic policy.[33]

As we have seen, in the pre-war years the German diplomats had long been convinced that one key to American diplomatic behavior lay in the Pacific. Even before the conclusion of the Tripartite Pact in September 1940, the United States was held

[33] Thomsen to Foreign Ministry 9/7/41, *StS/USA*/III/12411. "Whoever possesses Iceland holds a pistol permanently pointing at England, America and Canada." S. E. Morison, *Battle of the Atlantic*, pp. 58–67. Quote from *New York Post* 10/10/41 in *The Undeclared War*, p. 333. Thomsen to Foreign Ministry 15/9/41, *StS/USA*/VIII/375809.

to have undertaken "the task of relieving the Western powers in the Far East and vigorously expanding their interests."[34] When the administration announced an embargo on scrap to Japan in the same month, the Chargé described it as another link in a lengthening chain of reprisals against the Japanese. American public opinion, already hostile to the Japanese, had greeted the move enthusiastically.[35]

The year 1941 witnessed a mounting German anxiety about Japanese-American relations. The details of this concern, the Japanese responses and attitudes on the matter, as well as the German attempts to influence the course of these relations will be discussed in detail in later chapters. It is sufficient here to note briefly the tendency of the information which the *Wilhelmstrasse* received during this fateful year from Washington and Tokyo concerning American policy toward Japan.

The picture was one of greatly increased popular suspicion of Japan and a growing determination by the administration, in spite of certain conciliatory gestures, to stop Japanese expansion. The German diplomats in America and Japan were much concerned with the negotiations which opened in Washington in February between Secretary of State Hull and the Japanese Ambassador, Admiral Nomura. Thomsen cabled his concern over Nomura's response to American probing of Japanese intentions in the event of an American war with Germany. Ambassador Ott from Tokyo defined American policy as an attempt to "make the Pact ineffective and neutralize Japan for the duration of the war."[36] Dieckhoff advised that Roosevelt was entirely insincere in his Japanese overtures. The real object as he saw it was to gain time and divide the Axis. Basically, he concluded, the Americans

---

[34] Tokyo to Foreign Ministry 16/10/39, *DGFP*/D/VIII, pp. 298–303.

[35] Thomsen to Foreign Ministry 28/9/40, *StS/USA*/III/22912.

[36] Thomsen to Foreign Ministry 21/2/41, *StS/USA*/V/244102. Ott to Ribbentrop 5/5/41, *UStS/Japan-Amerika*/24892. See articles by Colin Ross, "Amerika Greift nach der Weltmacht," cited in Chapter 2, and Adam von Trott, "Die Fernostpolitik der Vereinigten Staaten," *Monatshefte fuer Auswaertige Politik*, Nov. 1940.

regarded Japan's Axis role as a bluff and intended to call it.[37]

American pressure on Japan regarding the German connection also took the form of attempts to persuade the Japanese that the institution of American convoys in the Atlantic did not constitute a *casus foederis* under the Pact. These pressures were supplemented in July by renewed economic measures. These were to be used as a kind of thumb screw: the quieter the Japanese were and the more independent of the Axis, the fewer the reprisals. The object here, Thomsen pointed out, was to restrain the Japanese within their own Pacific area. Furthermore, Thomsen added, the Americans were convinced that their intimidation was working.[38] Dieckhoff felt that the Hull-Nomura talks, reconvened on August 8, were an alibi that Roosevelt desperately needed. He explained that it would be easier for the President to carry the country into war against Japan than against Germany and saw in the discussions a dilemma for the Reich: if the negotiations succeeded, the Americans would have freed their Pacific flank; if they failed, it would be a good excuse for a Pacific war. Neither alternative offered much advantage to Germany, he declared.[39]

Ott cabled on October 2 that the talks which could only have led to a temporary *modus vivendi* had bogged down because of American inflexibility on the question of complete Japanese withdrawal from China. Thomsen came to the same conclusion and warned that Roosevelt was utterly determined to force Germany into an act of aggression in order to release Japan from any obligation to enter a German-American war. The arrival of Special Minister Kurusu to join the talks in November had been accom-

[37] Tokyo Embassy to Foreign Ministry 5/5/41, *DGFP*/D/XII, p. 715. Memo (Dieckhoff) 10/5/41, *DGFP*/D/XII, p. 752.

[38] Tokyo Embassy to Foreign Ministry 15/5/41, *StS/USA*/VI/245155. The steps in the American economic offensive against Japan are summarized in *FRUS*/Japan/II, pp. 201–273. The following embargoes had been placed: arms 14/12/37, industrial goods 20/12/39, raw materials 2/7/39, scrap 30/9/40. Thomsen to Foreign Ministry 26/7/41, *StS/USA*/VII/373762. Thomsen to Foreign Ministry 1/8/41, *StS/USA*/VII/37384.

[39] Memo (Dieckhoff) 4/9/41, *UStS/Japan-Amerika*/24992. Tokyo Embassy to Foreign Ministry 13/9/41, *StS/Japan*/IV/60606.

panied, according to Thomsen, by a "drumfire of propaganda" in the press to discredit the Axis, and drive home the point that any concession to Japan would only be a comfort to Germany. The following day the talks were reportedly at "a dead stop." Events were now moving rapidly. Thomsen cabled on November 27 that American-Japanese relations had suddenly entered a "very critical stage" since Hull had presented a virtual ultimatum.[40]

On December 1, Thomsen stated that American policy aimed to gain time and intimidate Japan, although Roosevelt wanted to avoid a Pacific war since this would not now be in the interests of the Allies. On December 3 Thomsen reported that the war of nerves had become so tense that a military collision was not unlikely. The Japanese, he asserted, were preparing for a rupture and an attack on Thailand was possible. On December 4, three days before Pearl Harbor, Thomsen described Japanese-American relations as "poised on a knife-edge."[41]

There were of course implications for Germany in much of the foreign policy which has been described. However, the state of German-American relations as such, the possibility of a rupture in those relations and the question of American entry into the war were of direct concern to Germany, and on these issues Berlin received considerable comment. In general Thomsen was well aware of the considerations which restrained American entrance: lack of preparation, the Pacific problem, public opinion and rapid German victories. However, in spite of these obstacles the reports from Washington and elsewhere did not by any means rule out the possibility of an American intervention. In June 1940, Thomsen passed on a statement by Roosevelt that if the Allies were defeated, the United States would be "sweet and

[40] Ott to Foreign Ministry 2/10/41, 4/10/41, *StS/Japan*/IV/60669, 60675. Thomsen to Foreign Ministry 16/11/41, *StS/USA*/X/44607. Thomsen to Foreign Ministry 27/11/41, *StS/USA*/X/44675.

[41] Thomsen to Foreign Ministry 1/12/41, 3/12/41, 4/12/41, *StS/USA/X/*44701, 44714, 44716.

polite and gracious toward Germany for two years," meanwhile building up her armed might regardless of cost or waste. For good measure Roosevelt had added that any direct or indirect German attack on the Western hemisphere would mean automatic war, regardless of the state of armaments. "I have," Thomsen noted, "no reason to doubt the authenticity of these statements."[42]

Although Roosevelt had squelched questions of American entry with a flat "This is definitely out," Thomsen was not at all sure that the matter ended there. On the contrary, a report in the Hearst Press that reckoned on American entry before 1941 Thomsen described as "not entirely unfounded."[43] The Chargé warned that although Pacific preoccupations were of increasing concern, Berlin ought to face the fact that America would do anything to aid Britain, injure Germany, arm herself and "then leave it to us to draw the conclusions." Roosevelt's comment to British Ambassador Lord Lothian that "only an incident can bring us in" was not of much comfort, since in Thomsen's view incidents on the high seas were now a decided possibility. Between June and December 1940 at least fifteen telegrams arrived in Berlin from European and Latin American embassies stressing the dangers of American entry. Memoranda by Woermann at Berlin suggest that this possibility was taken seriously at the *Wilhelmstrasse* in 1940.[44]

In the early months of 1941 the Washington reports tended to stress the problems facing the administration on the question. In May, Thomsen reported that the Americans intended to pursue

[42] Thomsen to Foreign Ministry 14/5/40, 18/5/40, *DGFP*/D/IX, pp. 340, 321. Thomsen to Foreign Ministry 11/6/40, *DGFP*/D/IX, p. 541.

[43] Thomsen to Foreign Ministry 19/6/40, *StS/USA*/II/12312. Thomsen to Foreign Ministry 22/8/40, *StS/USA*/III/22733.

[44] Thomsen to Foreign Ministry 18/10/40, *DGFP*/D/X, p. 508. Thomsen to Foreign Ministry 19/12/40, *StS/USA*/IV/62265. See for example: Brussels to Foreign Ministry 24/1/40, *DGFP*/D/VIII, p. 693. Rio to Foreign Ministry 2/7/40, *StS/USA*/II/12374. Rome to Foreign Ministry 21/10/40, *StS/USA*/III/23024. Memo (Woermann) 10/10/40, *StS/USA*/III/22989. Memo (Woermann) 21/10/40, *DGFP*/D/X, p. 353.

a two-fold policy regarding Germany. First there would be resistance to German mastery of the sea. But this was difficult since the American line of resistance had now been pulled back from Europe to a line from Greenland through Iceland to the Azores and Cape Verde islands. Thomsen saw only one conclusion to be drawn from this: that the idea of an expeditionary corps had been abandoned. The second aspect of American policy, Thomsen suggested, was United States naval patrol aid in delivering goods to England from new advanced positions. However, Thomsen doubted that American unpreparedness would permit Roosevelt any immediate intervention unless Germany seized Dakar or the chain of islands in the east Atlantic. During the same month, Dieckhoff was far less conditional in his view of American entry. He declared it to be "incontrovertible" that the American regime was preparing to enter the conflict and that it would not shrink from such a step once it had overcome certain domestic considerations.[45]

By the spring, Thomsen's reports on American policy toward Germany were also more pessimistic. The requisition of Axis ships in American ports and the blocking of Axis funds in American banks indicated to Thomsen that American hostility was to continue unabated. When the United States ordered the closure of German consulates in June Thomsen wired that while Roosevelt was unwilling to break relations himself, this move proved his willingness to "face the consequences of his policy unhesitatingly and make Germany responsible for any rupture." By July Thomsen found the administration more determined to have "war with Germany as quickly as possible," with American naval provocation the most likely cause. There would be no formal declaration of war, Thomsen argued, because there was no need of one.[46] Roosevelt's main difficulty remained the problem of

[45] Thomsen to Foreign Ministry 28/5/41, *StS/USA*/VI/24092. Memo (Dieckhoff) 22/5/41, *StS/USA*/VI/245191.

[46] Thomsen to Foreign Ministry 8/5/41, 14/5/41, *StS/USA*/VI/245074, 245428. Thomsen to Foreign Ministry 16/6/41, *DGFP*/D/XII, p. 1034. Thomsen to Foreign Ministry 10/7/41, 13/7/41, *StS/USA*/VII/373642.

making American influence felt rapidly enough to salvage the Allies.[47]

While Thomsen stressed both the possibility of American entry against Germany and the difficulties and problems which might restrain it, a more alarmist tone was apparent in the diplomatic reports from elsewhere. According to the Embassy in Budapest, for example, a State Department official had assured the Hungarian Ambassador in Washington that America was "determined to enter the war and see Hitler defeated even if it meant reducing Europe to ruins and regardless of whether England falls or not." This was in April, and five months later a report from Lisbon predicted American entry "within the week."[48] There were many other examples. Conversations with Japanese and Italian diplomats at Berlin suggested American attempts to have Germany fire the first shot, while intelligence sources warned of a "piecemeal engagement" of American forces.[49]

All of these reports had to be balanced against the almost frivolously optimistic dispatches of the Military Attaché in Washington on this subject and also had to be placed in the context of American actions. It is entirely likely that the *Wilhelmstrasse* gave greater weight to Thomsen's reports than to those from other sources regarding American affairs, and indeed the memoranda of the Foreign Ministry suggest that this was the case.

Policy recommendations by the diplomats in Berlin and Washington regarding German response to these American policies followed a consistent line. Almost without exception these memoranda called for restraint and the avoidance of anything which would exacerbate an already tense situation.

[47] Thomsen to Foreign Ministry 10/8/41, *StS/USA*/VII/376696. Thomsen to Foreign Ministry 4/12/41, *StS/USA*/X/44723.

[48] Budapest to Foreign Ministry 16/4/41, *StS/USA*/V/244409. Lisbon to Foreign Ministry 15/9/41, *StS/USA*/VIII/375811.

[49] Memo (Woermann) 15/5/41, *StS/USA*/VI/245156. Memo (Woermann) 11/6/41, *UStS/Japan-Amerika*/24945. Informationsstelle III 6/8/41, *StS/USA*/ VIII/375560.

State Secretary Weizsaeker in a note following the outbreak of war urged that everything be done to keep America neutral. To further this goal, it was suggested that a German Ambassador be returned to Washington in order to provide a listening post and strengthen German interests in the hemisphere. (Ribbentrop's reaction to this was a scribbled *"ausgeschlossen"* [out of the question] on the margin.) Weizsaeker opposed any *démarche* to Roosevelt on repeal of the Neutrality Acts since it would serve no purpose and might be interpreted as internal interference. His response was favorable to a more general declaration to the Americans that Germany had no war aims against the United States and that the war at sea would be pursued according to international law.[50]

Thomsen was also sensitive to anything which smacked of interference with American domestic affairs. German propaganda should confine itself to generalities about respect for the Monroe Doctrine and perhaps the futility of the First World War. Any overt endorsement of the isolationists, attacks on the President or even excessive criticism of the British were to be entirely avoided.[51]

Dieckhoff was especially concerned lest Germany be maneuvered into firing the first shot as a result of American provocation. In a long memorandum in January 1941 he addressed himself to the problem of what might be done to keep America out. There was to this end no substitute for rapid and sweeping German military victories which would render the whole question of American intervention academic. In any event, the Germans should take a strong, self-assured and calm attitude toward the Americans. He warned against any act or word which might substantiate the "German menace" myth in America. Americans were, he wrote, the most unpredictable people in the world. They could "with incredible speed be put into a mood which

[50] Memo (Weizsaeker) 17/9/39, *DGFP*/D/VIII, pp. 53–85.
[51] Thomsen to Foreign Ministry 24/9/39, *DGFP*/D/VIII, pp. 127–129. Thomsen to Foreign Ministry 16/5/40, 31/3/40, 13/6/40, *DGFP*/D/IX, pp. 351, 358, 559. Memo (Dieckhoff) 21/6/40, *StS*/*USA*/II/12326. Thomsen to Foreign Ministry 1/5/41, *StS*/*USA*/VI/245031.

precludes sound judgment." The President was a past master at
just such manipulations but even he needed material for it. The
Germans must at all costs not supply him with this material. It
was, he concluded, highly improbable that Roosevelt could compel war "if we remain ice-cold and calm."

Thomsen felt by April that adhering to this advice had already
upset Roosevelt's timetable. He and Dieckhoff continuously
warned against diplomatic retaliation or severing of relations.[52]
Far from weakening his position, Thomsen felt that the Atlantic
incidents made German restraint all the more imperative, and the
dispatches and memoranda on the subject retained this line un-
swervingly down to Pearl Harbor.[53]

The general tenor of the dispatches from Washington noted
in the pre-war years had thus been maintained in the crucial
period before American entry. Unfortunately, however, the
diplomatic pouches to Berlin contained other messages from the
Embassy, usually labeled "top secret" and flatly contradicting
much of the analysis and advice offered by Thomsen and Dieckhoff.

[52] Memo (Dieckhoff) 9/1/41, *DGFP*/D/XI, p. 1061. Memo (Dieckhoff)
21/7/41, *DGFP*/D/X, p. 259. Thomsen to Foreign Ministry 16/4/41, *StS/
USA*/V/244416. Memo (Dieckhoff) 17/6/41, *UStS/USA*/Unneutrales Ver-
halten/II/26480.

[53] Thomsen to Foreign Ministry 18/7/41, *StS/USA*/VII/373694. German
consuls did not, however, always follow this line. In June 1940, for example,
the consul in New Orleans aroused a furor when he warned that Germany
would not forget that "America aided her enemies while she was fighting for
her life." *NYT* 15/6/40.

CHAPTER 7

General von Boetticher's America

WHILE THE DIPLOMATS supplied the *Wilhelmstrasse* with sobering descriptions and cautious recommendations, quite another picture of America was being painted by the Military and Air Attaché, General Friedrich von Boetticher. We have already had a glimpse of this prior to the war. Boetticher's broad conception of his job enabled him to depart from the strictly military side of things and range freely over the whole field of American politics. Basing his observations on an allegedly unique relationship with high American military authorities, Boetticher's America was a country divided between a sober, moderate, patriotic and pro-German "General Staff" on the one hand and the politicians and press dominated by Jewry and the warmongers on the other. From this curious analysis, he formulated the view that American military intervention was out of the question and in any event could not divert the tide of German victory. These voluminous reports aroused the despair of Thomsen, the hostility of Dieckhoff, the suspicions of Weizsaeker and the admiration of Hitler.

We have already seen that prior to the war the General had remarked on the great and moderating influence of the American "General Staff" on Roosevelt and the State Department.[1] It was not until after the outbreak of war, however, that Boetticher

---

[1] Boetticher to OKW Ausland, OKH Attacheabteilung, RLM Attachegruppe 28/4/39, *DGFP*/D/VIII, p. 158. Boetticher's reports, countersigned by Thomsen, were usually sent to the above offices with copies to the Foreign Ministry. They will be abbreviated "Boetticher." Typically, Boetticher used the German term *Generalstab*, which inevitably suggested a false comparison between American and German military organization and tradition.

detailed for his superiors the precise outlook of the military leaders. He was glad to report that it was in fact thoroughly defensive.[2] Pacific problems and vast unpreparedness precluded in their mind any military action in Europe. There was great uncertainty regarding Japan and a consequent necessity to strengthen the Pacific defense "in deep echelon."

This was being accomplished by sending bombers to Manila, strengthening the fleet and air force at Pearl Harbor, concentrating naval striking power in California and reinforcing the Panama garrison. A mobile land force was being established to protect the United States itself, according to Boetticher. In fact, industrial pressure was compelling a defensive policy throughout. Since the "General Staff" was becoming ascendant over the politicians and cautious in outlook, American defensive armament was bound to take full priority over any expeditionary force or even military aid to the Allies. His conclusion was that the Americans were substantially unprepared materially or psychologically for military intervention in any form. Moreover, the General found "understanding for Germany" in military circles whose opinions were favorably compared with the "State Department's sterile attitude of hate and the impulsive policies of Roosevelt."[3] Thus even before 1940, the outlines of Boetticher's America had become clear.

As the tense months rolled by, the General found nothing to disturb his thesis. There was, for example, the matter of aircraft production. In April 1940, Boetticher reported on aircraft delivery promises to the Allies, which were ascribed to the need to boost Allied morale and to relieve domestic unemployment. Industry could not be expected to expand much for the time being and the fulfillment of even basic American defense needs would not materialize before the summer of 1941. American generals were reported to be opposed to all involvement outside the Western hemisphere. Thus, in the General's words, "the General Staff

[2] Boetticher 1/10/39, *DGFP*/D/VIII, p. 179.
[3] Boetticher 1/12/39, *DGFP*/D/VIII, p. 470.

has again shown its objectivity in the face of much political bait-
ing."[4]

In May, Boetticher believed that the military commanders had
achieved the same level of influence as the State Department on
Roosevelt's decisions. An early entry of the United States into
the war could now be definitely ruled out if the hemisphere was
not directly threatened. The idea that America would enter if
England was threatened was dismissed as a "slogan."[5] There was
in fact a great oceanic anxiety in America, Boetticher conceded,
but the point at issue was the Pacific, not the Atlantic. Although
even the military had warned of some possible deterioration of
German prestige in America if Hitler should attack through the
Low Countries, yet there was no cause for alarm, the Attaché
suggested, because it was also known that even the Scandinavian-
Americans had not been too unfavorably influenced against Germany by the Norwegian invasion. "People here," he concluded
cheerfully, "have shown sympathetic understanding."

The struggle between soldier and politician in America was
always stressed. The Attaché reported that the generals were
playing "the leading part" in American foreign policy, though
he conceded that the influence of "political babblers has by no
means been eliminated."[6] For example, military leaders were
now entirely pessimistic about an Allied victory. Only the pluto-
crats held out any hope. This favorable change of opinion Boetticher ascribed to Hitler's personal presence in the field of combat
and to comparisons now openly made in America between the
Fuehrer and George Washington. Furthermore, this was only
the beginning for the American people, who were unfortunately
still confused by "vague and unwholesome propaganda." These
comforting trends were but "harbingers of a new mode of
thought" revealing itself in the army and the people, though not
in the press.

[4] Boetticher 4/4/40, *DGFP*/D/IX, p. 73.
[5] Boetticher 11/5/40, *DGFP*/D/IX, p. 329.
[6] Boetticher 16/5/40, *DGFP*/D/IX, p. 353.

This popular awakening had caused apprehension among "the Jewish wirepullers" (one of the General's treasured clichés) and to conceal this anxiety they had launched two propaganda tricks: first, they had invented a German "threat" to the Azores, Greenland, Bermuda and Latin America. Second, they had conjured up an espionage scare. However, all was to turn out for the best because objectivity remained in the "General Staff" and the people would not go beyond their military leadership. One can scarcely imagine a formula better calculated to appeal to Hitler's peculiar political mythology than of the *Volk* rallying around soldierly leadership and rejecting the Jewish-plutocratic press and politicians in the national interest.

On May 24, Berlin received further details of Boetticher's America. Regarding what he liked to call "that American element so valuable to us," he could not in this report have been more optimistic. American military writers had effectively punctured British propaganda in regard to German military weakness, and events had put the military point of view in the ascendancy over the politicians. Almost lyrically, he added: "It is just as if a fresh breeze of the German spirit were blowing across to America from the battlefields of northern France and Belgium." People were now quite resigned to the defeat of the Allies and there were rumors of a German seizure of the British fleet. Symptomatic of this encouraging tendency was the attempt of the business community in America to adjust to the prospect of a German victory. If dangers to their confidence were avoided by Germany, these circles would gain the upper hand. If, however, there were disturbing incidents, the Jews and Freemasons would take over. "That is, after all," he concluded, "the American mentality."[7]

Events in June did not shake the Attaché's confidence. The entry of Italy into the war had been accurately adjudged in military quarters and thus there was no cause to worry about American reaction. Nor did Roosevelt's rearmament speech in that month disturb the General's optimism in the least. Through such

[7] Boetticher 24/5/40, *DGFP*/D/IX, p. 425.

"fanfare" and "pompous declarations," the administration sought to intimidate the Axis by having diplomatic missions in Washington convey to their government the imminence of American intervention.[8]

During the election campaign that summer Boetticher was evidently unhappy about pronouncements of the administration. In August he felt compelled to announce that "the Jewish element now holds key positions in the American armed forces." General John Pershing, for example, had become "a puppet in the hands of Roosevelt, which means the Jews." Inevitably Pershing was compared to "the greatly gifted [Col. Charles] Lindbergh." Set on this course, the administration was thus creating "a militarized state with Roosevelt as dictator."[9] He was not, however, in the least disturbed by the destroyer deal. It was, he asserted, no cause for alarm since the United States had "a long way to go" as yet in the direction of military preparation. The whole thing was a gimmick to buttress the British. Roosevelt, after all, had not kept past promises of aid and both Congress and the navy were opposed.[10] When contrary to Boetticher's predictions the deal was consummated, the Attaché made no further comment on the matter.

In the late summer and early fall of 1940, Boetticher's dispatches reveal a decidedly less optimistic tone and some little concern regarding a more active and expansionist American policy in certain areas, notably the Caribbean and Africa. In mid-August he called attention to American moves regarding French possessions in the Western hemisphere which included the preparation of American landing forces. More ominous in Boetticher's view was the establishment of an American consulate

---

[8] Boetticher 12/6/40, *StS/USA*/II/12257. Boetticher 16/5/40, *DGFP*/D/IX, p. 352.

[9] Boetticher 20/7/40, *DGFP*/D/IX, p. 254. Boetticher 4/8/40, *StS/USA*/II/12553.

[10] Boetticher 10/8/40, *DGFP*/D/X, p. 456. Boetticher opposed any protest regarding the rumored deal since this would just give an opportunity to the "influential Jew hatemonger clique" to charge internal interference.

in Dakar, symbolizing American concern in that area.[11] The first aim of American policy, Boetticher wrote in September, was to bring to a diplomatic or military solution the situation in the Pacific, if possible by using British naval forces. "Washington leads and London complies," he announced. Negotiations regarding Singapore, Port Arthur and Pacific bases had in view the disposal of the Japanese as a preparation for Atlantic operations. All of this, he explained, "would free the seas for a large-scale imperialist policy in the Atlantic." Specifically, the object of such a policy would be to bring West Africa under American influence, to control communication between Latin America and Europe, to procure Atlantic bases and to cement an alliance with Canada. Such dabbling in other areas, concluded the General, constituted a kind of one-way Monroe Doctrine which was altogether characteristic of the "boundless conceit of the Americans."[12]

In addition, the Attaché's office sent at this time the first of three warnings (the other two in July and November 1941) which, quite contrary to the usual line, placed a high value on the scale and quality of American military preparations.[13] This may have been brought on by some criticism which had been voiced against his reports earlier in the summer, by the destroyer deal or by the disappointingly strong defense line the Republican candidate was taking in his campaign speeches. It is also possible that these particular reports were written by the more realistic assistant Air Attaché, Captain Riedel.[14]

In any event, by October the reports from the Attaché had

---

[11] Boetticher 14/8/40, *DGFP*/D/X, p. 479.

[12] Boetticher 24/9/40, *DGFP*/D/XI, p. 177.

[13] Boetticher 14/9/40, *DGFP*/D/XI, p. 78. The other two reports are dated 12/7/41 and 5/11/41. In both of these the comment on American strength is brief and buried in dispatches the general tone of which must have conveyed exactly the opposite impression.

[14] This latter explanation was given to the author by Dr. Thomsen in the course of a conversation in Hamburg on November 8, 1963. Thomsen also remarked that in general Boetticher was quite impervious to persuasion about anything.

resumed their previous tone. In a dispatch entitled "On the effect of the Tripartite Pact on American defense policy," he held that the Pact had confirmed the concern of the armed forces that the United States was faced with major military defeat if policies did not become harmonized with military strength. The Pact had brought the dilemma of American policy to a head. The retaliatory embargo against the Japanese was a pointless gesture of the "shopkeeper's soul"; pointless because of Japanese stockpiling, the existence of other Pacific raw material sources and the injurious effects on the American economy. The Pact had, the General now boasted, convinced the "General Staff" that American advantage lay with an Axis victory.[15]

Increasingly, the General saw American policy as a gigantic bluff. The attempt was being made, for example, to give the impression that the American navy would strike at once if Japan did not yield. In furtherance of this fraud there had been a call-up of naval personnel, the loan to China, newspaper reports of the superiority of the American fleet over the Japanese and a possible recall of Americans from Japan. This great Pacific hoax would be supplemented by an insistence in the press that England could hold out. Naturally, the armed forces rejected such nonsense. The fact was, reported the Attaché, that the government was by no means united and was seeking a face-saving formula, since the fleet would require at least a two-year build-up to be in any condition to face Japan.[16]

In his final dispatch of 1940, Boetticher stressed once again the excessive burden on the American armaments industry. In spite of vigorous efforts and "dictatorial" regulations, there was only limited productive capacity for war materials, planes and engines; there was a lack of machine tools and skilled workers. There would necessarily have to be some reduction of targets, and the year ended for the Attaché with the great tension between gen-

---

[15] Boetticher 28/9/40, *DGFP*/D/XI, p. 209. Boetticher 2/10/40, *DGFP*/D/ XI, p. 237.
[16] Boetticher 9/10/40, *DGFP*/D/XI, p. 273.

eral and politician unresolved; with "diametrically opposing forces working against each other to determine America's fate."[17]

The new year brought little new for Boetticher. Indeed the heightening tension actually demonstrated his case. Roosevelt simply had no idea of how slow American mobilization would be; the Pacific distraction ruled out any possibility of a repetition of 1917. Thus Germany need take no notice of Roosevelt's "hollow chatter" since "it is always the same." In the ensuing months the General sent along to Berlin a number of general surveys of American policy all coming to the same conclusion: America could not and would not intervene although American policy was ambitious and imperialistic. In May, this policy was described as concerned with the Atlantic, Greenland and the Portuguese islands; the narrows between West Africa and Brazil; the African west coast and the Indian Ocean. The Americans would try to rescue Singapore, limit the Japanese and cut the main Pacific communication lines. However, he wrote, none of these would affect German plans if she achieved rapid victory. "This war," he said, "is a race with time."[18]

In June he described the United States as "desperate" to avoid war due to the Japanese question, military unpreparedness and the shipping problem. The anti-war faction now had the upper hand completely, he announced, and this would frustrate Roosevelt's plans.[19] In July Boetticher reported that "the wirepullers" around Roosevelt had hoped that England would fight and bleed until the moment when the United States could step in and administer the *coup de grâce* to a battered Axis with minimum effort. However, the victories of the Fuehrer and the firmness of the Japanese had destroyed all of these fond illusions. "The primitive strategists" (another of the General's ill-defined but

[17] Boetticher 16/10/40, *DGFP/D/XI*, p. 307. Boetticher 7/12/40, 15/12/40, *StS/USA*/IV/62188, 62246.
[18] Boetticher 11/1/41, *StS/USA*/IV/62345. Boetticher 16/2/41, 18/2/41, *StS/USA*/V/244087, 244090. Boetticher 10/5/41, *StS/USA*/VI/245098.
[19] Boetticher 17/6/41, *StS/USA*/VII/373560.

oft-repeated descriptions) had now to revise their plans and adjust themselves to greater commitments which they could not
possibly fulfill. "They move," he said, "in a fog and are doped
with clichés and massive self-inflation." And this, he concluded,
is what happened when politicians dabbled in military affairs.[20]
He made no comment about military attachés who dabbled in
politics.

In addition to these lengthy general commentaries, Boetticher
also concerned himself with the specifics of American policy
during 1941. In these comments his differences with Thomsen
and Dieckhoff became especially clear. In February, he directed
his attention to the Lend-Lease project. It was, of course, a
project of "the Jewish wirepullers" and was opposed by the
military leaders. The whole object of Lend-Lease, as Boetticher
saw it, was to free Roosevelt from internal legal ties. He admitted that activity had become intense: lists were being com-
piled, needs estimated, Anglo-American cooperation thrown into
gear. However, the Lend-Lease program and related activities
were, Berlin was assured, no cause at all for alarm. America faced
vast problems in fulfilling such a program in view of her own
defense needs, the problem of where to concentrate deliveries
and inadequate transportation. Thus, "everything is bluff and
disguise and the truth about American plans lies in my reports,"
he reassured his superiors.[21]

As the implementation of Lend-Lease became a fact, Boetticher
saw no reason to be disturbed. Although in their overweening
presumptuousness Americans now saw themselves as arbiters of
the world, it was clearly all a matter of bogus gestures designed
to persuade the world of America's imminent entry. After all,
Boetticher argued once again, 1941 was not 1917. Germany was
now master of Europe and this deprived the Americans of any
possible front. There was no available air power, and shipping

[20] Boetticher 7/7/41, *StS/USA*/VII/373619.
[21] Boetticher 26/2/41, *DGFP*/D/XII, pp. 161-164. Boetticher 25/5/41, *StS/
USA*/VI/245158.

losses would be too great. The air force was "antiquated" and the Axis alliance decisive.

Of course, Boetticher felt compelled to point out, there was the possibility that Roosevelt, erratic and Jewish-influenced, might react to incidents and this constituted an "X" factor. However, the "coldly calculating General Staff" naturally saw things as they were and this was now to be distinguished from the attitude of the navy, which had evidently joined the forces of evil in Boetticher's scheme of things. Only in the army could one find "the quiet and impressive personalities" which Germany should treasure.[22] Thus was Lend-Lease reduced in the spring of 1941 to "a trick," an "empty gesture" and "an admission of weakness" which could not possibly influence the outcome of the war.[23]

The contradictions in American policy had in 1941 become even more acute. Foremost among these was the promise to reinforce England without the possibility of fulfilling the promise. "Neither maneuvers nor fiery presidential words nor declarations of so-called experts," Boetticher felt, could remove the horns of this dilemma or rescue them from the other quandaries which had resulted from the failure of the administration to take note of military and economic realities. Thus the more Roosevelt spoke of Greenland, the Azores, Dakar and other areas, the more he threatened to use American convoys and other provocations, the more assured Germany could be of American weakness. Roosevelt's gestures and words could be entirely dismissed, Boetticher advised, as "crude exaggeration and pure bluff."[24]

Increasingly Boetticher placed his reliance in the generals during the final year. He now conceived it to be "our most decisive

---

[22] Boetticher 11/3/41, *DGFP*/D/XII, p. 266. This description of the navy as interventionist as compared to the isolationist army and air force also reached the *Wilhelmstrasse* in a dispatch from Lisbon quoting the American Military Attaché in that city. Lisbon to Foreign Ministry 14/11/40. *StS*/*USA*/IV/6208.

[23] Boetticher 12/3/41, 14/3/41, *StS*/*USA*/V/244231, 244237. Boetticher 26/3/41, *DGFP*/D/XII, p. 365.

[24] Boetticher 26/3/41, 4/4/41, 11/4/41, 16/4/41, 1/5/41, 15/5/41, *StS*/*USA*/ V/244312, 244248, 244395, 244410; VI/245033, 245158.

task" to influence this group and encourage them. In May he was able to report on the successes of this body. Working with Lindbergh and the "Hoover circle," the military leaders had been able to slow rearmament and compel Roosevelt to readjust his more far-reaching plans. The warmongers, he announced, were in retreat and the "intelligent and quiet advice of the General Staff" was gaining the upper hand. And this was being achieved in spite of Secretary of War Stimson ("a flunky of Roosevelt") and the imperialistic tendency of the navy, which "cannot do enough to whip up public opinion."[25] He was even complacent about the various incidents in the Atlantic involving American ships during 1941. Neither the sinking of the *Robin Moor* nor the attack on the *Greer* overly disturbed him. He simply ruled out the possibility that these things could have been deliberate or could bring America in since the country was too weak and divided to take advantage of such a situation. Naval weakness also rendered American threats to Africa and the Portuguese islands, which Boetticher had earlier regarded with some concern, improbable and hollow.[26]

The proclamation of national emergency was for the Attaché an attempt by Roosevelt to appear as a great leader, but the entire speech was "overshadowed with anxiety" since America could do nothing against the Axis. It merely proved how decisively the initiative lay with Germany. He saw no need at all to alter his earlier estimates of American potential since an acceleration of the American armaments industry was "out of the question." "His speech is, therefore, not an expression of American strength, but a confession of England's serious difficulties," which the United States could not alleviate. Finally, all of the talk of America's now proceeding to the acquisition of forward

---

[25] Boetticher 12/3/41, *StS/USA*/V/244231. Boetticher 17/9/41, *StS/USA*/VIII/375826. Mussolini also had unkind things to say about the American navy at this time, when he characterized it to Ribbentrop as "dilettantish" and "for purposes of sport." "Like the British army," he added. Memo (Ribbentrop-Mussolini meeting) 20/9/40, *DGFP*/D/XI, p. 119.

[26] Boetticher 13/6/41, *StS/USA*/VI/245414. Boetticher 7/9/41, *StS/USA*/VIII/375752. Boetticher 24/7/41, *StS/USA*/VIII/373720.

strategic positions was waved aside as "just another cliché."[27]

The entry of Russia into the war was to be welcomed because it would sharpen the contradictions of American policy. Roosevelt could promise the Soviets "the blue from heaven" but nothing would materialize. By October, the "primitive strategists" and the Roosevelt clique had been proved wrong in their faith in Russian resistance, while the military men who saw the German drive as "a master plan of German leadership and soldierly invincibility" had been proved right.[28]

Japanese-American relations were also treated by Boetticher in these final months. His theme here was quite simple: the American fleet was split, and even if it had been united it could not defeat the Japanese navy. Since the American dilemma in the Pacific was "insoluble," Japan and the Axis had an open field for their activities free from American interference. "Japan," he wrote in October, "can do what she wants in the Far East without American military intervention." His only fear was that the Japanese would be intimidated by American gestures and fail to perceive the sham of American policy.

The plain fact of the matter was that America not only wanted but absolutely had to seek agreement with Japan in order to gain time to build her two-ocean fleet. Moreover, he insisted, there was no hope whatever of America becoming the "arsenal of democracy" without access to Far Eastern raw materials. Hence there was "a war of nerves between Japan and the U.S.A." So long, Boetticher believed, as Japan did not attack the Philippines, however, America would not fight, preferring as she did to rely on bluff and intimidation. Convinced of Japanese gullibility in these matters, Boetticher took it upon himself to tutor them and was, he reported, able to convince the Japanese Military Attaché

[27] Boetticher 29/5/41, *StS/USA*/VI/245252. Mussolini's comment on the declaration of national emergency was typically distasteful: "Never has a nation been guided by a paralytic." *NYT* 28/5/41.

[28] Boetticher 6/8/41, 22/8/41, *StS/USA*/VIII/375567, 375654. Boetticher 8/10/41, *StS/USA*/IX/422126.

that American policy was all "a glittering façade."[29] Finally regarding Japanese-American relations, Boetticher on November 15 urged Berlin to disregard rumors of war if the Hull-Kurusu talks failed. Indeed, the General declared himself highly "amused" at such tactics of bluff since "we have known for two years that America cannot commit herself in the Pacific."[30]

True to his policy of interpreting every American word and act in the direction of Anglo-American solidarity and involvement in the war as a sign of weakness and division, Boetticher dismissed the Roosevelt-Churchill meeting in August out of hand. It could at most prolong the war but not affect the outcome. Filtered through the General's curious logic, the meeting was in fact "the greatest admission of Anglo-American military weakness" and an effort to conceal the fact that Germany had won the race for time. The Atlantic Charter was therefore simply so much "grousing, boasting, chatter and incitement" (*Schimpferei, Grosssprecherei, Rederei, Hetzerei*).[31]

In the final few weeks, Boetticher's reports became almost smug. American military support for a continental invasion by Britain would always be blocked by the armed forces. Such an adventure could not even be contemplated before 1944. These doubts in high military places and this conviction of German victory had now infected wider circles with misgivings about the anti-Axis line of American policy. Recognition was growing everywhere that Russia was finished, that Japan was successfully blocking American policy and that American production could never catch up to German production. Anglo-American policy was held to be "fully under the spell of German victories," while reports of American counter-moves in the Pacific were described

*

29 Boetticher 14/8/41, 23/8/41, *StS/USA*/VIII/375628, 375669. Boetticher 30/7/41, *StS*/USA/VII/373776. Boetticher 17/9/41, 21/9/41, *StS*/USA/VIII/375826, 375844.
30 Boetticher 15/11/41, *StS*/USA/IX/422366.
31 Boetticher 6/8/41, 14/8/41, 2/9/41, *StS*/*USA*/VIII/375566, 375628, 375726.

as "nonsensical and fantastic." Barring a possible but unlikely erratic act by Roosevelt, Boetticher gave Berlin a final assurance that American entry was *"ausgeschlossen."*[32]

In estimating the General's reports it is not asserted that his views were either entirely eccentric or wholly inaccurate. The faith in a rapid German victory upon which he based many of his judgments was a belief widely held in Washington and elsewhere at that time. Hull, for example, certainly had doubts about the British ability to hold out. There was in fact considerable vacillation on the convoy issue, and the production problems involved in fulfilling Lend-Lease requirements were considerable.[33] Furthermore, we have seen that regarding American hemispheric sensitivity the General was consistently apprehensive and his warnings were every bit as urgent as Thomsen's against German tampering, or the appearance of it, with Latin America. Thomsen and Boetticher were not far apart in their emphasis on the Japanese factor, and the underestimation of isolationism in America which marked the diplomatic reports may even have been partially corrected by Boetticher's observations.

Yet the overall impression of these numerous, lengthy and repetitious dispatches remains clear: it is one of great exaggeration of the cautiousness and especially the political influence of American military leaders and gross underestimation of American industrial potential, coupled with an almost frivolous disregard for the impact of American intervention against Germany. The picture of America Boetticher gave to Berlin was inaccurate, naïve and, from the point of view of German policy planning, dangerously distorted.

Of the accuracy of his reports, General von Boetticher himself revealed not the slightest doubt, however. In May 1940 he wrote

---

[32] Boetticher 17/10/41, 18/10/41, StS/USA/IX/422172, 422189. Boetticher 4/11/41, StS/USA/IX/422291. Boetticher 20/11/41, StS/USA/X/44640.

[33] See discussion in Langer and Gleason, *The Undeclared War*, pp. 436–444, 515, 569–574. See alleged comment by U.S. Military Attaché in Lisbon regarding pessimism about English chances. Lisbon Embassy to Berlin 14/11/40, StS/USA/IV/162081.

that "thanks to my connections, I have always sent exhaustive reports of which not one has contained an error of any importance." In a letter to the Chief of the German General Staff "personally" Boetticher stated that "I have never overestimated my activities, but I may be permitted to report that my dispatches have never required alteration."[34] Not only were his reports accurate, they were also unique. Other diplomats in Washington failed to see the fraudulence of American policy and were in their innocence actually impressed by the possibilities of American influence in the war. This was, he suggested in March 1941, especially true of the Soviet and Japanese envoys. Their problem was, he complained, that they lacked the overall view. "How foolishly," he wrote on another occasion, "even the naval, military and air attachés at the embassies accept American propaganda regarding the productive capacity of American industry. How inaccurately their respective governments are informed."[35]

Weizsaeker, Dieckhoff and Thomsen were less impressed. Following Boetticher's glib assurances regarding American reaction to the German attack on Scandinavia, Weizsaeker expressed to Thomsen his considerable doubt about so cheerful a reaction to German aggression in America. "I request you now to study the press again and see to it that reports by the Wehrmacht Attaché where, as in this instance, they touch on the political field, are coordinated with your views."[36] Thomsen in his reply spoke of a "harmonious relationship of confidence" between himself and Boetticher which did not preclude differences of opinion on facts. The General was, he added, "an extraordinarily sensitive personality" and it had to be borne in mind that the General placed a high evaluation on his sources of information and on the amount of influence which the military had upon American policy. His telegrams expressed the mood of some high military officers,

---

[34] Boetticher 24/5/40, *DGFP/D/IX*, p. 424. Boetticher 1/8/41, *StS/USA/* VII/373785.
[35] Boetticher 26/3/41, *DGFP/D/XIII*, p. 365. Boetticher 11/4/41, *StS/USA/* 244395. Boetticher 16/5/40, *DGFP/D/IX*, p. 353.
[36] Weizsaeker to Thomsen 19/4/40, *DGFP/D/IX*, p. 208.

therefore, and not that of other more decisive factors in American policy. "I try," he added, "to counteract this."

Following these rather vague statements, Thomsen got to what was probably the root of the matter. Since the outbreak of war, Thomsen explained, Boetticher had come to regard the importance of his position as greatly increased. "He has now the unusually high rank of commanding general," Thomsen noted. On the occasion of his forty years of service,

> He received a personal telegram of recognition from the Fuehrer which justified him in concluding that his activity here is appreciated in the highest quarters. This is all the more reason why I should acknowledge that General von Boetticher upholds my authority in every respect.[37]

The matter of Boetticher's political reporting was not settled by this exchange, however. A year later, in April 1941, Weizsaeker complained to Thomsen that the Wehrmacht Attaché continued to report about political matters and that he overclassified his reports. The State Secretary wondered if Thomsen could not "in a comradely way" persuade the General not to overstep his field.[38] Boetticher responded to this "comradely" advice by reminding the *Wilhelmstrasse* that he was acting on direct instructions from the Fuehrer.[39]

By May, as the General's political reporting continued unabated, even Ribbentrop was moved to complain, reminding Thomsen that he, as head of mission, was responsible for the political content of the dispatches and that political reporting was "no business of Boetticher's."[40]

[37] Thomsen to Weizsaeker 24/4/40, *DGFP/D/IX*, p. 231.

[38] Weizsaeker to Thomsen 3/4/41, *StS/USA/V/244344*. Boetticher almost inevitably sent his reports *citissime* even when they contained the most ordinary and routine information. Since these reports were also verbose, this put a great burden on the Embassy's coding facilities. (Thomsen in conversation with the author, Hamburg, 8/11/63).

[39] Boetticher to Weizsaeker 10/4/41, *StS/USA/V/244388*. Thomsen to Foreign Ministry 23/5/41, *StS/USA/VI/245200*. Thomsen has told the author that such an open break might have resulted in his own recall and had a damaging effect on the already strained relations between Germany and the United States.

[40] Ribbentrop to Thomsen 26/5/41, 27/5/41, *StS/USA/VI/245208, 245229*.

If Thomsen felt some need for caution regarding Boetticher's reports, Dieckhoff in Berlin was less restrained in his critique. In a series of memoranda he took strong issue with most of the General's interpretations. In January 1941 he attacked Boetticher's view that American entry into the war would make no difference as "erroneous." On the contrary, the former Ambassador warned that if America entered Roosevelt would assume full powers and command of industrial mobilization. Even with their own defense needs, he continued, the amount the Americans could make available to England would increase and none of this was changed at all by Pacific diversions. Moreover, South America would back Roosevelt and American entry would raise doubts in neutral minds about Germany's ability to win the war. Peace with England Dieckhoff held to be possible; but peace with England and the United States would be out of the question.[41]

The former Ambassador's interpretation of Lend-Lease was entirely at variance with Boetticher's, and in June Dieckhoff denied categorically that the "General Staff" had any decisive role in American policy or influence with Roosevelt. He added that the whole question of military preparedness in America was secondary in the light of the experience of 1917. In July he pressed his criticism of the Attaché's reliance on the military. It simply was not a true picture, he maintained, since the generals had to "go along with the President" and not the other way around.[42]

In a letter to the author, Boetticher denied that his reports had been politically colored. "I had to do with political matters only in so far as they touched upon military questions. The responsibility for all political questions lay with the appropriate officials

There is evidence, however, as will be discussed below, that Ribbentrop was not entirely displeased with the General's reports, at least in their depreciation of American military strength.

[41] Memo (Dieckhoff) 9/1/41, *DGFP*/D/XI, p. 1061.

[42] Memo (Dieckhoff) 6/6/41, *DGFP*/D/XII/, p. 973. Memo (Dieckhoff) 4/7/41, *StS*/*USA*/VII/373609.

of the Embassy."[43] Nevertheless, other post-war testimony confirms the considerable suspicion of the Attaché's reporting at the *Wilhelmstrasse*. Testifying at the diplomats' trial in 1949, Woermann noted his own resistance to the misleading impressions of the dispatches, which he found "unreliable." Kordt has a similar appraisal in his memoirs, while Weizsaeker testifying in his own defense affirmed that although the reports were circulated for the record, he found them "repulsive" in their language and worrisome because of "the exaggerated statements."[44]

It is not clear what effect the reports had in military circles. Weizsaeker wrote to Thomsen that Boetticher's information was "of special value" to General Halder, although there is no mention of this in the Halder diaries. The General's opinions were also recorded from time to time in the German naval war diaries and they may have had some influence on German admiralty views regarding the United States. This will be discussed in a later chapter. William Shirer recalls that some of the members of the OKW expressed their doubts about Boetticher's accuracy to him. This doubt was also evidently entertained by at least one member of the State Security Office.[45]

Yet, both the language and the content of the reports could not but have commended themselves to the Hitler-Ribbentrop viewpoint. With the well-known tendency of the Fuehrer to read nothing that did not flatter his instincts, and the reluctance of his colleagues to show him evidence of a contrary nature, it may well be assumed that Boetticher's comments did in fact reach the Reichschancellor. But we need not merely assume it. There is more specific evidence that the fantasies of Boetticher formed one of the bases of Hitler's opinion of the United States and its

[43] Letter, Boetticher to author, 24/6/63. The author had invited the General to make a full commentary on these matters.

[44] Woermann testimony, *Case 11*/XXIII, p. 11233. *Wahn und Wirklichkeit*, p. 142. Weizsaeker testimony, *Case 11*/XVIII, pp. 8063, 8079.

[45] Weizsaeker to Thomsen 3/4/41, *StS/USA*/V/244344. *OKM-KTB*/A/IX/25/5/40, 2/10/40, 15/10/40; XXI/19/5/41; XXIV/2/8/41. Shirer, *Third Reich*, p. 749. Schellenberg, *op. cit.*, p. 125.

policies. We have already seen Boetticher's and Thomsen's af-
firmations of this. Walter Tannenberg, the former First Secretary of the Washington Embassy, testified in his post-war interrogation that the Thomsen dispatches were not shown to
Hitler by Ribbentrop but the Boetticher reports were shown to
him by General Keitel. Kordt has confirmed that the telegrams
of the Attaché were read by Hitler "with the greatest interest."
Weizsaeker testified at his trial that "the most dangerous thing
about these reports and the thing that gave us most misgivings
was that Hitler and Ribbentrop liked to read them."[46] Finally,
Hitler expressed his personal confidence by receiving Boetticher
immediately upon his return in January 1942 and greeting him
with the words: "You have reported courageously. You have not
made us nervous."[47]

We cannot judge the effect of all of this diplomatic reporting
until we have discussed the actual impact of the United States
upon German policy. We may assume at this point that Ribbentrop was aware at least of the outlines of the picture presented by
Thomsen, Dieckhoff and the others. Although reluctant to do so,
it seems likely that Hitler had to display some greater interest in
America than he had done before the war. But he was not a man
to abandon his prejudices lightly and we need not doubt that his
impression of American intentions and capacities was the result of
a highly selective process. His own statements certainly suggest
this and, as we shall see, his policies tend to bear this out. Yet the
reality of American power was bound in these final years to
break, if only occasionally, through the fog of misconceptions.
   It was in fact the America of economic and of growing military strength, of marked hostility to Nazi Germany, of determination under a resolute President to resist the conquest of
Europe and England by Hitler to the limit of its capacity — it

[46] Tannenberg interrogation as quoted in Trefousse, "Failure of German Intelligence," *MVHR*, June 1955. Letter, Kordt to author, 9/7/63. Weizsaeker
testimony, *Case 11/XVII*, p. 8064.
[47] Kordt recalled this statement in a letter to the author, 9/7/63.

was this America, which had been pictured by the diplomats since the 1930's, rather than the distant, weakened, decadent and militarily inadequate country conjured up by Hitler and supported by Ribbentrop and Boetticher which the Fuehrer had to face in December 1941. But even before the outbreak of hostilities, as the war with England lengthened, the truth of the matter had become clear if Hitler had cared to perceive it. Had he been able to rouse himself from his maps of the Soviet Union, he might have seen that the United States had already become a factor in German foreign policy, had already intruded itself into his political world. Neither his distrust of the harassed *Wilhelmstrasse* nor his self-righteous assurances to all who cared to listen that it could not be so were sufficient to alter this reality, although his efforts to escape the implications of American power were reflected in the confusion of the German response. Hitler continued to hover between myth and reality, and the tensions between these two views of the United States rendered the German reaction to America contradictory and in the long run self-defeating.

PART III

The United States and
German Foreign Policy

CHAPTER 8

America and Hitler's Continental Policy

HITLER'S ATTITUDE toward America, we have observed, reflected his political assumptions and strategic limitations. The racial and cultural prerequisites for national power which excluded liberal democracy, his "infantryman's mentality" which so dismayed Ernst Hanfstaengl; his reliance upon *Lebensraum* in Eastern Europe as the answer to the German question and his tendency to concentrate on immediate European problems, all stand revealed in his contemptuous statements about the United States. The diplomatic reports as far as the Fuehrer was concerned appear to have been gestures in futility. But this is not the whole story. For Hitler, after 1939, had to conduct a war and, for all of his self-delusion, this required some estimation of the forces arraigned against him. These forces included, indirectly but persistently, the United States and it was the country more accurately portrayed in the diplomatic reports.

In his fortress Europe, gratefully surrounded by all the old familiar political and strategic factors, Hitler could believe himself relatively safe from American power. Here there is scanty evidence of America in Hitler's plans. Here he could concentrate on his *Drang nach Osten*, on the final solution of the Russian question which would bring in turn the solution to everything else, including the need to deal with the incomprehensible British and the impudent Americans. It was to be a race between the inevitable conquest of Russia and the staying power of the Anglo-Saxon bloc. Pending this triumphant day, Hitler fought a rearguard holding operation in the Atlantic and, through his Japanese ally, in the Pacific. His policy in these two areas would be different. In the Atlantic, where he could see little connection with the Russian operation (Barbarossa), his stance was cautious. But Japan was located on the Soviet Eastern flank. Here he was prepared to take greater risks. Through both policies he became increasingly entangled with the United States, with a power which was not even supposed to exist in world politics.

Hitler's foreign policy contained, in varying combinations, elements both of planning and opportunism. For the most part he grounded his plans and seized his opportunities in Europe. His continentalism served as a standard by which he judged and manipulated even those policies and factors which lay outside Europe. Additional evidence of this will be seen in the following chapters dealing with naval and Far Eastern policy, areas in which America entered German strategic calculations in a significant way. But was America a direct factor in German continental policy as well? We have seen in an earlier chapter that in the early years Hitler speculated on a continental role for the United States and that in 1933 he greeted Roosevelt's disarmament proposals, taking the occasion to "welcome the possibility of bringing the United States into European relations as a guarantor of peace."[1] However, this sentiment was never repeated and, in spite of the warnings from Washington, Hitler came, as we know, to assume American isolation as a constant of international relations. The answer to the question, then, is that Hitler and his diplomats were aware of American influence in Europe both actual and potential but that, for various reasons, that country never assumed great importance in the years under consideration.

An awareness of American foreign policy is suggested by the use which Hitler and his associates made of it from time to time to justify German actions. The Versailles Treaty ("no greater subjugation than this can ever be inflicted on the chieftains of the Sioux tribe"), the "betrayal" of the Fourteen Points, non-recognition of Manchuria and withdrawal from the League of Nations

[1] *Zweites Buch*, pp. 100–125; speech of 16/5/33, Baynes, *op. cit.*, p. 1055.

were early examples of this.[2] Later, during the Czech crisis, Hitler, both in public and in private used the Monroe Doctrine to defend German policy ("We Germans support a similar doctrine for Europe"). Moreover, the American "short of war" stance regarding Britain was held up as a proper attitude for Japan to adopt against the Western powers for the sake of Germany.[3] The justification of German policy through dubious parallels to the actions of other countries was, of course, a well-known propaganda ploy of the Fuehrer.[4]

In the same way, Hitler was well aware, as we have seen, of Roosevelt's various appeals and speeches about the European situation and reacted to them, though not in a manner to suggest that he took the American President very seriously. There is, for example, no reason to believe that the American appeals at the time of Munich either influenced Hitler to call the conference or affected the course of events. Ambassador Wilson recorded in his diary in October the impression that Roosevelt's first message may have had the effect of calling Hitler's attention to the might and power of the United States, but added, "I cannot honestly convince myself that the second message had any appreciable influence on events." According to French sources, Hitler's first reaction to Roosevelt's non-aggression appeal of April 1939 was to refuse to reply to "so contemptible a creature." When he did reply, the contempt was all too apparent. ("With all due respect to Mr. Roosevelt's insight into the needs and cares of other countries. . . .")[5]

---

[2] Speech 28/4/39, Baynes, *op. cit.*, pp. 1635-1656. Neurath to Tokyo Embassy 18/1/34, *DGFP*/C/II, p. 385. Memorandum for Italian Ambassador 12/2/34, *ibid.*, p. 470. "I resolved to follow the example of the U.S.A.," Hitler said, regarding the League in his speech of April 28, 1939. Baynes, *op. cit.*, p. 1641.

[3] Speech 28/4/39, Baynes, *op. cit.*, p. 1646. Ribbentrop testimony, *IMT*/X, p. 427. Welles was told that Germany regarded Eastern Europe as her Mexico. Memo 29/2/40, *DGFP*/D/VIII, p. 818. *OKM-KTB*/C/VIII — 11/2/41.

[4] See for example his comparison of the Sudetens to the Palestinian Arabs. Speech 12/9/38, Baynes, *op. cit.*, p. 1437.

[5] Wilson, *op. cit.*, pp. 57, 58: diary entry for 22/10/40. Discussion in *The Challenge to Isolation*, pp. 32-35. Bullitt telegram 18/4/39, *ibid.*, p. 87.

According to Ribbentrop, Roosevelt's final appeals in August 1939 forced Hitler to alter his timetable and he recalled Hitler's "annoyance" at the President for this change. But although some have suggested that Hitler as early as 1938 had reckoned on the possibility of American power in the scales against Germany, there is no evidence to support the picture of an American factor in Hitler's continental calculations in the years before the war, nor in the crucial weeks prior to its outbreak.[6]

After September 1939, Hitler became well aware that English hopes rested increasingly on American support. He complained to the American businessman Mooney in March 1940 that peace was being delayed by the English refusal to give us hope of aid from others, "for example the United States." This factor was at first minimized by his confidence in a quick conquest of the continent followed by a deal with the English, before American aid could become effective.[7] It was then pushed aside pending the successful completion of Operation Barbarossa. In any event, the growing Anglo-American unity was not regarded by Hitler as a strictly continental problem and will be examined in the context of naval policy and relations with Japan.

Regarding other areas of Europe, we have already learned that the *Wilhelmstrasse* was aware of American influence in Europe, especially in France, Spain and the Balkans, as well as in Africa. Hitler also mentioned United States influence in discussing these areas from time to time, but, again, not in a way that suggested anything other than a subsidiary consideration. For example, he expressed to Admiral Darlan in May 1941 some fear that Amer-

---

[6] Ribbentrop, *op. cit.*, pp. 117, 152. Assmann, *Deutsche Schicksalsjahre*, p. 578. See for example the Halder notes regarding the two meetings at the Obersalzburg of August 14 and 22, 1939, at which there was no mention whatever of the United States.

[7] Hitler-Moore conference 4/30/40, *RAM*/F14408. *Mein Kampf*, p. 128. Halder, *Diary* 18/12/40, V, p. 74. Ribbentrop testimony, *IMT*/X, pp. 287, 237. Ribbentrop, *op. cit.*, p. 27. Raeder testimony, *NCA*, sup. B, p. 1438. Hitler-Henderson meeting 25/8/39, *DGFP/D/VIII*, p. 280. For Hitler's dismissal of American aid see: Hitler-Ciano conference 1/10/39, *DDI*, ser. 9/1, p. 431. Conference of 23/11/39, *IMT/XXVI*, p. 327. Conference of 1/4/41, *DGFP/D/XII*, p. 789. Hitler-Mussolini conference 3/6/41, *DGFP/D/XII*, p. 940.

ican imperialism would force France to cede African territory to the United States. It was, he pointed out, up to France to prevent this. Walter Schellenberg of the State Security Office maintained that Hitler had speculated on possible American operations in Africa and in the Spanish and Portuguese islands, even before the war.[8] Spanish Foreign Minister Serrano-Suñer found Hitler much concerned about possible American action in this area, and in July 1941 the Fuehrer remarked that "when the U.S.A. occupies the Spanish and Portuguese islands I will rush into Spain; I will send panzers and infantry divisions into North Africa."[9]

Although the attack on the Soviet Union fundamentally represented a reversion to Hitler's original goals, a return to the initiative after the English stalemate and the final link in the chain of continental domination, there is some evidence that the United States was a subsidiary factor in the decision to attack. On January 8, 1941, Hitler told his admirals that "if Russia collapsed, Japan would be greatly relieved; this in turn would mean increased danger to the U.S.A." At the time of the attack he told Mussolini that America would have less inclination to enter the war with the defeat of Russia. When the attack was underway, Hitler was recorded as saying that "a victorious campaign on the Eastern front will have a beneficial effect on the whole situation and probably also on the attitude of the U.S.A."[10]

But if America had been a direct and general influence on German operations in Europe before 1942 one would have expected considerable mention of the fact in the military plans, directives, memoranda and diaries. An investigation of these sources, however, yields meager results, as far as the air force

---

[8] Hitler-Darlan conference 11/5/41, *DGFP*/D/XII, p. 767. Schellenberg, *op. cit.*, p. 58.

[9] Serrano-Suñer, *op. cit.*, p. 247. Hitler comment of 25/7/41 in Hinsley, *op. cit.*, p. 151.

[10] Fuehrer conference 8/1/41, *FCNA*/1941, pp. 8–13. Hitler to Mussolini 21/6/41, *NSR*, pp. 329–353. Fuehrer conference 9/7/41, *FCNA*/1941, p. 92. See Weinberg, *Germany and the Soviet Union*, pp. 115, 170.

and army are concerned. There is some evidence supporting Goering's post-war claim to have been concerned about American airpower. Ambassador Wilson had the distinct impression that the *Luftwaffe* Chief was taking due account of American potential.[11]

Some support for Goering's concern in the matter may be found in the curious affair of the American oil millionaire, W. R. Davis. It appears that Davis, a man with ambitions and connections in American politics, was from 1939 to 1941 active in assisting the German navy to obtain oil from Mexico before the United States and Germany were at war.[12] In the course of these activities, he evidently met Goering on several occasions in September 1939. He may also have met Hitler at that time. The nature of his conversations with the *Reichsmarschall* is not definitely known, but Davis apparently suggested Roosevelt's mediation in the European war. According to the report he gave Assistant Secretary of State Adolph Berle, Goering, whom he pictured as the real governor of Germany, expressed great interest in a settlement sponsored by the United States and based upon a restoration of the Versailles losses as well as "a new economic arrangement." Goering, as Davis explained it, was very concerned about America's role in the future of the European continent. The State Department was apparently unimpressed and nothing came of the matter.[13] On the other hand when State Security Chief Schellenberg spoke to Goering of the possibility of American power on the continent, the *Luftwaffe* Chief told him to see a psychiatrist.

Schellenberg insisted after the war that there was in fact a considerable concern with the possibilities of an American continental intervention in military intelligence circles. He cited the example of Admiral Canaris, Chief of Military Counter-Intelli-

[11] Goering testimony, *IMT*/IX, p. 363. Wilson to Roosevelt 2/5/38, Wilson, *op. cit.*, pp. 29, 30.

[12] *OKM-Marine Attache/Amerika*/Witthoeft to OKM 23/5/41.

[13] Langer and Gleason, *The Challenge to Isolation*, pp. 247, 254. Rogge, *op. cit.*, pp. 239–254. Tansill, *Backdoor to War*, pp. 558–561. See also *Das Politische Tagebuch Alfred Rosenbergs*, p. 101.

gence, for whom this was "a constantly recurring theme." Jodl also stated after the war that "America was granted an exceptional position for a long time," but this is not borne out by the entries in his own diary nor in his strategic proposals.[14]

There are scattered references in other military sources. Halder noted in his diary at the time of the destroyer deal that "America's interest to bail out Britain is becoming increasingly obvious," and there were a number of remarks, which will be examined in a later chapter, pointing to the United States as the target of the Tripartite Pact. In this same month, August 1940, the army high command asked the admiralty for its views on the possibility of an American landing in West Africa, and in May 1941 in connection with plans for Operation Isabella (the occupation of Portugal) an OKW directive mentioned the possibility of a British grab for Spain to offset Balkan reverses and in order to offer "the U.S.A. favorable conditions for her entry into the war." General Warlimont, General Jodl's deputy at the OKW, in November 1940 attempted, unsuccessfully, to promote Franco-German military cooperation in order to avoid a war with Russia and "influence the United States in our favor."[15] But these scanty and tangential references simply underscore the absence of the United States as a factor in German land and air strategy on the European continent through 1941. Colonel Hossbach, in recalling the more significant meetings with the Fuehrer at which long-range plans were discussed, affirmed that there was "not one word of the real military and political situation and the position of the United States."[16]

The one military officer who took America strongly into account from the start was General Ludwig Beck, Chief of the

---

[14] Schellenberg, *op. cit.*, p. 216. Jodl testimony, *IMT/XV*, p. 397.

[15] Halder, *Diary* 23/8/40, IV, p. 169. *OKM/KTB/A/XIII — 10/9/40*. Directive OKW 7/5/41, *DGFP/D/XII*, p. 73. W. Warlimont, *Inside Hitler's Headquarters*, p. 125.

[16] Hossbach, *op. cit.*, p. 190. The United States is mentioned very briefly on only three occasions in the *Fuehrerweisungen fuer die Kriegsruehrung.* (W. Hubatsch, ed.)

Army General Staff until his resignation in September 1938. Opposed to the plans to resolve the Czech question by force, Beck in the spring and summer of 1938 wrote a number of blunt and very pessimistic memoranda which contained frank predictions of disaster for Germany if she took the course of "National Socialist adventures." Central in Beck's gloomy analysis was the assumption that an attack on Czechoslovakia would inevitably involve not only England and France but America as well; that the United States was already a member of a potential anti-German coalition. On May 5, in a note entitled "Observations regarding the present military and political position of Germany," he recalled that in the World War America had been the supply base for England and France and expressed doubts of Germany's ability to sustain a long war even if America only supplied her enemies with raw materials and food deliveries.

Three weeks later Beck put the case more strongly. "Germany," he wrote, "stands today opposite a coalition of Czechoslovakia, France, England and America, whose cooperation in the event of war is already closer today than in 1914."[17] In his "Testament" of July and August, Beck returned to these themes. America was already in some areas the armaments supplier of England. He predicted that American aid would be developed to the fullest extent and be supplemented by propaganda and political support as well. American public opinion was ready, he warned, and the country twenty times more powerful than it had been in 1914. He concluded:

> If America threw its powerful war potential in the scales on the side of England and France (and that we must unfortunately assume to be probable), then the opponents of Germany will receive an increase of power especially for a longer war against which Germany can put up nothing.[18]

It is not entirely clear how much of the contents of these

[17] W. Foerster, *op. cit.*, pp. 83–119.
[18] *Ibid*, p. 114.

memoranda got to Hitler, although he was certainly aware of Beck's general point of view. Neither the author nor the contents would have been valued very highly by the Fuehrer in any event and at a meeting on August 10, 1938, Hitler made abundantly clear to his military advisors that notwithstanding the defeatism (*Miesmacherei*) of the General Staff, he would proceed with his plans. America was not mentioned and Beck's resignation followed a week later.[19]

It is not difficult to see why America was so seldom considered in the continental plans of the Reich. We have already noted expressions of the most complete contempt on the part of Hitler for American military talents and his acceptance of the Boetticher line regarding American arms production. In an earlier chapter, we saw that American military intervention in the first war had come to be regarded by Hitler as a farce, American rearmament as "lies pure and simple," American production claims as "gigantic exaggerations."[20] As Germany secured her continental fortress it is not at all surprising that Hitler simply dismissed as militarily inconceivable the prospect of an American invasion. Without such an invasion there could be no role for American power on the continent, in Hitler's view. There is every evidence that this certainty was shared by leading Nazi officials. The Foreign Minister told Molotov in November 1940 that an American entry was "of no importance at all for Germany" since "Germany and Italy would never again allow an Anglo-Saxon to land on the European continent." Thus any invasion attempt was doomed to complete failure from the start.[21] To an Amer-

---

[19] S. Westfal, *Heer in Fesseln*, p. 39, and Foerster, *op. cit.*, p. 49, both emphasize that Hitler rarely received Beck and that "every point of contact was absent." The conference of August 10 in Jodl, *Diary* 10/8/38. See also discussion in Goerlitz, *History of the German General Staff*, pp. 328–330. Beck became involved in the conspiracy against Hitler in July 1944 and was forced to commit suicide when it failed.

[20] Hitler-Mussolini meeting 4/10/40, *DGFP*/D/XI, p. 248. Hitler-Mussolini conference 3/6/41 *DGFP*/D/XII, p. 945. Halder, *Diary*, III, 14/9/40, 15/10/40, 30/3/41. Doenitz testimony, *IMT*/XIII, p. 373.

[21] Ribbentrop-Molotov conference 12/11/40, *DGFP*/D/XI, p. 533.

ican visitor Ribbentrop described an American invasion as "a full-standing catastrophe," "completely laughable" and "absolute lunacy." Goebbels, Hess and others expressed the same opinions.[22]

It is difficult, then, to escape the conclusion that American influence on the European continent was recognized in Berlin, but that at the highest political and military levels it was not regarded as a substantial factor. Some influence on timing or urgency and as subsidiary support for more immediate and obvious arguments is the most that may be said for America as a military and political factor in the directly continental aspects of German policy. Only as the solution of continental problems became involved in maritime and Far Eastern considerations was Hitler compelled, reluctantly, to have a second look at the United States.

As far as Europe was concerned, when, in spite of expectations, America did enter the war, the OKW was not surprisingly thrown into considerable confusion. General Jodl telephoned his deputy, Warlimont, on the day following Pearl Harbor and requested information on the possibility of American moves in Europe. Warlimont could only reply that "so far we have never even considered a war with the United States and so we have no data on which to base this exercise." Jodl's reaction ("see what you can do") led Warlimont to comment that "this and no more was the beginning for our headquarters of a German strategy against America."[23]

[22] Ribbentrop-Cudahy conference 4/5/41, *RAM*/F90199. Ribbentrop-Ciano conference 19/6/40, Ciano, *Diary*, p. 375. Goebbels statement in Thomsen to Foreign Ministry 2/5/41, *StS/USA*/VI/245043. Hess interrogation *NCA*/VII, p. 664. The Japanese were convinced of German feelings of security in the matter. Joint conference 12/7/40, *IMTFE*/XIV, p. 6200.

[23] Warlimont, *op. cit.*, p. 208.

CHAPTER 9

Hitler and the German Navy

THE EUROPEAN WAR, in the years from Poland to Pearl Harbor, slowly escalated into a world struggle. Hitler was not able to confine the struggle to the familiar theater of operations. The United States was a primary factor in the expansion of the war into two less comfortable areas: the Atlantic Ocean and the Far East. The story of the United States and German naval policy in the years from 1939 to 1941 is essentially the story of Hitler's struggle to avoid the implications of this unexpected turn of affairs; of his continued relegation of the battle of the Atlantic to a holding action when in fact, as his Admirals tried to persuade him, it had become a major field of conflict.

In setting the background for these events, we must briefly note three general factors in the years before 1939: Hitler's personal disposition toward the navy, the German naval tradition which the Fuehrer inherited when he came to power and the actual plans and preparations made by the *Kriegsmarine* down to 1939.

Hitler, as we have noted earlier, was not a naval enthusiast. He regarded the old *Hochseeflotte* of the World War as "a parade piece," "a romantic toy" and "a target for enemy shooting practice." Hanfstaengl was not the only one to notice his discomfort at sea and in the presence of maritime considerations. His submarine chief, Karl Doenitz, has written that "for Hitler the war at sea was something strange and sinister." The Leader himself once admitted: "On land I am a hero, at sea I am a coward."[1]

[1] *Zweites Buch*, pp. 48, 171. *Mein Kampf*, pp. 128, 892. A. Martiensen, *Hitler and His Admirals*, p. 4. K. Doenitz, *Memoirs*, p. 403.

Hitler saw the navy's role as an auxiliary to land operations. At the first meeting with his naval chief, Admiral Erich Raeder, he made this quite clear. "The role of the navy," he wanted the Admiral to know, "lies in the framework of its responsibility toward a European continental policy." This line was unchanged seven years later when he told his assembled military chiefs that "only a final solution of all land problems will enable us to accomplish our tasks in the air and on the sea."[2] This view was not to be confused with any balanced grasp of the relations between land and seapower. Admiral Raeder has written, and others have supported the conclusion, that Hitler "had little real appreciation for the indirect pattern of seapower and the continental pressure it can exert on the enemy from a favorable geopolitical position." All Hitler was interested in, according to the Admiral, was "the comparative speed, size, armament, and fire power of ships and drawing theoretical conclusions therefrom. He was quite unaware of the implications of sea strategy such as bases, dependency on sea importations, allies, and geographical position."[3]

One need not conclude from this that Hitler was totally without knowledge or tactical sense in naval matters. He did in fact have a considerable interest in technical facts about naval craft, he was certainly aware of the problems of blockade and some of his critique of an excessive reliance on commerce raiding (the *guerre de course*) had much to commend it.[4] What is certainly true is that he often failed to grasp the implications of naval power, to understand the problems faced by his admirals, or even to interest himself in any sustained way in the condition or

---

[2] E. Raeder, *My Life*, pp. 166, 287. Raeder testimony, *IMT*/XIV, p. 22. Halder, *Diaries*, VI, p. 41. See also Jodl, *Diary* (1780–PS), 27/1/38.

[3] E. Raeder, *op. cit.*, p. 271. Further discussion in S. Morison, *op. cit.*, pp. 5–8. S. Roskill, *The War at Sea*, I, p. 490; F. Ruge, *Der Seekrieg*, p. 30. For an army view, Jodl, *Diary* (1780-PS), 27/1/38.

[4] Raeder, *op. cit.*, p. 271. For warnings about the blockade see Schmundt Memorandum 23/5/39, *NCA*/VII, p. 849. For critique of the *guerre de course* by Hitler see his reaction to the Graf Spee incident as described in Raeder, *op. cit.*, p. 290.

prospects of his fleet. He admitted frankly to his submarine chief that he lacked "an overall picture of these things and was uncertain about them."[5]

It should also be mentioned that Hitler's interest in the navy, while never great as such, was bound to fluctuate at various times according to the potential enemy he had in mind. So long as France and the Soviet Union were the targets, he could afford to neglect his fleet and follow his continental inclinations. When during 1938, however, England became the likely target Hitler must have seen, reluctantly, that a war with England meant a war at sea. That he did perceive this will be shown below.

Hitler's indifference to naval affairs certainly stemmed in part from his intense interest in maps. A casual glance at the geographical position of Germany would be discouraging to any German with naval ambitions for his country and Hitler, as we know, had few maritime inclinations in any event. Admiral Raeder was not the first to have noticed that nature had given England an incalculable naval advantage over Germany. "Without firing a single shot," Hitler's naval chief wrote, "it had cut us off almost completely from all communications overseas." In spite of this, or perhaps because it has made the German navy something of an artificial creation, there has been no lack of thought given by Germans to their naval affairs.[6]

The strategic heritage which earlier thinkers handed on to Hitler's naval chiefs was confused and contradictory. The dream of Germany as a full-fledged naval power capable of using its fleet strategically to carry the fight to the enemy and gain command of the sea had come up against the sobering realities of geography and the numerical superiority of the British navy. Admiral von Tirpitz himself, although the principal figure associated with German high-seas ambitions in the Wilhelmian era,

---

[5] Doenitz testimony, *IMT*/XIV, p. 90.
[6] See Hitler's comments on this in *Zweites Buch*, p. 147. Raeder, *op. cit.*, p. 285. See also J. Maerz, *Die Seeherrschaft*, p. 47. H. Rosinski, *Strategy and Propaganda in German Naval Thought*, Brassey's Naval Annual, 1945, p. 125.

had found himself involved in a naval competition with England which he could not win. He was thus compelled to moderate his vision and evolved in place of a fleet capable of offensive military action one of sufficient size to dissuade the enemy from attacking it at all due to the risk of serious losses which would be incurred as the price of victory. This was the so-called "risk theory": an effort to prevent the war politically which he could not win militarily.[7]

Nor did the experience of the First World War clarify the situation or produce a basic strategic theory for the future. There was, however, in the 1920's a considerable amount of criticism and examination of these issues within naval circles, including some suggestions for a fundamental reduction of the scope of naval activities and repudiation of any doctrine of strategic offense for Germany on the high seas. In 1926, a memorandum was prepared by a Captain Wegener which did not go this far, but sought instead to bring the earlier and more ambitious viewpoint of Tirpitz up to date. Critical of German naval operations in the World War, Wegener termed his refurbished command of the sea "command of communication." One authority is certain that Wegener's book was Hitler's "naval bible" while the Captain himself became an unofficial, confidential advisor.[8]

If Hitler's naval thinking stopped here, the evolution toward a fundamentally revised conception of the German naval future continued in some circles. The tendency among naval thinkers in the 1930's was toward abandonment of the fleet as a military unit and the recasting of its role into that of a commerce raider. The champion of this *guerre de course* was Captain Waldeyer-Hartz. In his article "Naval Warfare for Tomorrow," published in 1936, the author urged separation of command of the sea from control of communication and promoted economic warfare rather than military considerations as the determinant of a new

---

[7] H. Rosinski, *German Theories of Naval Warfare*, Brassey's Naval Annual, 1940, p. 90.

[8] *Strategy and Propaganda*, p. 137. Rosinski's appraisal of Wegener's influence in *ibid.*, p. 144.

naval strategy. He predicted that the attack on and defense of trade rather than the destruction of the enemy fleet would become the primary objective of the German navy in the future.[9] This would require the wide dispersal of German naval power along the lines of communication throughout the seven seas, and he asserted that the distinction between merchantmen and men-of-war was bound to disappear.

These views evidently found much favor in the Naval High Command during the 1930's. Admiral Assmann, the official historian at the Naval High Command (OKM), for example urged acceptance of England's inevitable command of the sea and equated naval war with tonnage war.[10] It was to be in the conduct of such a *guerre de course* after 1939 that the United States emerged as a powerful consideration in German naval policy. However, as we shall see, the OKM was at odds with Hitler concerning Atlantic policy and these disagreements may have been partially rooted in the Fuehrer's failure to share with his admirals this particular view of Germany's maritime future. There is some reason to suppose on the face of it that in spite of his concession to Britain of her command of the sea, this restricted, commercial outlook might not have been congenial to Hitler's strategic mentality. To the extent that he gave his attention to naval affairs at all, it is likely that the subordination of military to economic factors and the absence of any decisive battle or dramatic stroke in the plan together with the detachment of the navy from its role in support of land operations on the continent, all were of dubious merit to the Fuehrer. The important fact is that all of these diverse conceptions passed through a fog of indifference and emerged only with reference and in subordination to more decisive issues. To his admirals these ideas were naturally of more direct significance.

*

[9] *German Theories*, p. 97.
[10] This is evident in Assmann's book *Deutsche Seestrategie. Strategy and Propaganda*, p. 142. Rosinski feels that the "economists" really won out and is critical of some of the results of this.

German naval policy in the period from 1933 to 1939 was naturally conditioned by the expectations regarding Anglo-German relations. According to Raeder, Hitler in 1933 expressed his strong desire to avoid "complications" with England. Naval expansion therefore was to be pursued not with the idea of competition with Britain, but rather "only to the extent demanded by a continental European policy."[11] His determination to reach a maritime accommodation with England by conceding British naval supremacy was symbolized by the Anglo-German naval treaty of 1935, which quantitatively restricted German fleet strength to one third that of Britain, and by further qualitative restrictions undertaken in July 1937.[12] There is no doubt that Hitler attached the greatest importance to these agreements and any objections from the navy were submerged by the political goal of an Anglo-German understanding.

Although Hitler had begun as early as November 1937 to include England among "the hate-inspired antagonists" of Germany, he also in 1937 reaffirmed his strong determination to live at peace with Italy, Japan and England and continued to deny any interest in "contesting England's claim to a naval position corresponding to her world interests."[13] It can be said, therefore, that prior to May 1938, naval planning was predicated on a probable clash with France, Russia and Czechoslovakia and the concern was primarily to build up the fleet to the full limits provided for in the two treaties with England. Following the "weekend crisis" in May 1938, however, in which Hitler felt himself to have been humiliated by the Czechs and by the English *démarche* on their behalf, Hitler announced his unalterable decision to "smash"

---

[11] Raeder testimony, *IMT*/XIV, p. 21. Also *NCA*/VIII, p. 684.

[12] R. Bensel, *Die Deutsche Flottenpolitik von 1933 bis 1939*, p. 30. "With the conclusion of the naval treaty, Hitler documented his will toward a continentally oriented foreign policy." Ribbentrop testimony, *IMT*/X, p. 233. Raeder, *op. cit.*, p. 178. Assmann, *op. cit.*, p. 118. R. Ruge, *The New German Navy*, Brassey's Naval Annual, 1937, p. 118. D. Watt, "The Anglo-German Naval Agreement of 1935," *Journal of Modern History*, June 1956.

[13] Hossbach Memorandum, *DGFP*/D/I, p. 23. *NCA*, sup. B, p. 1438. Raeder denies that he ever even entertained such hopes. *IMT*/XXXIV, p. 775.

Czechoslovakia. This crisis was probably decisive in Hitler's change of heart regarding England, a change which was bound to have fundamental effects on the navy.[14]

It now fell upon the *Oberkommando der Marine* to draw up a plan of naval construction in accordance with the changing foreign policy perspectives. Some balance clearly had to be struck between an interim fleet for specialized raiding operations and a balanced fleet for strategic purposes which could only be produced over a period of years. Raeder in his memoirs has insisted that Hitler "had assured me that the fleet would not be needed before 1944 at the earliest" and that the Fuehrer "never so much as intimated" an early war with England. At the launching of the battleship *Tirpitz* in April 1938, Raeder has recalled that Hitler specifically reassured him on this point, and testified at Nuremberg that this was repeated as late as August 22, 1939. Doenitz supported Raeder in the view that the German navy had not been told of a specific enemy.[15]

Nevertheless, the navy clearly was thinking by this time of possible war with England ultimately. In March 1938, Raeder addressed German shipbuilders regarding the new construction plans which aimed to create "the necessary means of power which he [Hitler] needs for the execution of his foreign policy tasks." He specifically designated France and England as opponents and mentioned as well that Russia and "a large row of overseas states" (the United States?) might become involved.[16]

Against such an array of potential enemies the strength of the German navy at that time could have given rise to few illusions about the results of a second battle of Jutland in the near future.

[14] *NCA*/V/743, Watt, "Anglo-German Naval Negotiations on the Eve of the Second World War," *Journal of the Royal United Service Institute*, May, Aug. 1958.

[15] Raeder, *op. cit.*, pp. 215, 270, 271. This in spite of the tone of the speech made on the occasion, which was so bellicose that Hitler ordered arrangements for direct transmission canceled at the last moment. Shirer, *Rise and Fall*, p. 467. *IMT*/XIV, pp. 48, 68. Raeder testimony. *IMT*/XIII, p. 249. Doenitz testimony.

[16] *IMT*/XXXIV, p. 188.

The inclination to the views of Captain Waldeyer-Hartz for a *guerre de course* was reinforced by these circumstances.[17] Raeder was interested therefore in an interim fleet to harass British communications by surface and submarine raids which would compel the enemy to divide his forces. But he was concerned as well about the construction of a balanced navy which might ultimately be able to give a good account of itself even against the British. Operating under the illusion that he had until 1944 at the earliest to complete his plans, Raeder and his colleagues drew up the Zebra or Z-plan for the construction of a fleet capable both of carrying on a *guerre de course* and of winning control of the sea, as well as serving as a "fleet in being." Capital ships including aircraft carriers and especially pocket battleships supported by cruisers and destroyers as well as submarines were to be in a position to carry out full-scale air, surface and undersea warfare against British commerce and diversionary operations against the British fleet by 1945. In October 1938, Hitler demanded of Raeder that "every ship built by us must be stronger than the corresponding English ship."[18]

Hitler approved the plan in January 1939, but rebuffed Raeder's suggestion that certain interim weaknesses be corrected for the short term in case war should break out earlier than anticipated.[19] Nevertheless the navy was unmistakably looming in Hitler's calculations by this time. In a memorandum for the Commissioner of the Four Year Plan, the Fuehrer commanded that "the expansion of the navy ordered by me shall have priority over all other tasks including the armament of the two other branches of the Wehrmacht." The next step was taken in April 1939, when Hitler renounced the Anglo-German naval treaty in

[17] H. Reinecke, *German Surface Force Strategy in World War II*, p. 182. Raeder, *op. cit.*, p. 272.

[18] D. Kauffmann, *German Naval Strategy in World War Two*, pp. 1–3. Raeder, *op. cit.*, p. 273; NCA/VIII, p. 691. Assmann, *op. cit.*, p. 122. Ruge, *Der Seekrieg*, pp. 26–31.

[19] Raeder, *op. cit.*, p. 273. A. Martiensen, *op. cit.*, p. 3. Martiensen feels that in general Hitler treated Raeder like a "technical advisor."

the course of his marathon reply to Roosevelt's demand for non-aggression guarantees.[20] Also in April with the formulation of the plans for Case White (the liquidation of Poland), the navy was directed to prepare for possible action against British shipping. However, Raeder was not unduly alarmed by this. In a memorandum the following month, he insisted that this was an isolated and precautionary measure "and should not on any account be regarded as the forerunner of a settlement by force of arms with an opponent in the West."[21]

Nevertheless, the navy began its deployment and the OKM disturbed the Foreign Ministry (not for the last time) by preparations for unrestricted submarine warfare in the event of hostilities. Submarines were to be grouped around the main British sea routes, pocket battleships to be used as an independent striking force in the North and South Atlantic, and the rest of the fleet would form the reserve.[22]

On August 4, operational orders were issued which contained an analysis of the political situation by the OKM: England and France would be the enemy in the event of war, the U.S.S.R. was uncertain and only Spain and Japan could be considered benevolent. There was no mention of America at all. In the event of war, contact with enemy warships was to be avoided if possible. However, there was to be disruption of communications and destruction of enemy merchant shipping by all means possible, though according to prize law and with respect for neutrals. These general principles were reasserted in directive number 1 of August 31 and the Z-plan was officially altered from the goal of a balanced fleet in six to eight years to a striking force for immediate use. Emphasis was now also shifted to support of

[20] Memorandum 27/1/39, *DGFP*/D/VII, appendix VII, p. 643. Baynes, *op. cit.*, pp. 1635–1656.
[21] *FCNA*/1939, p. 3. Directive 3/4/39. *IMT*/XXXIV, pp. 428–458. Memo 16/5/39, *FCNA*/1939, p. 2.
[22] Memo (Albrecht) 3/5/39, *Auswaertiges Amt, Buero des Unterstaatssekretaers, Akten betr. Seekrieg* (hereafter *UStS/Seekrieg*/I/33833. For description of these preparations see Martiensen, *op. cit.*, p. 14.

German military operations against Poland and the defense of the German coast.[23]

Whether or not Raeder and his colleagues had really been so surprised at the outbreak of war, there can be no question that the German fleet was totally unprepared for its tasks in September 1939 and that there was considerable gloom at the Naval High Command. "The U-boat arm is still much too weak to have any decisive effect on the war. The surface force can do no more than show they know how to die gallantly."[24] This unpreparedness has been variously ascribed to Versailles limitations, restricted shipyard capacity and the fact that armies take less time to build and Hitler was in a hurry. However, the heart of the matter probably lies in Hitler's preoccupation with his land operations and his relegation of the navy to a low priority until a late date.

It is to be noticed that the United States was conspicuous by its absence as a factor in pre-war German naval planning. Whatever may have occurred to naval leaders from time to time in this regard, there was no mention of America as a possible enemy in the memoranda, plans and directives concerning naval matters with the possible exception of Raeder's indirect reference to "a large row of overseas states" during his speech to the shipbuilders in 1938. There was nevertheless in the long run and inherent in the plan for a dispersed attack on Britain's far-flung communication lines which Hitler's precipitate action forced upon his navy, a lurking danger of conflict with America on the high seas. Once Britain's determination to hold out had tarnished the hope of a

[23] Operations order 4/8/39, *FCNA*/1939, p. 10. Directive 1, 31/8/39, *FCNA*/ 1939, pp. 5-9.
[24] There is no evidence that the naval command ever presented the situation to Hitler in such starkly pessimistic colors. *Oberkommando der Marine, Kriegstagebuch* (hereafter *OKM-KTB*), C/VII, Memo 3/9/39. Assmann, *Deutsche Seekriegsfuehrung* (in Balanz des Zweiten Weltkriegs), pp. 117, 118. Doenitz Memo 1/9/39, *FCNA*/1939, p. 12. Doenitz testimony, *IMT*/XIII, p. 249. The navy as of September 1 consisted of two old battleships, two battle cruisers, three pocket battleships, eight cruisers, twenty-two destroyers and fifty-seven submarines, of which a good number were not seaworthy. S. Roskill, *op. cit.*, vol. I, pp. 51-61, and appendix G, pp. 990-992.

short war or a quick deal, neither Hitler's absolute preference for land warfare nor his refusal to take proper account of naval factors nor his reluctance to think in terms beyond Europe could save him from an involvement, however reluctant, under conditions and in areas distasteful to him, with a country whose significance for Germany he had previously dismissed from calculation.

CHAPTER 10

The United States and German Naval Policy

HITLER'S continental prejudices which played their role in naval unpreparedness at the outbreak of the war were equally apparent after it had started in the priority which he assigned to securing the continent and to the needs of the land and air forces by which he meant to achieve this goal. In his willingness to concede British seapower as a desirable complement to German land power, however, he failed to understand, as Hinsley has pointed out, the end to which this maritime strength had often been applied: namely, the prevention of precisely the kind of continental hegemony which he hoped to establish.[1] Nevertheless, these persistent general assumptions were now reinforced by a more specific consideration which led him to restrain his admirals. This new factor was the United States.

The usual image of a cautious General Staff urging moderation on an impulsive Fuehrer is most certainly not an accurate portrayal of Hitler's relations with his admirals, with regard to either naval policy in general or the United States in particular. Indeed, the opposite is the case here and the picture of a moderate, hesitant Fuehrer seems so askew, so out of line with the popular image of Hitler as a war lord, especially in view of his announced contempt for American power, that we shall have to return to the problem at the end of our discussion of the battle of the Atlantic.

*

[1] Hinsley, *op. cit.*, p. 26.

In spite of post-war testimony disclaiming all intention of involving the United States in the conflict,[2] the records of the Fuehrer conferences on naval affairs, the admiralty memoranda and the naval war diaries reveal a continuous drive by the OKM to lift the restraints on naval action and in favor of a green light to sweep the seas of commerce bound for the Allies. In their advocacy of this course, Hitler's naval advisors showed no undue concern for American reactions and in fact were pressing for a policy which would have resulted in the almost certain engagement of United States naval forces in combat.

Hitler's response to these requests (in which he was seconded by the Foreign Ministry) was in general to refuse the suggestions outright, to delay decisions on them or to grant small concessions. His justification for this caution included both the general necessity of securing the continental base first as well as specific and repeated reference to the problem of America. Indeed, it was precisely when the suggestions made to him seemed to impinge in some way on American interests that Hitler was most adamant in rejecting them. In this, it need not be assumed that Hitler's caution necessarily stemmed from a realistic appraisal of the facts in distinction to the recklessness of his admirals. Hitler's views may well have been grounded in indifference and confusion, and it is entirely possible that an unrestricted, full-scale war against England's commerce pursued from the start, as the admirals suggested, might have compelled a rapid British capitulation and thereby also removed the only real basis for an American entry to the continent. The point here is merely that there did exist a tension in naval policy between the OKM on the one hand and Hitler and the Foreign Ministry on the other and that the most significant factor underlying this tension was the United States.

These problems in naval policy along with the emergence of the United States as a factor became apparent during the final months of 1939. Less than a week after the outbreak of war,

---

[2] Raeder, *op. cit.*, p. 347. Weizsaeker testimony, *IMT*/XIV, p. 278. Doenitz testimony, *IMT*/XIV, pp. 264–266. Ruge, *Der Seekrieg*, p. 178.

Hitler and his advisors agreed that because of American neutrality ("at least outwardly") there would have to be an initial policy of restraint until the situation was clarified. This restraint was to involve a withdrawal of some submarines, the sparing of passenger ships and abstaining from offensive acts against France.[3] By September 23, Raeder was, however, already becoming impatient. He indicated that the navy's policy ought to be gradual removal of restrictions but without undue notice. He pressed especially for the lifting of restrictions against France and Britain and for increased submarine construction. Hitler agreed to some of these suggestions, and by the end of September directives allowed for greater leeway in attacking Allied shipping, although neutrals and passenger vessels were to be spared.[4]

The Foreign Ministry was not entirely pleased with the prospect of an intensified war at sea, and the source of their concern was the United States. In a memorandum to the OKM on September 27, Woermann of the Political Department urged that neutrals should be carefully warned about radio reporting, evasion tactics and unlighted ships and that the area of operations should be limited "so the Americans cannot say we are conducting war against them." Woermann suggested that the navy avoid "brutal" submarine warfare until American neutrality legislation was clarified and it could be determined if American passengers might be on board any of the proposed targets.[5]

This caution from the *Wilhelmstrasse* was contrary to the inclination of the OKM. By October, Raeder was ready to remove all the wraps as far as England was concerned. He urged upon Hitler that the naval war should proceed "at once and with the fullest intensity." Even the threat of America's entry into the war, which appeared to Raeder as certain if the war continued,

---

[3] Fuehrer conference 7/9/39, *FCNA*/1939, pp. 16, 17. Directive 3, 9/9/39, *DGFP*/D/VIII, p. 41.

[4] Fuehrer conference 23/9/39, *FCNA*/1939, pp. 18–24. Directive 4, 25/9/39. The subordination of the navy to the other services was indicated at this time in Directive 6, 9/10/39, *DGFP*/D/VIII, p. 249.

[5] Woermann to OKM/27/9/39, *UStS/Seekrieg*/I/33890. Woermann memo 3/10/39, *DGFP*/D/VIII, p. 203. Memorandum (Weizsaeker) 17/9/39, *ibid.*, p. 53.

was not to give rise to restraints, which would only prolong the conflict. Hitler was recorded as "agreeing entirely with this." However, when it came to specific measures, such as a higher priority for submarine construction, Hitler shied off, promising only to look into the matter.[6]

The anxiety of the Foreign Ministry was again aroused. Weizsaeker reminded Ribbentrop that a decision regarding unrestricted naval warfare was as much political as military. The State Secretary wondered if it was worth bringing new opponents into the war, without really possessing the submarines required to bring England to her knees. He wanted the Foreign Ministry kept better informed on naval matters. Ribbentrop himself took up the matter of the neutrals and the war at sea on December 27. He held the consequences of sinking American and other neutral shipping of such great political importance that he reserved to himself reference to the Fuehrer in this "as in the general problems of intensifying the war at sea."[7]

Recognizing the shadow of the United States in Hitler's pronounced reserve in these matters, Raeder presented him with a memorandum on November 10 which explained the point of view of the OKM concerning the United States. Referring to the neutrality laws as a "shackle on the most war loving of American presidents," the memo agreed that naval action should not provide Roosevelt with an excuse to break this shackle. However, the naval command was sure that the war with Britain on the high seas could be intensified without provoking the United States, although the final stage of intensification might have to be delayed until the German fleet had sufficient strength to deal with an American intervention.[8] Hitler was evidently not impressed, for although directives during November gave increased

---

[6] Fuehrer conference 10/10/39, *FCNA*/1939, pp. 25, 26.

[7] Weizsaeker to Ribbentrop 14/10/39, *UStS/Seekrieg*/I/33909. Weizsaeker was evidently supplied with further details some days later. Memo (Weizsaeker) 17/10/39, *UStS/Seekrieg*/I/33911. Memo (Eisenlohr) 27/12/39, *UStS/Seekrieg*/I/34157. Memo (Ritter) 16/11/39, *UStS/Seekrieg*/I/33986.

[8] Fuehrer conference 1/11/39, *FCNA*/1939, pp. 37, 38. Fuehrer conference 10/11/39, *FCNA*/1940, p. 39. *NCA*, sup. A, p. 89.

latitude to the navy, the rights and sensibilities of neutrals (and among these the United States was specifically cited) were to be rigorously observed.[9] The results of the final conference in 1939 left the situation unchanged. Raeder's efforts to have Hitler issue a bellicose proclamation of warning that if Britain violated international law Germany would retaliate by sinking all ships in the combat area was turned down flat. As Jodl recorded in his diary for December 30, "Neutrals who behave correctly and are not in convoy are not to be molested."[10]

German naval policy in 1940 was strongly influenced by Hitler's perplexity regarding Great Britain and this inevitably led him into the problem of the United States which he was now compelled to see as a primary factor in the English refusal to come to terms. Hitler's equivocation about Britain stemmed partially from his uncertainty about why the British continued to fight a hopeless war and partially from his reluctance to make full use of the navy to compel her to realize her position. Thus there was dithering about the battle of the Atlantic and about the cross-channel invasion of England (Operation Sea Lion), the lost opportunity at Dunkirk and constant searching for more congenial continental alternatives (seizure of Norway and France, plans to attack Gibraltar and the U.S.S.R.). Anxious for a quick decision, yet unwilling to unleash his navy to carry the main thrust in precipitating this decision, Hitler injected an element of self-defeat into German naval policy in 1940.

This policy was evolved amidst tension caused by the continuing pressure of the OKM to release itself from the restraints of continental priorities and a mounting concern about the effects of American policy. United States interest in the Mediterranean and Africa, the inconveniences imposed by the Pan American security zone and the aid to England (especially the destroyer

[9] Directive 9, 29/11/39, *DGFP*/D/VIII, p. 463.
[10] Fuehrer conference 30/12/39, *FCNA*/1939, pp. 66–68. Jodl, *Diary* 30/12/39 (PS-1811).

deal and the announcement of Lend-Lease), which the navy thought might be really decisive in a long war — these were the problems posed by America which were continuously circulated in OKM memoranda and brought repeatedly to the attention of the Fuehrer in order to advance the cause of intensified naval warfare. Hitler would have none of it.[11]

Raeder expressed these anxieties to Hitler in January. He criticized the High Command of the Armed Forces (OKW) as being too influenced by the "continental idea" and requested stronger support of naval activities from the *Luftwaffe*. He insisted that Britain was the prime enemy and complained that the navy's hands were tied by the higher production and personnel priorities assigned to the other services. Hitler was reported to be "quite unmoved" by all of this. He merely reiterated his desire to secure the continental base first and justified his priorities.[12] Rebuffed on these points, Raeder a month later requested that the navy at least be allowed to fire on all unlighted ships in American waters and that operations be authorized in the territorial waters off Halifax. The Fuehrer rejected these requests as well "in view of the psychological effect on the U.S.A." When Hitler also denied proposals to send submarines into the Mediterranean, Raeder could only refer to the results of this conference as "a real setback," and inform the American Naval Attaché at Berlin that orders had been issued to avoid all contacts with American ships.[13]

That Raeder had not prevailed in his demands for more consideration of the navy became even clearer as the plans for events in the West (Case Yellow) were evolved in the spring of 1940. The subordinate role of the navy in these land-air operations was made clear. This raised once again the differences between navy and air force in regard both to the countries to be occupied (the

[11] A discussion of this is in Hinsley, pp. 60–95. Roskill, *op. cit.*, I, p. 240.

[12] Fuehrer conference 26/1/40, *FCNA*/1940, pp. 6–8. See also Raeder, *op. cit.*, pp. 283, 284.

[13] Fuehrer conference 23/2/40, *FCNA*/1940, pp. 11–13. Memo 27/2/40, *OKM/Marine Attache/Amerika*.

navy opposed occupation of the Low Countries and favored the acquisition of submarine bases off the west coasts of France and Norway) and the weapons to be used.[14] The United States appeared as a factor even in these tactical disputes. In the conference of May 7, Hitler supported the *Luftwaffe* in the disagreement over the vulnerability of the battleship to air attack because he felt "it might affect the plans of the U.S.A." The navy was, however, promised some greater freedom of action, and in June Hitler assured his admirals that after the fall of France the fleet would be granted a higher priority. This happier day for the navy was of course constantly deferred pending the securing not merely of France, but, as we shall see, of the whole continent including Russia.[15]

Meanwhile, in the Norwegian campaign Hitler had used his navy more directly in the securing of the continent. It had been necessary in this case to overcome the Fuehrer's reluctance to rely on naval action to secure a military objective. As one of his naval advisors testified after the war, "to carry out an operation across so great a body of water was strange to him." Following this operation, however, Norway became something of an *idée fixe* as a point for Anglo-American invasion. Hitler came to place it above North Africa or the Atlantic in the priority of tasks for the navy.[16]

In June and July naval planning was focused on preparations for the cross-channel invasion of England, Operation Sea Lion. In this episode, Hitler's uncertainty was matched by that of his naval advisors. Hitler was evidently as unhappy at the general prospect of such a massive naval operation as his admirals were appalled at the technical details, and he showed enthusiasm only

[14] Fuehrer conference 29/3/40, *FCNA*/1940, p. 46. Specifically, the navy was to tend to mining, canal operations, seizure of islands and the disruption of channel communication. *IMT*/XXXIV, p. 425; Jodl memorandum 7/10/41.

[15] Fuehrer conference 7/5/40, *FCNA*/1940, pp. 47, 48. Directive 13, 24/5/40. *DGFP*/D/IX, p. 428. Circulatory note 6/6/40, *UStS/Seekrieg*/II/34324. Fuehrer conference 7/6/40, *FCNA*/1940, p. 55.

[16] Puttkammer testimony, *Case 11*/LIII, p. 25807. Fuehrer conferences 9/7/41, 22/1/42, *FCNA*/1941, 1942, pp. 91, 98.

when the invasion appeared the best method of achieving the rapid victory over England which he so desired. Even at this point, the operation was probably regarded as much as a threat or a *coup de grâce* administered to an England already prostrate from air attack.[17]

In the debates over the actual arrangements, the tension between Hitler and the OKM as well as between the OKM and the other services became acute. Raeder even wondered in fact if a blockade might be substituted for the invasion idea, since the task allocated to the navy in Operation Sea Lion was "out of all proportion to the navy's strength and bore no relation to the tasks set out for the army and air force." Hitler offered little comfort as he sided repeatedly with the other services on questions of timing, date of attack and type of front to be established. By August Hitler was clearly thinking of alternatives to this dubious venture and in September the whole thing was postponed indefinitely.[18] There is no direct evidence that the United States figured in Hitler's calculations regarding Sea Lion beyond the sense of urgency in a quick liquidation of English resistance before American aid fully materialized.[19] However, in the consideration of alternatives to the invasion, the American role reappeared strongly.

As Sea Lion faded and other possibilities for striking at England became necessary in the autumn of 1940, four geographical areas emerged or re-emerged as focal points of OKM concern:

[17] In a directive of July 16, the words "if necessary" were inserted before the plans for an actual occupation of Britain. Fuehrer conference 16/7/40, *FCNA/* 1940, p. 47. Raeder, *op. cit.*, p. 331. See first two chapters of R. Wheatley, *Operation Sea Lion*. Hinsley, *op. cit.*, pp. 78–83. For an army view see Halder, *Diaries*, vol. III, 30/7/40, pp. 138–140; 14/9/40, p. 196.

[18] Fuehrer conferences 20/6/40, 11/7/40, *FCNA/*1940, pp. 59, 64–65. The directive for preparations was issued 2/7/40, *FCNA/*1940, p. 61. Fuehrer conference 19/7/40, *FCNA/*1940, p. 69. Fuehrer conferences 31/7/40, 1/8/40; directives of 1/8/40, 16/8/40, *FCNA/*1940, pp. 75, 77–80, 81, 82. Fuehrer conferences 27/8/40, 7/9/40, 17/9/40, *FCNA/*1940, pp. 90, 93, 99, 101.

[19] In the Fuehrer conference for July 21, in the context of a discussion of Sea Lion, mention was made of the need to consider the role of the United States and Soviet Russia carefully in deciding upon a policy to bring the war with England to a rapid conclusion. *FCNA/*1940, p. 72.

the Mediterranean, Africa and the Spanish and Portuguese islands, the Atlantic and the Western hemisphere. In each of these areas, American influence was considered to be a factor of some importance. Hitler was not indifferent to these alternatives, but he was becoming much preoccupied after July 1940 with his own continental alternative to Sea Lion: Operation Barbarossa, the invasion of Russia. Thus he tended, for example, to place a greater reliance on France and Spain in the Mediterranean and limit the German commitments. These differences of priority became clear in the discussions with his admirals. On September 9, the navy urged attacks on Gibraltar and Suez as alternatives to Sea Lion since, in the navy's view, Britain had to be "excluded from the Mediterranean." Furthermore, these operations had to be prepared "before the United States steps in." It was, the navy warned, not a secondary matter, but a primary blow against Britain. Raeder took up the argument two weeks later when he described the Mediterranean to Hitler as "the pivot of their empire" and asserted the importance of a German stroke, again before the Americans intervened.[20]

American interests were seen as a more direct factor in Africa and the Spanish and Portuguese islands. The OKM did not rule out the possibility of American military action in this area. In the course of a lengthy memorandum entitled "The Problem of the U.S.A." presented at a conference in September, a warning was sounded about a possible American occupation of the Spanish and Portuguese islands and of British and French West Africa. A preventive German occupation of the Canaries was suggested along with the use of the French fleet in defense of French colonies.[21] The decisive importance of North West Africa was

[20] Fuehrer conference 7/9/40, *FCNA*/1940, p. 93. Fuehrer conference 26/9/40, *FCNA*/1940, pp. 104, 105. Raeder also expanded upon the inability of the Italians to take Suez and Gibraltar without German aid. See also Raeder, *op. cit.*, p. 336.

[21] These areas had long been of interest to German naval thinkers. See for example the article by Gadow "Marinepolitische Umschau," in *Nauticus*, 1938, p. 8. Raeder stressed the importance of Dakar to Hitler at the Fuehrer conferences of 20/6/40 and 11/7/40, *FCNA*/1940, pp. 58, 65. An entry in the naval

constantly stressed by Raeder, who foresaw Anglo-American-Gaullist cooperation in this area. Hitler agreed with the general dangers both to the Mediterranean and North Africa, but beyond vague references to agreements with France and Spain, he had little specific to offer. The Fuehrer told Mussolini on November 20 that his object in the African-Mediterranean area was "to expel the British fleet from its refuge," but Raeder still confessed his "grave misgivings" about German policy there in view of the Anglo-Saxon threat.[22]

The aspect of American policy which the German navy was bound to watch with the greatest apprehension, however, was the steadily more intimate relation of the United States and England and the problems this would raise for naval operations in the Atlantic. The admiralty was uncertain about American motives in this respect. American naval ambitions were viewed as definitely expansionist and were taken to include the hope of inheriting British naval and imperial power. Thus as the German naval command saw it, in extending aid to Great Britain, the United States may have been acting either from American interests or with the idea of creating an Anglo-Saxon condominium on the high seas.[23] Whatever the motive or final end, the OKM was clearly as impressed as Thomsen and Dieckhoff had been by the degree of American commitment to England as symbolized by the destroyer deal ("an openly hostile act against Germany"), and the conviction grew that English resistance was largely a matter of reliance on this commitment. Although some doubt was expressed about American ability to deliver the required supplies immediately, the naval staff termed American aid a

war diary expressed similar concern over American interest in the islands. *OKM-KTB*/A/XIII — 3/9/40.

[22] Fuehrer conference 26/9/40, *FCNA*/1940, p. 105. Fuehrer conference 14/11/40, *FCNA*/1940, pp. 126–128. *OKM-KTB*/A/ — 18/11/40, 23/11/40. Hitler to Mussolini 20/11/40, *Les Lettres*, p. 84. Fuehrer conference 27/12/40, *FCNA*/1940, p. 135.

[23] Fuehrer conference 21/7/40, *FCNA*/1940, p. 71. *OKM-KTB*/A/XIII — 3/9/40, 2/9/40. Fuehrer conference 7/9/40, *FCNA*/1940, p. 94.

"vastly important" factor in the long run as the United States, Great Britain and Canada grew closer together against Germany.[24]

By December 1940 the admiralty was pressing the point that American aid to England and the prospect of far more to come made the rapid defeat of that country more urgent. By decisive strokes against England, according to one entry in the war diary, Germany would be able to convince the Americans that aid to Britain was "a total loss." Was it not time, therefore, to employ "the sharpest use of every available weapon in order finally to shatter British resistance and compel them to sue for peace"?[25] Roosevelt's announcement of Lend-Lease in December seemed to substantiate all of this. It was the view of the naval command that this measure had "the most far-reaching consequences for England's continuation in the war," since it would enlist "the entire enormous armaments capacity of the United States" in the service of Germany's enemies. Conjuring up a gloomy picture of ships, food, planes and even fleet units flowing across the Atlantic in ever-increasing quantities, the German admirals flatly labeled the move "an entry into the war without the politico-military complications of an official declaration." They wondered if "the political leadership of the Reich ought not to adopt at least diplomatic counter-measures." Nothing was now so important, the memorandum concluded, as that supplies from America be stopped and England brought to surrender with all speed.[26]

These thoughts in the war diary were conveyed to Hitler by Raeder in the course of the final Fuehrer conference of 1940 on

---

[24] Fuehrer conference 21/7/40, *FCNA*/1940, p. 71. *OKM-KTB*/A/XIII — 3/9/40. Morison feels that the destroyer deal was of the greatest importance in convincing the OKM of the direction of American policy. Morison, *op. cit.*, p. 34. According to a later analysis by the OKM, this event marked the dividing line in American policy between neutrality and belligerency. Appendix to Fuehrer conference 10/7/41, *OKM-KTB*/C/VII, p. 191. *OKM-KTB*/A/XIII — 3/9/40. *OKM/KTB*/A/XIV — 21/10/40. Fuehrer conference 7/9/40, *FCNA*/1940, p. 94.

[25] *OKM/KTB*/A/XVI — 2/12/40.

[26] *OKM-KTB*/A/XVI — 20/12/40.

December 27. Warning, among other things, that ships from America could more than replace those lost through the present restricted submarine operations, that material deliveries had increased "tremendously" and that aircraft production in the United States could provide England with vast reinforcement, Raeder that day presented the strongest case for concentrating all German effort against Britain with "the utmost speed and urgency." He declared himself opposed to the attack on Russia prior to the defeat of England and complained that the urgency of this was not properly recognized by the OKW. He summed up his views pointedly: *"the* problem is British supply lines; *the* weapon, the submarine."* Once again Hitler expressed his general agreement, and once again undermined it with talk of having to secure his continental base first. Once that had been done, he gave Raeder the now familiar assurance, the navy would come into its own. When Raeder, who must have been close to despair at this point, reminded Hitler that this left them right back where they had been earlier in the year, the Fuehrer waved him aside with vague references to "new political factors." Raeder had to be content to concentrate what submarine and surface forces he had on the Battle of the Atlantic, as best he could.[27]

Finally, the Western hemisphere itself and American entry into the war were matters which began to interest the German naval planners later in 1940. Particularly irksome was the Pan American security zone, which had been declared by the Pan American Congress in September 1939. This establishment of a three-hundred-mile zone around the Americas within which belligerent ships were not to operate had not been well received from the start, although directives had gone out ordering respect for the zone.[28] Recognizing the strategic importance of the

[27] Fuehrer conference 27/12/40, *FCNA*/1940, pp. 138–140. This included preparation of French and Norwegian bases, deployment of reconnaissance craft and supply ships and the establishment of three commands under shore control: Group North (North Atlantic), Group West (Channel and West Atlantic) and submarines. Martiensen, *op. cit.,* p. 104.

[28] OKW to Foreign Ministry 18/6/40, *DGFP/D/IX*, p. 616. Ruge charac-

hemisphere to the United States, the admiralty was nevertheless worried by the resultant hampering of cruiser operations, and the attention of the Fuehrer was directed to this situation at a conference in November. It was also pointed out that since the United States had quite abandoned the neutrality which was the only justification for the zone, German surface ships should be authorized to engage in hostilities within the zone. Hitler declined to grant this authorization, adding merely that he might review the situation in the future. In December 1940 the question was raised again. There could, it was felt, now be no talk of American neutrality after the destroyer deal and therefore the zone had lost its original justification.[29]

Regarding an actual American entry, it has already been shown that in the view of the German naval authorities the American drift from neutrality had by this time proceeded so far that it constituted a *de facto* state of war with Germany. Nevertheless, there was some comment in the war diary for 1940 referring to a more formal involvement. Earlier commentary on this reflected the Boetticher line regarding the influence of the "General Staff" and uncertainty about Japan as obstacles to American entry. However, by August the outlook was more pessimistic: "All signs indicate that the U.S.A. will be ready for war at the beginning of 1941 and at this time, if not earlier, will enter the war."[30]

---

terized the zone as "a novelty in international law." Ruge, *Der Seekrieg*, p. 178. The Foreign Ministry urged caution on the grounds of South American sensibilities as well. Memo 22/5/40, *DGFP*/D/IX, p. 371.

[29] Fuehrer conference 7/9/40, *FCNA*/1940, p. 94. *OKM-KTB*/A/15 — 19/11/40. The restricted activities of the cruiser *Admiral Scheer*, for example, had been raised at the Foreign Ministry. The Ministry memo indicated that Raeder had understood the political need for these things, but had raised military objections. Memo (Ritter) 9/11/40, *DGFP*/D/XI, p. 505. Appendix to Fuehrer conference 14/11/40, *OKM-KTB*/C/VII, p. 246. *OKM-ATT*/SKL Memorandum 2/12/40.

[30] *OKM-KTB*/A/II — 3/10/39. *OKM-KTB*/A/IX — 22/5/40. *OKM-KTB*/A/XII — 29/8/40, 6/8/40.

Hitler and the Battle of the Atlantic

FORMER ADMIRAL WAGNER testifying at Nuremberg after the war stated that "all naval decisions in 1941 were taken with an eye to the effect on the U.S.A."[1] The Admiral was quite correct in his statement, although this consciousness of American power did not lead German naval authorities into any undue caution in the policies they advocated. During this final year before the outbreak of formal hostilities, many of the problems which had emerged in 1940 continued to be of concern to the OKM. The disputes with the *Luftwaffe* and resentment over the subordinate role of the fleet formed frequent complaints.[2] Anglo-American influence in Africa was also mentioned increasingly in the Fuehrer conferences and repeatedly in the war diaries. Any American foothold in this area was regarded as "most dangerous" and steps were urged to forestall such an eventuality.[3]

But it is obvious that by 1941 the navy regarded the bridge of supplies which had been thrown across the Atlantic to be the very crux of the war at sea. The American occupation of Iceland, the implementation of Lend-Lease and the Roosevelt order

[1] Wagner testimony, *IMT*/XIII, p. 476.

[2] Fuehrer conferences 18/3/41, 25/7/41, *FCNA*/1941, pp. 32, 94. Assmann feels that inadequate air support was the primary cause of the failure of the submarines. Assmann, "Why U-Boat Warfare Failed," *Foreign Affairs*, July, 1950, p. 665. See discussion of production priorities in Milward, *The German Economy at War*, pp. 37, 43.

[3] Fuehrer conferences 18/3/41, 22/5/41, 10/7/41, 25/7/41, *FCNA*/1941, pp. 33, 51, 92, 107. *OKM Marine Archiv Voelkerrecht II Handhabung der Neutralen: USA, 1941* (hereafter *OKM/Handhabung*), 2/4/41. *OKM-KTB/A/XX* — 19/4/41, XXI — 87/5/41, XXIII — 16/7/41, XXVI — 31/10/41. There was also a certain concern expressed about the fate of the French Fleet. Fuehrer conference 8–9/141, *FCNA*/1941, p. 11.

to "shoot at sight," all against a background of continuing incidents between German and American ships, seemed to the OKM to have extinguished any real distinction between the status of the United States and Great Britain. The navy insisted, therefore, as before but now with increased urgency, on the need to lift all restrictions on naval warfare. These suggestions were however swallowed up by Hitler's absorption with Operation Barbarossa and the admirals were waved aside once again with vague promises of decisive maritime action following the defeat of the Soviet Union.

For the German admirals, then, the enemy remained England reinforced by America. Indeed, for some, America was the more important of the two. "The antipode of Hitler is increasingly Roosevelt," was the formulation of this view in the naval war diary in January.[4] The appearance of American aircraft in bombing attacks on Germany, the repair of British ships in American yards and the reconnaissance and radio reporting activities against German shipping were symptoms of what the admiralty considered, just as the diplomats did, a *de facto* military alliance of the Anglo-Saxon powers. A joint Anglo-American defense line from Gibraltar to Singapore was predicted, and this cooperation had become so close by the end of the year that both before and after the attack on Pearl Harbor the entries in the war diary noted that formal American entry could make little difference.[5]

Naval circles may have felt an initial optimism early in the year about carrying their viewpoint in the OKW and with Hitler. Early directives spoke of renewed efforts against England and held out hope of freedom from "earlier concepts" in the

[4] *OKM-KTB*/A/XVII/ — 20/1/41.
[5] Fuehrer conferences 4/2/41, 18/3/41, *FCNA*/1941, pp. 21, 32. *OKM-KTB*/ A/XXII — 19/6/41.   *OKM-KTB*/A/XXVII — 11/11/41.   *OKM/KTB/A/* XXVIII — 6/12/41. Post-war German commentary on this aspect of American policy may be found in Assmann, *Deutsche Seestrategie*, pp. 158–161. See also Doenitz, *op. cit.*, chap. 11.

struggle. Hitler, in his directive of March 5, saw the navy's task as assisting in the "swift conquest of England in order to keep America out of the war." Raeder was even authorized by Hitler to give a press interview where, amidst much publicity, he denounced American policy ("Grand Admiral Raeder warns the warmongers in the U.S.A.").[6] But when the navy sought specific measures of relief from restraint in its actions against Britain which might involve the U.S.A., Hitler was as adamant as ever. Offending America was a risk he was just not prepared to take prior to a solution of the Russian problem.

Specifically, the navy called for the abandonment of immunity granted to American ships and the freedom to attack these vessels according to prize law, as well as alteration of the German respect for the Pan American security zone. The issue of applying prize law was urgently but unsuccessfully raised in April. In addition, probably as a result of Roosevelt's announcement that month of the extension of the security zone together with measures for increased Anglo-American cooperation in the Atlantic,[7] the navy produced a number of papers defining its position. One such report in May cited the disadvantages of German policy up to that point: American shipping was unmolested on direct routes, American activity was serving the enemy as an intelligence source, British ships were able to disguise themselves as Americans. If, on the other hand, prize law were applied to America, the shipping tonnage against Germany would decline, the Americans would be forced to seek delays and detours, the American fleet would not be in a position to provide full protection and British vessels would no longer be able to disguise themselves. As to the question of American lives, the navy admitted that it could not

---

[6] Directives 23 (6/2/41), 24 (5/3/41), 25 (25/3/41), DGFP/D/XII, pp. 42, 220, 363. *OKM-KTB*/C/VIII — 23/5/41. Appendix to Fuehrer conference 22/5/41, *ibid*.

[7] Fuehrer conference 18/3/41, *FCNA*/1941, p. 32. *OKM-KTB*/A/XX/ — 12/4/41. For description of this see Langer and Gleason, *The Undeclared War*, p. 435. Coast-guard cutters were sent to England in March, *ibid.*, p. 424. Watson, *op. cit.*, pp. 386–391.

guarantee these, though all efforts would always be made. Finally, if the political situation precluded this step, it was held to be "absolutely necessary" that fleet units be authorized at least to take in United States steamers in order to prevent disguise and to demonstrate the gravity of the situation.[8]

Three weeks later in an appendix to the Fuehrer conference of May 22, a memorandum was prepared entitled "The present problem of conducting the war at sea in the Atlantic in view of the position of the U.S.A." Citing American aid as the "life blood of England" and the "crux of the battle of the Atlantic," the memorandum then enumerated the problems of the navy in these circumstances, adding the strengthening of patrols and the conversion of merchant ships into attack aircraft carriers to the other examples of American involvement. The navy also called it "inexcusable" that the United States government allowed American citizens including women and children to travel on belligerent ships.

Because of political considerations, the report complained, the navy was not allowed to engage United States ships nor conduct commercial war against the United States nor use weapons except in self-defense. "In the long run, this must be regarded as an unsatisfactory solution." The navy must at least be able to fire at unlighted ships. What distinction, the report went on, could now possibly be drawn between war and peace? The alternatives were clear: either continue the present policy giving the United States a free hand and simply abandon the battle of the Atlantic or clarify the issue by applying prize regulations against American merchantmen; by firing on United States naval vessels if they threatened German ships; by attacking all unlighted ships without warning as well as American merchant ships in convoy; by firing on neutral ships impeding German operations. To these suggestions, Hitler merely remarked that Roosevelt's position was weak and "under no circumstances" should Germany risk an American entry through naval incidents. At most, the Fuehrer would consider sending a warning, but as

[8] Operation orders 5/5/41, 20/5/41, *OKM-KTB*/C/VIII.

for the rest of the program, it was to be shelved pending "American developments."[9]

On May 27, Roosevelt declared the "unlimited national emergency" with strong overtones of further threats and incidents on the high seas ("if the Axis fails to gain control of the sea they are lost"), only slightly softened by failure to announce the expected institution of convoys.[10] The navy, therefore, undeterred by Hitler's previous indifference, found it necessary to press its case during the summer of 1941 in view of what it considered to be a deteriorating situation. In July, after noting that "only respect for higher political considerations" restrained them from attacking American ships, the *Seekriegsleitung* (operational command) declared itself to be "completely clear on the point that American activity had led to an extraordinary aggravation of the submarine war." The report warned that if this continued, "ruthless recognition" of the situation would be in order and appropriate measures taken.[11] These suggestions again fell on deaf ears. The review of directives issued on September 17 to the submarine command again excepted American warships and merchantmen from the targets available. Neither lack of lights nor radio activity were to be considered a release from this prohibition.[12]

In addition to the pressure to apply prize regulations to the Americans, Hitler's naval advisors also continued to urge modification of German policy toward the now extended Pan American security zone. The matter was discussed by Ribbentrop and Hitler in April, and Hitler expressed grave reservations even

---

[9] Appendix to Fuehrer conference 22/5/41, *OKM-KTB*/C/VIII, p. 102. Hitler refused again at the Fuehrer conference of 6/6/41, *FCNA*/1941, p. 87. See also *OKM-KTB*/A/XXII — 7/6/41. Hitler's tendency to wait and see how American Atlantic policy developed was not entirely unjustified at this stage since the policy did in fact vacillate. The escorting of ships had, for example, been withdrawn on April 20 and the orders to transfer fleet units from Pearl Harbor to the Atlantic had been rescinded. Watkins, *op. cit.*, p. 390. *The Undeclared War*, p. 446.

[10] Speech 27/5/41, *PPA*/1941, p. 181.

[11] *OKM-KTB*/A/XXII — 22/6/41, 29/6/41. Appendix to Fuehrer conference 25/7/41, *OKM-KTB*/C/VIII, p. 206.

[12] Directive 17/9/41, *OKM-KTB*/C/VIII, p. 242. *OKM-KTB*/A/XXV/ — 9/9/41. Appendix to Fuehrer conference 13/11/41, *OKM-KTB*/C/VIII, p. 279.

about sending a protest note regarding the zone.[13] Raeder felt constrained by military considerations to renew his appeals that German operations within the zone be authorized to compel the enemy to spread his forces. It would, he indicated, suffice merely to give the navy operational freedom in the area and no note or announcement would be required. The United States could hardly complain since the British had paid no attention to the zone from the start. Acknowledging that operations off Canada were probably too provocative, Raeder nonetheless recommended that Germany recognize a zone no wider than twenty miles. Hitler was evasive until August when he flatly rejected any German operations within the zone.[14]

There were two specific incidents in American policy, in addition to the general tendencies noted above, which apparently alarmed the OKM more than anything which had happened since the destroyer deal: the occupation of Greenland and Iceland and Roosevelt's order to "shoot at sight" announced on September 11. The navy took the Greenland incident seriously. "This step should on no account be underestimated," was the warning in the war diary. The Greenland move along with American interest in Iceland and Africa was pictured as the foundation for "a first-rate security system" for supplying goods to England. It was "completely beyond doubt" that this would be injurious to the German effort in the Atlantic. The Iceland occupation was regarded even more seriously. The move, in the view of the navy, had created an immense burden on Germany and might serve as a precedent for similar operations against Dakar and the Azores. Did this not really constitute an American entry into the war and should it not be so considered?[15]

[13] Ribbentrop felt that if everything were done to save American lives it would be worth the risk. Rintelen to Weizsaeker 12/4/41, *StS/USA/V/244401.*
[14] Fuehrer conference 4/4/41, *FCNA/*1941, p. 45. Fuehrer conferences 26/8/41, 17/9/41, *FCNA/*1941, pp. 103, 109. Appendix to Fuehrer conference 6/6/41, *OKM-KTB/C/VIII,* p. 160.
[15] *OKM-KTB/A/XX* — 11/4/41, 26/4/41. *OKM-KTB/A/XXIII* — 3/7/41, 8/7/41.

This question was raised at the Fuehrer conference of July 10, 1941. Hitler, with Barbarossa going well, declined to be alarmed and stressed again his anxiety to avoid incidents and postpone an American entry "for at least one or two months."[16] He was left, however, with a memorandum summarizing the navy's interpretation of the matter. The Iceland affair, according to the report, had had the "strongest and most damaging effect" on the German war effort. The air reconnaissance and convoying activities along the routes to Iceland meant a direct American intrusion into the German blockade area. The way was open to incidents and provocations. The navy advised retaliation by attacking without warning American merchantmen and even, if need be, warships who found themselves in the blockade zone. If, the memorandum argued, the Fuehrer could agree that the Iceland occupation was in fact tantamount to a declaration of war, then the blockade zone could reasonably be widened to include the entire North Atlantic, the Pan American security zone reduced for German operations, prize law applied, American warships treated like the enemies they were and Japan encouraged to distract American attention to the Far East. Hitler was unimpressed, contenting himself with the bland hope that the British might be resentful of American influence in Iceland.[17]

On September 11, Roosevelt delivered his famous "shoot at sight" speech. Referring to German submarine actions as "piracy, legally and morally," the President had called for "active defense" and orders had been given to American naval vessels to "shoot at sight" any German ship caught in American defensive waters. This was the other move in United States foreign policy in 1941 which seemed to make a special impact on the German admirals. It was characterized as nothing less than "a localized declaration of war" and an act which could inflict "exceptionally strong injury" on Germany's Atlantic effort and commercial shipping

---

[16] Fuehrer conference 10/7/41, *FCNA*/1941, p. 91.
[17] Appendix to Fuehrer conference 10/7/41, *OKM-KTB*/C/VIII, p. 170. Fuehrer conference 25/7/41, *FCNA*/1941, p. 94.

since American defensive waters seemed to include "practically the entire western Atlantic." Submarines under these circumstances should either be given permission to attack or be withdrawn. To yield would simply bring on further provocation and it was now necessary to demonstrate to the Americans "that the German navy did not fear incidents."[18]

These ideas, recorded in the war diaries, were expressed to Hitler in the conference of September 17. Raeder warned his chief that Germany had now to expect offensive acts "at every encounter." "There is," he explained, "no longer any difference between British and American ships." He then went on to make a variety of detailed suggestions, which left only non-threatening American warships, traveling alone, exempt from German attack.[19] In spite of Ribbentrop's post-war assertion that Hitler was "greatly excited" by Roosevelt's speech, the Fuehrer ordered no change in policy at least until mid-October, and Ribbentrop himself, while denouncing the speech as "a tissue of lies" about a matter that had "not the slightest connection with any threat to America," assured his Japanese counterpart that in the Atlantic Germany would pursue a policy of "prudence" (*Besonnenheit*).[20]

The reaction of the OKM to the various incidents involving German and American ships in the Atlantic suggests that in pressing for a more aggressive policy the German naval command was well aware of the risk involved. The significance of repeated contact and the possibility of a full-scale confrontation with American naval forces were not overlooked by the admiralty. However, they were also highly doubtful that the policy of

[18] For discussion of this speech see Langer and Gleason, *The Undeclared War*, pp. 744–746. Text in *PPA*/1941, p. 441. Ciano recorded that the speech had made "a great impression." *Diary* 25/10/41, p. 390. *OKM-KTB*/A/XXV — 13/9/41.

[19] Raeder's new proposals called specifically for attacks on all escorting vessels in any operational area. All neutral ships except unconvoyed neutrals outside the blockade were to be sunk without warning.

[20] Ribbentrop testimony, *IMT*/X, p. 296. Fuehrer conference 17/9/41, *FCNA*/1941, p. 109. Appendix to Fuehrer conferences 17/9/41, 29/9/41, *OKM-KTB*/C/VIII, pp. 237, 249. Ribbentrop to Tokyo Embassy 13/9/41, *StS/USA/*III/373804.

avoiding incidents under all circumstances would in fact keep America out. At best this line was considered problematical.[21] Raeder, for example, found satisfaction in the encounter between a German U-boat and the destroyer *Greer*, while the sinking of the U.S.S. *Robin Moor* demonstrated that Germany meant business, that as he put it, "firm measures are always more effective than apparent yielding."[22] However, in a Fuehrer conference three weeks before Pearl Harbor at which these matters were discussed, in spite of the apparent willingness of the OKM to run the risk of further incidents, it was decided that the navy was to retain the policy of restraint "in keeping with strategic necessity." Even if the Neutrality Acts were totally repealed (as Raeder suggested was likely), Hitler was firm: the orders would stand and would only be changed "according to developments," whatever that meant.[23]

Had the German navy any fear that such incidents might lead to a formal American entry? Apparently not, since mention of such a possibility is scanty. The belief that a rapid victory over Britain would render American intervention academic and some reference to the restraints of public opinion and the Japanese appear in naval thinking during 1941, and this doubtless encouraged some to believe that America could not enter.[24] However, the impression is that by this time the navy was quite simply in-

---

[21] See for example *OKM-KTB*/A/XX — 26/4/41. For example a war diary entry for April states that "*if* the German refusal to be provoked *does* weaken Roosevelt's hand, then Hitler's continental policy is correct." (Emphasis mine.) *OKM-KTB*/A/XX — 27/4/41. Again in May the "hope" is expressed that the soft line will strengthen American public opinion and keep America out. *OKM-KTB*/C/VII — 7/5/41.

[22] Fuehrer conference 21/6/41, *FCNA*/1941, p. 88. Roosevelt's reaction to the *Robin Moor* incident was in fact moderate. *The Undeclared War*, p. 456. The navy's viewpoint was also given to the Foreign Ministry. OKM to Foreign Ministry 12/9/41, *StS/USA*/VIII/375787. Hitler found the behavior of the submarine commander at the *Greer* incident "exactly right." *OKM-KTB*/A/XXV — 9/9/41.

[23] Fuehrer conference 13/11/41, *FCNA*/1941, pp. 119, 120.

[24] *OKM-KTB*/A/XXVI — 1/10/41, 21/10/41. Admiral Witthoeft-Emden, the Attaché in Washington, had cabled in April that an American entry was certainly "always possible." Witthoeft to OKM 24/4/41, *OKM-Att.*

different to the question. In naval terms, as Raeder brought out repeatedly, the war was on, whatever the juridical status of the two countries. His object throughout the year was to compel Hitler to recognize this fact.[25]

On this particular aspect of German policy at least, Hitler continued to be supported by the Foreign Ministry, and Raeder's conferences with the diplomats seem to have been as unrewarding as those with the Fuehrer. The Ministry was, for example, considerably alarmed at the *Robin Moor* incident and the navy's attitude toward it. Reasserting the view that such matters were diplomatic as well as naval, a memorandum on the subject concluded with the sentiment that the Foreign Ministry "must not be pushed by the navy." Two weeks before Pearl Harbor, even while urging an aggressive course upon the Japanese regarding America, the navy was warned by Ribbentrop that naval forces were to be especially careful outside the Pan American neutrality zone so that political problems with America could be avoided. Any yielding to provocation, he warned, would only give the Americans renewed opportunities. Submarines, in case of doubt, were to err on the side of restraint in order that hostilities between the two countries could be avoided.[26]

There remains the final question: why did Hitler restrain his admirals? On the face of it, the picture of a hesitant Fuehrer speaking the idiom of international maritime law seems almost incredible. Was this the result of a realistic appraisal of the implications of American power for Germany? There is little evidence for this. On the contrary, Hitler's stated contempt for the world position of the United States forms a startling contrast to his posture of extreme caution about offending that country on the high seas. If he had so little regard for a threat from the

[25] Hitler did tell Cudahy on May 23, 1941, that American convoys meant war. *DGFP*/D/XII, p. 854.

[26] *OKM-KTB*/C/VIII — 10/4/41. Weizsaeker to Ribbentrop 12/4/41, *StS*/*Krieg*/X/443236. Weizsaeker to Ribbentrop, *DGFP*/D/XII, p. 519. Memorandum (Ritter) 25/11/41, *UStS*/*Seekrieg*/I/34041.

Americans, why was he evidently so fearful of provoking them? We are here confronted with one of the real paradoxes in Hitler's conduct of foreign and military affairs, and this ironic element becomes even clearer in the context of the reckless course he freely urged upon the Japanese. Some of this element of inconsistency is probably irreducible, and with a man like Hitler it would not do to try and iron it out completely. However, a number of relevant factors may be usefully recalled at this point.

First, Hitler's restraint in the battle of the Atlantic was no doubt in part a reflection of his general hesitancy about maritime affairs and his uncertainty about overseas matters. Secondly, the inconsistency of his response was a function of his surprise at the unexpected entry of this discounted country into his strategic world after 1939. Thirdly, Hitler's naval policy may well reflect his inability to accept or at least enthuse about the *guerre de course* to which his navy had been reduced by his own pre-war neglect. But most of all, his unusual caution regarding the Atlantic was the result of his *Lebensraum* fetish; of his inability to take his eyes from his maps of the Ukraine; of his fixation with the acquisition of a continental base. Through June 1940, this had meant France. Now he had returned to his original continental objective: the Soviet Union. He made it perfectly clear that anything else was an annoyance and a distraction. The Barbarossa obsession also provides a clue about the seeming inconsistency of his naval and Far Eastern policies as far as America is concerned, since Japanese activity on the Russian Eastern flank was obviously of greater relevance to Germany's own plans for that country. For his admirals, however, the Russian operation remained a kind of strategic sound barrier. Only let this victory be his, he assured them, and his continental plans would be complete. He could then turn his navy loose on the Anglo-Saxons. This priority he repeated to his admirals at tedious length throughout 1941.[27]

[27] Ruge shares the conviction that the Russian obsession was at the root of Hitler's Atlantic reticence. *Der Seekrieg*, p. 181.

At the first naval conference of the final year, Hitler admitted that if Germany were forced to fight the United States and Russia simultaneously "the situation would then become very complicated." However, he was cheered by the thought that the completion of Barbarossa would remove not only the Russian but the American threat as well. Though these expectations may have been something of a rationalization for his obvious relish at having a land operation at the head of his priorities once again, all provocations of America were definitely to be avoided pending the liquidation of the Eastern question.[28] In the Fuehrer conference of June 21, Hitler demanded avoidance of naval incidents with America until Barbarossa was well underway. The effects of the collapse of Russia on Japan was, he felt, bound to deter the Americans. Thus the order went out: "The Fuehrer desires absolutely to avoid any possibility of involvement with the U.S.A. until the development of Barbarossa becomes clear, i.e. for a few more weeks."[29] These "few more weeks" were repeated again in July with the assurance that the Americans would be so impressed by the magnitude of the German victory over Russia that all thought of intervention would be killed. At the conference of July 25, Hitler told Raeder that while he agreed with much of the navy's analysis of the situation he wanted to avoid an American declaration of war while the Eastern campaign was in progress. In any event, it would be over before American aid could be effective. After that, moreover, he reserved "the right to take serious action against the U.S.A. as well . . ." In spite of the mounting incidents which, according to Ribbentrop, "gradually convinced the Fuehrer that sooner or later they would bring the United States into war against us," the references to keeping America at bay until the liquidation of Russia continued for the remainder of the year, even as the few weeks became a few months.[30]

[28] Fuehrer conference 8–9/1/41, *FCNA*/1941, p. 13.
[29] Fuehrer conference 21/6/41, *FCNA*/1941, p. 90.
[30] Fuehrer conference 10/7/41, *FCNA*/1941, p. 91. Fuehrer conference

Hitler's policy of restraining his navy did not of course prevent the entry of the United States prior to victory over Russia, and the problem of fighting both of the two formerly neutral colossi simultaneously, which he had admitted would be "very complicated," became eventually very complicated indeed. As we shall see in the following chapters, Hitler partially brought this state of affairs down on his own head by urging upon the Japanese a more intransigent policy regarding the United States than he was willing to allow to his own navy. Yet he continued to cling to his priorities even in these altered circumstances and persistently followed the ever-receding mirage of continental security as the goal which would provide all that was required to deal with the maritime powers. Hitler's admirals, who had been no more successful than Hanfstaengl in washing "the dust of the infantry" from the Fuehrer's eyes, heard in August 1942 once again the old familiar refrain: "When our aim in the East, namely the creation of a blockade-proof *Lebensraum*, is achieved, we must still fight the naval war against the Anglo-Saxons to the end."[31]

25/7/41, *FCNA*/1941, p. 94. Ribbentrop testimony, *IMT*/X, p. 295. Fuehrer conference 17/9/41, *FCNA*/1941, p. 109. *OKM-KTB*/A/XXVI — 1/10/41.

[31] Fuehrer conference 29/8/42, *FCNA*/1942, p. 53.

CHAPTER 12

Germany and Japan Prior to the War

THE UNITED STATES became for Adolf Hitler not only an unwelcome Atlantic distraction but a factor which forced his attention to the Pacific as well. Indeed, the American impact on German foreign relations was no doubt greatest in the Far Eastern area, and Hitler's reaction to this influence formed an interesting counterpoint to the naval policy described in the previous chapter.

Emerging vaguely as a by-product of German preparations for a war against the West in the months prior to the attack on Poland, America loomed increasingly in German calculations in the Pacific. By the summer of 1940 it had become the central issue of German-Japanese relations, the target of the Triangle Pact signed in September of that year and the primary subject of Nazi policy in Asia down to Pearl Harbor. There is no evidence that, prior to the Munich conference in September 1938, the United States played any significant role in this aspect of German policy, although Japanese considerations of America no doubt indirectly affected the course of German affairs in the Far East. However, the curious pattern of the German relationship with Japan, the divergent perspectives, the maneuvering to extract different meaning and purpose from pompous, insubstantial agreements, all of this had already emerged by the outbreak of the European war. We must therefore have this background clearly in mind in order to understand the fateful role which America played in German policy toward Japan in the years before Pearl Harbor.[1]

[1] Useful accounts of this period may be found in Presseisen, *German-Japanese*

There was little real foundation for close German-Japanese ties prior to the establishment of the Third Reich. Contacts with Japan were neither especially close nor cordial. The influence in Japan of German science, the Germany army and the political system of Bismarck were counteracted by events of the Wilhelmian and Weimar period: German participation in European pressures against the Japanese in China in the 1890's, Kaiser Wilhelm's obsession with the "yellow menace," Japanese possession of former German islands after the World War as well as a certain pro-Chinese orientation in diplomatic, military and commercial circles at Berlin. Many of these factors continued to play a role during the Nazi period.

On the other hand, there were those in Germany who had long advocated close German-Japanese relations as a geographical imperative. As early as 1913, the future geo-politician Karl Haushofer envisaged a German-Russian-Japanese combination in control of the heartland and able to provide an antidote to Anglo-Saxon domination. Haushofer, who may have influenced Hitler through Rudolph Hess in the 1920's and who became a figure of some importance as director of the *Institut fuer Geopolitik* in the following decade, expressed his theories regarding the Far East fully in his *Geopolitik des Pazifischen Ozeans*. Stressing the need for continental control of the Eurasian heartland, Haushofer saw Japan as a natural partner for Germany along with Russia in the formation of an unconquerable bloc. Japan and Germany, he went on in terms Hitler and Ribbentrop were to employ later, shared the same enemies. "They long to break the same chains," and this was for Haushofer the reason why Germany must not lose contact with the Pacific.[2]

Relations, chap. I, F. Iklé, *German-Japanese Relations*, chap. I, and most impressively in T. Sommer, Deutschland und Japan zwischen den Maechten, chaps. 1–3. F. C. Jones brilliantly relates Japanese foreign and domestic policies before 1937 in chap. I of *Japan's New Order in Asia*.

[2] See Presseisen, *op. cit.*, pp. 15–17, K. Haushofer, *Geopolitik des Pazifischen Ozeans*, p. 133. Haushofer's actual importance in the Third Reich is a matter of dispute. His continentalism and expansionism would have been more congenial to the Fuehrer than his rejection of racism and his Russophilia.

Hitler's own attitude to Japan prior to 1933 was expressed in *Mein Kampf,* where he classified the Japanese among the "culture-bearing" rather than the "culture-creating" races. The Japanese, he was sure, were absolutely dependent upon Western culture and technology. He could not, however, hate these people since they had been victims, like Germany, of the Versailles system and of the Jews, who feared their commercial competition.[3] In addition, although the yellow menace was not a primary Hitlerian rallying cry, racial factors probably cannot be eliminated from Hitler's outlook toward the Japanese. This came out later in moments of anger.

In the actual development of German-Japanese relations between 1933 and 1936, three features emerged: a considerable amount of ideological and political speculation about a possible Japanese role in German foreign policy; a number of political, cultural and propaganda gestures toward closer ties; little diplomatic activity in this direction in spite of many rumors to the contrary. Certainly, Japanophile sentiments were prominent in Nazi circles at this time. Haushofer, now writing in the *Voelkischer Beobachter,* explained that Japan's experience "impresses upon us the immense superiority of the fascist form of life in the struggle for existence." Alfred Rosenberg, the Nazi ideologue, and the prominent journalist Dr. Joachim von Leers found no racial objection to the Japanese in international affairs. "We cannot," von Leers pointed out, "expect that in politics all our friends will do us the favor of acquiring blue eyes and blond hair."[4] There was a certain ideological comfort to be found in the Japanese political system which, though never acquiring the totalitarian aspect of Nazi Germany, was illiberal, anti-communist and chauvinistic. In addition, geo-political arguments stressed the value of having some connection with a power on

---

3 *Mein Kampf,* pp. 398, 399, 931.
4 For the Haushofer pronouncements see *Voelkischer Beobachter* 19/6/33, 17/1/33, 6/4/33. The von Leers article in *Die Tat,* September 1934, quoted in Presseisen, *op. cit.,* p. 66. Rosenberg evidently shifted from an earlier position on the subject. *Ibid.,* p. 8. See also Rosenberg, *op. cit.,* p. 30.

the Soviet Pacific flank.[5] However, it was the joint German and Japanese position outside the League of Nations which evidently drew the attention of many to a common political bond. Here were two powers not only with anti-communist governments and expansionist tendencies, but also isolated from organized international society and cast by that isolationism in the role of revisionists. Thus Germany and Japan occupied in some eyes the strange position of being both anti-revolutionary (opposed to communism) and anti-status-quo (opposed to the League of Nations).[6]

There is some evidence that Hitler himself took an early interest in Japan as a factor in German foreign policy. According to Erich Kordt, after the Manchurian adventure Hitler showed an interest in the Japanese army, "whose war-like spirit inspired him." When Japan left the League, Kordt wrote further, "Hitler's sympathies for that country were fully aroused." Hitler himself in 1935 told General Ott, who was to be German Military Attaché and later Ambassador in Tokyo, that he thought Japanese military pressure on Russia's Eastern front would limit Soviet activity in Europe.[7] It will be noted that Hitler's interest here was not in the acquisition of German influence in the Far East as such, but rather in the role Japan might play in the politics of the European continent. More specifically, Hitler was already drawing a direct line between a Russo-German war and an activist Japanese policy; just the sort of connection, it will be recalled, he was unable to perceive between Barbarossa and the battle of the Atlantic.

[5] Some Japanese also admired the Nazi system in the early years. See the statement by Matsuoka 4/3/33, Presseisen, *op. cit.*, p. 32. Dodd reported on this argument. Dodd, *Diary* 17/10/33, p. 63. See also *SIA/*1933, pp. 175–179.

[6] *Voelkischer Beobachter* 17/1/33, 6/4/33; *Nicht aus den Akten*, p. 122.

[7] *Nicht aus den Akten*, pp. 122–123. Both Kordt and Dirksen believe that it was Hitler himself who first had the idea of concluding a pact with Japan. Dirksen, *op. cit.*, p. 142. Ribbentrop testimony, *IMT/X*, pp. 239–241. General von Blomberg told Dirksen that Hitler was definitely interested in the role Japan might play in German foreign policy. Poole, *op. cit.*, p. 135. Conference with Ott 10/3/35, reported in Sommer, *op. cit.*, p. 20.

In other circles, however, this interest in Japan was not shared. Many leading diplomats were outspokenly pro-Chinese and business circles in Germany tended to share this bias due to large German economic interests long established in China and the flourishing barter trade which then existed between the two countries. There was also considerable Sinophile sentiment in the German army, since German advisors were playing a significant role in organizing the Chinese armed forces.[8]

Against this background of renewed interest as well as of tension between pro-Chinese and pro-Japanese factions in Berlin which was to persist, German-Japanese rapprochement proceeded tentatively in non-diplomatic areas. There were technical exchanges, fleet visits and cultural contacts along with expressions of mutual regard and approval of policy.[9] And there were endless rumors, echoed in American quarters, of more substantial and ominous military connections.[10] However, there had in fact been no noticeable rush into more formal arrangements until, against the background of the Franco-Russian alliance, the enunciation of the popular front by the comintern, the rapprochement between Germany and Italy following the Abyssinian campaign and the Spanish Civil War, negotiations were opened which culminated in the Anti-Comintern Pact of 1936.

The Anti-Comintern Pact and the German attitude toward the Sino-Japanese war which broke out in 1937 amply illustrated the

[8] Dirksen, *op. cit.*, pp. 144, 145. Dirksen to Foreign Ministry 4/1/34, *DGFP*/C/II, p. 298. Weizsaeker, *op. cit.*, p. 140. Buelow to Trautman 12/10/34, *DGFP*/C/III, p. 480. Memo (Buelow) 7/3/35, *DGFP*/C/III, p. 988. Kordt wrote of the old rule of the Foreign Ministry to keep out of the Far East. *Nicht aus den Akten*, p. 12. Von Neurath testimony, *IMT*/XII, p. 635. Presseisen, *op. cit.*, pp. 75, 147–163. Statement by Ott to Sommer, Sommer, *op. cit.*, p. 8.

[9] Dirksen, *op. cit.*, p. 153. *SIA*/1934, p. 667. Iklé, *op. cit.*, p. 13. Dodd, *Diary* 17/3/35, pp. 222, 223. J. Grew, *Ten Years in Japan*, p. 155; Presseisen, *op. cit.*, p. 45.

[10] See for example Report from Military Attaché to Hull 17/5/34, Hull, *op. cit.*, p. 244. See also *SIA*/1933, p. 114. Dodd, *Diary*, pp. 255, 248, 256, 301. The American embassy in Tokyo reported along the same line, Grew, *op. cit.*, p. 155. *FRUS*/1935/III, pp. 181, 311, 481–482.

defective and equivocal basis of the German-Japanese connection.[11] In spite of Ribbentrop's typically extravagant statement at the signing ("an epoch-making event"), the contract which emerged with its vague agreement to exchange information about cominform activity and its provision for a standing commission to accomplish this purpose was certainly anything but a sweeping military alliance.[12] The Pact contained in fact the seeds of a reversal of the traditionally pro-Chinese German policy in the Far East, thus exchanging a position of real influence in that area for mere dependence on a country which she could not easily either intimidate or control. Moreover, talk of an internal communist threat in either Germany or Japan was on the face of it so far-fetched that the Pact could only evoke thoughts of ulterior motives and secret agreements in the minds of those who might otherwise have considered joining an anti-communist front. As in the case of the later Tripartite arrangement, the Pact was probably largely a matter of bluff and propaganda. But there was never even complete agreement on who was to be bluffed and what the propaganda was to cloak. While in Japan the target remained Russia and there was anxiety about its effect upon Britain and America, in Germany Hitler made clear by November 1937 that he already had in mind the intimidation of England as well, while the United States was apparently of no concern at all.[13]

As to the propaganda value of the arrangement as a cloak for expansion, the problem was that this expansion was bound sooner

[11] For German origins of the Pact see Hitler speech in August 1936 in *Vierteljahreshefte fuer Zeitgeschichte*, 1955/2, pp. 184–210. For Japanese response, Memo (Hirota) 30/6/36 and Five Ministers Conference 7/8/36, *IMTFE*, Exh. 216, in Presseisen, *op. cit.*, p. 95.

[12] Ribbentrop's statement at the signing in *DIA*/1936, pp. 299–300. The secret protocols attached added little in the way of real obligation. See Weinberg, "Die Geheimen Abkommen zum Antikominternpakt," *Vierteljahreshefte fuer Zeitgeschichte*, 1954/2/April. Ott testimony, *Case 11*/XXI, p. 10165.

[13] Hitler did not even rule out England's joining the Pact. He told Ribbentrop to "bring England into the Anticomintern Pact . . . that is my greatest wish." Sommer, *op. cit.*, p. 32. Ribbentrop testimony, *IMT*/X, pp. 266–270. Ciano, *Diary* 1/11/37, 2/11/38, pp. 27, 188.

or later to involve the interests of countries such as the United States, with which one or the other partner did not wish hostilities. Revisionist powers may unite in their grudge against the established order, but the vision of a corrected order to say nothing of details of timing, priority and area of operations may all reveal painful differences. This is what plagued German-Japanese relations from the start.[14] Japan feared any European involvement and Germany wanted to avoid Asian complications. The Pact was well described by a Japanese newspaper as "a frame in which any picture may be painted."[15] The major partners could not agree on the picture: for the Japanese it was a Pacific seascape; for Hitler, the landscape of continental Europe.

The discrepancies became evident when Japan attacked China in July 1937. Germany's futile neutrality proclamation and abortive mediation attempt merely demonstrated how little control Berlin could exercise over her newly found Far Eastern partner.[16] Ambassador Ott's call in January 1938 for an "adjustment of German-Japanese relations to the present situation" was echoed by Hitler the following month. "I cannot agree," he said, "with those politicians who think they do Europe a service in harming Japan . . . I do not consider China strong enough either spiritually or militarily to deal with Bolshevism."[17] Germany now yielded rapidly to Japanese demands: Manchukuo was recog-

[14] See Grew to State Department 13/11/37, *FRUS*/Japan/II, p. 160, in which the American Ambassador pictured the Anti-Comintern Pact as an alliance of have-nots against haves, with anti-communism as a window dressing.

[15] Dirksen to Foreign Ministry 8/9/37, *DGFP*/D/I, p. 757. Tokyo Embassy to State Department 18/5/39, *FRUS*/Japan/II, p. 1. Memo (Ribbentrop) 7/8/37, *DGFP*/D/I, p. 750. The American Military Attaché in Berlin noted this in a report of 1/2/38, *FRUS* /1938/I, p. 14. *The Japan Advertiser* 7/11/37, in Sommer, *op. cit.*, p. 92.

[16] Report (Trautmann) 27/1/37, Auswaertiges Amt, *Pol VIII/Japan-Deutschland*, I/131261. Weizsaecker to Tokyo Embassy 28/7/37, Memo (Weizsaecker) 30/7/37, *DGFP*/D/I, pp. 743, 744. Dirksen to Foreign Ministry 31/7/37, *Pol. VIII/Japan-Deutschland*/II/130859. Memo (Weizsaecker) 1/12/37, *DGFP*/D/I, p. 787. Foreign Ministry to Tokyo Embassy 10/12/37, 24/12/37, *DGFP*/D/I, pp. 800, 808.

[17] Tokyo Embassy to Foreign Ministry 26/1/38, *DGFP*/D/I, p. 826. *DIA*/ 1938/II, pp. 8, 9. (Hitler statement).

nized, military advisors and materials withdrawn from China, and in June Trautmann, the Ambassador at Nanking who had fought for a pro-Chinese policy, was recalled. These moves, however, did not evoke the least generosity on the part of Japan toward German requests for economic privileges in North China.[18]

Thus the pattern had emerged fully revealing the essential weakness of the German relationship with Japan which many had foreseen as a consequence of yielding the one real area of German Far Eastern influence (China) to follow the will-of-the-wisp of Japanese friendship. Hitler's interest was not in the Far East as such but rather on the use to which an Asian connection might be put in future European struggles. The revisionist frame was still there, but there was as yet no agreement on the picture. As the war in Europe grew nearer in 1938 and 1939, it became increasingly urgent for Hitler that the picture conform to his continental requirements. As Britain became the leading obstacle to his ambitions, however, we may notice the first vague inclusion within the frame of German-Japanese relations of the United States.

The year 1938 marked a turning point in German foreign relations. The shift from preparation to execution, Hitler's assumption of full control symbolized by the nomination of Joachim von Ribbentrop to the Foreign Ministry and the emergence of Britain as a prime potential enemy were all bound to effect German relations with Japan.[19] From January 1938 until the early summer of 1939, undeterred by the problems revealed during the Sino-Japanese war, Hitler tried to forge the Anti-Comintern Pact into a military alliance. He succeeded in this goal only

[18] Foreign Ministry to Nanking Embassy 21/2/38, *DGFP*/D/I, p. 839. Memo (Weizsaeker) 27/4/38, *DGFP*/D/I, p. 855. Memo (Wiehl) 26/4/38, *DGFP*/D/ I, p. 856. Foreign Ministry to Trautmann 24/6/38, *DGFP*/D/I, p. 883. German requests are found in memos of the economic department 29/6/38, 6/7/38, 28/7/38, *DGFP*/D/I, pp. 886, 888, 890.
[19] See Ribbentrop's "Notes for the Fuehrer" 2/1/38, *DGFP*/D/I, p. 162, for the Foreign Minister's emphasis on England. Also, Ciano, *Diary* 24/10/37, p. 24.

with Italy, however, and, growing impatient with the Japanese, he turned to Eastern Europe. He thus entered the war not in alliance with his anti-comintern partner, but rather in agreement with communist Russia.

Japanese caution about these German moves for a military alliance did not deter Ribbentrop from enthusing on the prospects to the Italians. These conversations are of the greatest interest to us, for in these the Foreign Minister first mentions the United States as a factor in German calculations in the Far East. In June 1938, Ribbentrop explained to Attolico, the able Italian envoy in Berlin, that "a plain open military alliance" would intimidate not only England and France, but the U.S.A. as well. He was certain that Japan would cooperate fully even if it meant war with China, Russia, England and the U.S.A. simultaneously.[20] On October 28, Ribbentrop arrived in Rome with the news that Hitler now regarded war as inevitable and intended to pursue an alliance with Italy and Japan relentlessly. Munich had demonstrated to the Fuehrer the weakness of the West and the isolationism of America. Now was the time to negotiate a genuine military pact to encourage this weakness and this isolationism. This would be, the Reich Foreign Minister insisted breathlessly, "the greatest thing in the world." The Italians were less enthusiastic at this time ("That Ribbentrop, always exaggerating" was Ciano's reaction), and only warmed to the idea after the new year.[21] By this time, however, the new Japanese government headed by Prince Konoye had become even more restrained in their attitude toward a pact.

Once again, each partner was seeking something quite different. The Germans were interested in the immediate diplomatic

---

[20] Ott to Weizsaeker 1/11/38, *DGFP*/D/IV, p. 685. See also Grew to Hull 12/10/38, *FRUS*/1938/II, p. 316. Ribbentrop-Attolico meeting 19/6/38, Toscano, *op. cit.*, pp. 24–28. Neither Attolico nor his chief were especially enthusiastic. Ciano to Attolico 27/6/38, *ibid.*, p. 29.

[21] Ribbentrop statement 28/10/38, *DGFP*/D/IV, p. 515. Ciano, *Diplomatic Papers* 28/10/38, pp. 242–247. Toscano, *op. cit.*, pp. 58, 59; D. Watt, "The Rome-Berlin Axis," *Journal of Politics*, Oct. 1960.

effect of an alliance rather than its military efficacy in a future war. It was to be a bluff which would provide the intimidation required to accomplish an Eastern solution without Western interference. Therefore, it had to be full, unqualified and well publicized. Moreover, we know from Ribbentrop's statements to Attolico and Ciano, cited above, that Western interference now included the United States.[22] For the Japanese, on the other hand, the enemy was still Russia and the need was to avoid unduly antagonizing the West, including the United States, and avoid a European entanglement.[23] Therefore, the Japanese pressed for reservations, allowing greater discretion in applying such a pact and specifically reassuring the United States.[24] It was, of course, German policy to oppose such qualifications which would destroy the whole *raison d'être* of a pact from the German point of view.[25] Although Japan watered down some of these reservations, German patience had become exhausted. Ribbentrop expressed his doubts about Japanese reliability, while Hitler found the Japanese "more and more incomprehensible."[26]

Although not giving up the Japanese relationship[27] Hitler now turned to other quarters for support. On June 21, Ott in Tokyo

[22] *DGFP*/D/VII, Appendix I, p. 1107. See Watt, "The Rome-Berlin Axis," p. 537.

[23] Ott to Foreign Ministry 28/1/39, *DGFP*/D/IV, p. 698. Ott to Foreign Ministry 14/2/39, *DGFP*/D/IV, p. 703.

[24] Oshima testimony, *IMTFE*/LXXVI, p. 34001. Ott to Ribbentrop 17/5/39, 7/6/39, *DGFP*/D/VI, pp. 522, 656. Ott also emphasized that the Japanese army favored while the navy and Foreign Ministry tended to oppose the pact. Ott to Foreign Ministry 24/4/39, 8/5/39, 17/5/39, *DGFP*/D/VI, pp. 317, 454, 572, 858. See also Grew to State Department 18/5/39, *FRUS*/Japan/II, pp. 161–162.

[25] Ribbentrop to Ott 26/4/39, 17/6/39, *DGFP*/D/VI, pp. 337, 735. Weizsaeker to Ott 2/3/39, *DGFP*/D/IV, p. 702. Oshima to Japanese Foreign Ministry 2/4/39, IMTFE/LXXVI, p. 34007.

[26] Ott to Foreign Ministry 27/4/39, *DGFP*/D/VI, pp. 346, 541. Ott to Foreign Ministry 17/6/39, *DGFP*/D/VI, pp. 757, 750. Ribbentrop to Ott 15/5/39. *DGFP*/D/VI, p. 494. "One does not understand here any longer what is actually happening in Tokyo." Ribbentrop to Ott 28/5/39, *DGFP*/D/VI, p. 559.

[27] The mission of Admiral Foerster to Tokyo indicated this fact. Weizsaeker to Ott 17/6/39, *DGFP*/D/VI, p. 737. Attolico thought that the Germans were simply going to let the Japanese relationship ripen in the course of events. Attolico to Ciano 29/5/39, *DDI*, ser. 8/VII, p. 37.

was ordered to suspend pressure for a treaty. The reason for this lay in the tangled web of negotiations then occurring in Moscow which led to the Nazi-Soviet pact in August.[28] Since Japan was in August 1939 capable neither of military nor diplomatic support, Hitler turned to the Soviets as a more operational alternative. By August 14, Hitler had made his decision. He spoke of the "defection" of Japan. "Japan," he said, "does not go with us without conditions. I have decided to go with Stalin."[29] He also reserved some choice Hitlerian invective for his erstwhile allies who were no longer the Aryans of Asia but rather "lacquered half-monkeys who needed to feel the knout." Confronted without warning by the alliance of her anti-comintern partner with communist Russia, Japanese shock was naturally profound.[30]

As to the role of the United States in German-Japanese relations during these months, we have already seen that America was not absent as a factor from the earlier German overture for a military alliance. In addition, since America was for Japan an obviously more important consideration than for Germany, the Germans were constantly having that country thrust at them during the negotiations.[31] Compelled to pay some attention to the American question in her relations with Japan, Germany disagreed with her partner on how best to handle an American

---

[28] Weizsaeker to Ott 21/6/39, *DGFP*/D/VI, p. 755. Ribbentrop had warned Oshima about the possibility of a German-Soviet arrangement in April, but the Japanese envoy did not take it seriously. Oshima testimony, *IMFTE*/XIII, p. 6079; Stahner testimony, *ibid*, LVIII, p. 24399.

[29] Halder, *Diary* 14/8/39, I, p. 6. Ribbentrop to Moscow Embassy 14/8/39, *DGFP*/D/VII, p. 62. *NCA*/VII, p. 752. See also Hitler's statement to Mussolini that the Japanese were only willing to sign a pact against the U.S.S.R. but he required something for use against the West at that time. Hitler to Mussolini 25/8/39, *DGFP*/D/VII, p. 281.

[30] Hitler statement 22/8/39, *IMT*/XXVI, pp. 338, 523. Ott reported "dismay" in Tokyo. Ott to Foreign Ministry 22/8/39, *DGFP*/D/VII, p. 251. Memo (Weizsaeker) 22/8/39, *DGFP*/D/VII, p. 253. Oshima referred to it after the war as "an act of extreme bad faith on the part of Germany." Oshima testimony, *IMTFE*/LXXVI, p. 34015.

[31] Ott to Foreign Ministry 14/3/39, 23/3/39, *DGFP*/D/IV, p. 703; VI, p. 81. Ott to Weizsaeker 5/7/39, *DGFP*/D/VI, p. 858. Ott to Foreign Ministry 10/8/39, 18/8/39, *DGFP*/D/VII, pp. 6, 119.

threat. In May, Ribbentrop directed Ott to point out to the Japanese that fear of America was no ground for delaying a pact since such an arrangement was the best method of keeping America out of the war. In rejecting any Japanese qualifications to the proposed treaty, Ribbentrop told Oshima that only a straightforward alliance would have the effect of deterring America and Soviet Russia from entering the war.[32] This emphasis on intimidation of the United States was also clear from the instructions given to Admiral Foerster, whose trip in July was to convince the Japanese navy that "only a perfectly clear alliance is calculated fully to ensure American neutrality."[33]

Thus had the United States emerged prior to the war as a factor, though not as yet a central factor, in German policy toward Japan.

[32] Ribbentrop to Ott 15/5/39, *DGFP*/D/VI, p. 454. Ribbentrop to Ott 17/6/39, *DGFP*/D/VI, p. 737. Memo (Weizsaeker) 16/6/36, *DGFP*/D/VI, p. 734.
[33] Weizsaeker to Ott 17/6/39, *DGFP*/D/VI, p. 737. Ott to Weizsaeker 5/7/39, *DGFP*/D/VI, p. 858.

CHAPTER 13

America and the World Triangle

IN THE MONTHS following the outbreak of the war, the Germans, while persistently disclaiming any Far Eastern interests, renewed their pressure upon Tokyo for an alliance. The drive for a military arrangement varied in intensity according to events in Europe and especially according to the attitude of England. When Hitler finally recognized that the war with England might be a protracted one after all, he ordered preparations for Sea Lion and stepped up the efforts for an arrangement with Japan which were to culminate in the Triangle Pact. The lengthening of the struggle with Britain had yet another effect on German policy: it moved the United States to the center of German-Japanese relations. Hitler's assumptions expressed in July and again in November 1939 that isolationist sentiment had rendered America "not dangerous"[1] were shaken in 1940 as American policies made it manifestly clear that war with Britain in the long run meant involvement with the United States.

Any activation of the German-Japanese connection was bound to involve the American factor, as Ambassadors Ott and Kurusu constantly stressed, because of the formidable role which that country played in Japanese calculations. America had, according to Ott, undertaken nothing less than "the task of relieving the Western powers in the Far East" and was "urgently espousing their interests." Germany had to take account of this in her drive for a closer Japanese relationship, since the Tokyo government

[1] Attolico to Ciano 3/7/39, *DDI*, ser. 8/XII, p. 34. Hitler statement 23/11/39, *IMT*/XXVI, p. 331 (789-PS).

was "still chasing after the phantom of a settlement with America."[2] As early as October 1939, Ott warned that it had to be a major feature of German policy to block a Japanese-American agreement. Weizsaeker had accepted this view by January 1940. In the course of an angry protest to the Italians about alleged efforts by the Italian Ambassador in Tokyo to promote Japanese-American understanding, the State Secretary declared it to be "injurious to German interests to exert influence upon Japan in order to bring about an understanding with America." In March, Hitler himself took a similar line with Mussolini. Japan, he told the Duce, was considered by Germany to be "a necessary counterweight" to the United States.[3] From this point on, scarcely an issue arose between the two countries which did not in some way involve consideration of America.

There was for example the question of the German attitude toward Japanese expansion. German victories in Europe had opened up in Tokyo new possibilities of release from economic dependence on the United States through seizure of new raw material sources to the south.[4] The Japanese became concerned about German attitudes toward such an expansion and began to press Berlin for a statement of disinterest.[5] Weizsaeker suggested to Ribbentrop in May 1940 that the Japanese be informed that the threat to the Dutch East Indies came from the Allies and the United States rather than from Germany. They were to be told,

[2] Ott to Foreign Ministry 16/10/39, 3/12/39, *DGFP*/D/VIII, pp. 298, 585. Memo (conference with Kurusu) 12/12/39, 1/2/40, *DGFP*/D/VIII, pp. 524, 729. Ott to Foreign Ministry 2/3/40, *DGFP*/D/VIII, p. 835. Stahmer to Foreign Ministry 10/5/40, *DGFP*/D/IX, p. 310.

[3] Policy report (Ott) 16/10/39, *DGFP*/D/VII, p. 298. Weizsaeker to Rome (January) *DGFP*/D/VIII, p. 678. Ciano, *Diplomatic Papers*, pp. 356, 357, Entries 10/3/40, 11/3/40.

[4] Stahmer to Foreign Ministry 10/5/40, *DGFP*/D/IX, p. 310. Ott to Foreign Ministry 10/5/40, *DGFP*/D/IX, p. 321. This problem had become acute with the relapse of the Japanese-American trade treaty on January 26 and the threat of further economic sanctions which had been voiced by Stimson. *NYT* 11/1/40.

[5] Memo (Kurusu conference) 1/2/40, *DGFP*/D/VIII, p. 729. Memo (Kurusu conference) 15/4/40, *DGFP*/D/IX, p. 175. Ott to Foreign Ministry 11/5/40, *DGFP*/D/IX, p. 327. Japanese ministerial meeting, *IMTFE*/XIV, p. 6197.

furthermore, that American activity in the Pacific had demonstrated the German theory of United States "collusion" with the
Allies.[6] Ribbentrop's disclaimer of interest in the Indies was at
least in part an attempt to encourage a confrontation with the
Anglo-Saxons by forcing the Yonai government either into an
expansionist and therefore ultimately anti-American direction
or into resignation at the hands of Japanese extremists.[7]

In requesting a similar German gesture regarding Indo-China
after the defeat of France, the Japanese stressed the "considerable
service" that she had done Germany in tying the American fleet
down in the Pacific. Ott in sending this request to Berlin added
that Germany could give "a friendly gesture" as a means of
sharpening Japanese hostility to Britain and America.[8] The presence of America in German thinking was made abundantly clear
by the Ambassador when he informed the Japanese that Germany
had no interest in Indo-China and Japan might feel free to proceed. However, in return for this Japan was to give a solemn
assurance that she would "keep America occupied in the Pacific
area" possibly by promising to attack the Philippines and Hawaii
in case America should enter the war against Germany.[9] This
was just what Japan had done, special Minister Sato told Ribbentrop in July. His country, he wanted the Foreign Minister to
know, had "been drawing the attention of the British, French and
American governments to herself" and this had facilitated the
German victories in Europe which in turn had opened up new
possibilities of cooperation. Was it not, Sato inquired, very much

[6] Weizsaeker to Ribbentrop 18/5/40, *DGFP/D/IX*, p. 375. The State Department was certainly concerned about the effect of German victories on the
Asian status quo. Memo (Hull) 16/5/40, *FRUS*/Japan/II, pp. 285–288.

[7] Ribbentrop to Ott 20/5/40, *DGFP/D/IX*, p. 385. He succeeded to the
extent that the German response was hailed in Tokyo and compared favorably
with Western equivocation. Ott to Foreign Ministry 23/5/40, *IMTFE*/XIV,
pp. 6161, 6162.

[8] Ott to Foreign Ministry 19/6/40, *DGFP/D/IX*, p. 617. Memo (Weizsaeker)
21/5/40, *DGFP/D/IX*, p. 654. See also Ott to Foreign Ministry 21/5/40,
DGFP/D/IX, p. 654. The Japanese were in fact negotiating with the United
States for a *modus vivendi* during June and July. Langer and Gleason, *The Undeclared War*, p. 592.

[9] Ott to Foreign Ministry 24/6/40, *DGFP/D/X*, p. 5.

to the mutual advantage of Germany and Japan to keep America confined to her hemisphere?[10]

However, for some weeks following the fall of France there was a suspension of German interest in a Japanese alliance and Ribbentrop was noncommittal regarding Sato's suggestions.[11] This was no doubt a reflection of Hitler's certainty that following the French collapse Britain would sue for peace. Such an event would of course have had a profound effect upon German-Japanese relations. On July 1 he told the new Italian Ambassador that he"could not conceive of anyone in England still seriously believing in victory." He told his generals on July 13 that Germany had no need for the collapse of the British Empire. "We would achieve something with German blood which could only benefit Japan and America."[12]

However, his patience was clearly running out and on the same day he expressed the collapse of his hopes ("I have been treated so shabbily") to Mussolini. When the British declined the offer expressed in his Reichstag speech of July 19, the prospect of a long war with England stretched before him and, as we have seen, the longer it lasted the more significant was the American role bound to be.[13] If he did not even yet entirely discard the vision of an ultimate Anglo-German understanding, it ceased at least to be an immediate strategic alternative. At the same time, although still nominally tied to the Soviet Union by the Non-Aggression Pact of August 1939, we know that Hitler was already contemplating a possible attack on that country.[14] Japanese activity in the Far East was of obvious relevance to such an attack and, although the Triangle Pact was to specifically exclude the U.S.S.R.

---

[10] Memo (Sato-Ribbentrop conversation) 9/7/40, *DGFP/D/X*, p. 162. Sato made clear Japan's need to proceed carefully regarding the United States, however.

[11] Sato to Arita 15/7/40, *IMTFE/XIV*, p. 6189. Weizsaeker had cabled Ott to delay any further approaches. Weizsaeker to Ott 25/6/40, *DGFP/D/X*, p. 5.

[12] Hitler conversation with Alfieri 1/7/40, *DGFP/D/X*, *p.* 82. Halder, *Diary* 13/7/40, IV, p. 115.

[13] Hitler to Mussolini 13/7/40, *DGFP/D/X*, pp. 226–229. Halder, *Diary* 31/7/40, IV, p. 141.

[14] Halder, *Diary* 31/7/40, IV, p. 141.

from its operation, this was hardly the sort of thing which would give Adolf Hitler pangs of conscience should a favorable opportunity for an invasion of Russia present itself. Thus we cannot entirely exclude the Soviet factor from Hitler's motives in activating the Japanese connection.

At the end of July he told his military advisors that Britain was relying on Russia and America. "If hope of Russia falls away, America will also fall away because the collapse of Russia increases Japanese effectiveness in Asia." Russia, he said, was the "east Asian dagger" of the Anglo-Saxons against Japan. His intention was to reverse this and make Japan the German dagger against America.[15] Hitler turned now once again to the Far East to assist him in the solution of his European problems. The effort must now be to block American support for England and the technique for this had been perceived some months before by American Ambassador Joseph Grew in Tokyo. "They [the Germans] aim to bring about a situation," he had written Secretary Hull, "where the entry of the United States into the war against Germany would ensure a similar clash with Japan."[16]

At the same time events in Tokyo were moving toward a favorable disposition to serious German-Japanese negotiations. On July 12 and 16 government meetings evolved plans for "harmonizing" Japanese and Axis policies.[17] In addition to general statements recognizing Germany and Japan as ascendant in their respective spheres of influence, great attention was paid to the problem of America. These decisions were followed by the fall of the moderate Yonai government and the installation of Matsuoka as Foreign Minister in the new Konoye cabinet. Whether motivated by fascist and anti-American tendencies, a desire to clear up the Chinese war rapidly or merely a particular concept of Japanese nationalism (Hitler thought he had "the hypocrisy of an American Bible missionary"), Matsuoka was correctly pic-

---

[15] *Ibid.*, p. 141.
[16] Grew to Hull 4/5/40, *FRUS*/1940/IV, p. 338.
[17] Joint Council Protocol 12/7/40 and 16/7/40, *IMTFE*/XIV, pp. 6191–6203.

tured by Ott as a man who would "seriously seek alignment with the Axis powers."[18] The stage was now finally set for the conclusion of the anti-American alliance which Grew had foreseen. The American envoy now was sure that Japan was "going hell bent towards the Axis" and the establishment of a new order in Asia which would involve "riding roughshod over the rights and interests and principles and policies of the United States and Britain."[19] The significance of America which Japan had long recognized had now been acknowledged by Germany as well. This mutual recognition brought the two countries into a military alliance although even this was insufficient to convert the formal arrangement into a genuine community of interest.

Despite a distinctly cautious tone in government circles in Tokyo, both Ambassador Kurusu and Foreign Minister Matsuoka assured the Germans of the more favorable disposition of the government toward the Axis and made specific inquiries about German reaction to Japanese plans for an Asian new order and to the possibility of a Japanese-American war.[20] The pro-Axis position of the new government, the hesitation over Sea Lion as a solution to the British question, the Ogdensburg declaration by President Roosevelt and the Prime Minister of Canada, the rumors of the destroyer deal and the desire to influence isolationist sentiment in America prior to the November elections, all now pushed Hitler into the final drive to seek a pact with Japan as quickly as possible.[21] Kurusu reported to Matsuoka on August

18 Ott to Foreign Ministry 23/7/40, *DGFP/D/X*, p. 278. Hull thought Matsuoka was "as crooked as a basket of fishhooks." Hull, *op. cit.*, pp. 902, 983. Grew to Hull 25/7/40, *FRUS/Japan/II*, p. 104; Hitler comment 3/6/41; *DGFP/D/XII*, p. 940.

19 Grew, *Ten Years in Japan*, p. 324.

20 "Outlines of Basic National Policy." Cabinet decisions of 26/7/40 and liaison conference of 27/7/40, *IMFTE/XIV/6271–77* and XXXIII/11794. See Grew Memorandum 26/7/40, *FRUS/Japan/II/105*. Memo (Weizsaeker) 1/8/40, 7/8/40, *DGFP/D/X*, pp. 391, 432. Ott to Foreign Ministry 2/8/40, 14/8/40, *DGFP/D/X*, pp. 393, 476.

21 For the effect on Hitler of the attitude of the new government, see Halder, *Diary* 1/8/40, 5/8/40, pp. 146, 150. The hesitation over Sea Lion is described in

13 that Ribbentrop was ready to negotiate and Special Envoy Stahmer was dispatched two days later.[22]

However, in spite of grandiose statements by Konoye and Matsuoka it is clear from the instructions given to the Japanese negotiators that the Japanese position was reserved.[23] General reference was made to mutual cooperation in the "establishment of the New Order in Europe and in Asia." Regarding the United States the goals were: to restrain that country within the Western hemisphere and in the event of one party finding itself at war with America to ensure that the other party assists "by all possible means." Japan also wished to be in a position to exert economic and political pressure on the United States. On these points there was no essential difference with the German position which had developed. However, future problems were contained in the provisos that peaceful means would be adhered to regarding America, and Japan would take military action against America only if the proper "external and internal circumstances" allowed it. Japan would reserve to herself the decision on these circumstances. This general rather than specific military commitment and the unwillingness to relinquish independence of action regarding the United States became a characteristic of Japanese policy down to Pearl Harbor. It nullified German efforts to intimidate the United States. As before, only a clear, public, straightforward military pact would have served Hitler's interests in Europe.[24]

---

the previous chapter. The effect of the Ogdensburg declaration and rumors of the destroyer deal was asserted by Kordt in *Case 11*/XV, p. 7420. The desire to influence the isolationists is found in *Wahn und Wirklichkeit*, p. 257, and in a statement by Ribbentrop to Ciano, *Diplomatic Papers* 19/9/40, p. 389.

[22] Kurusu to Matsuoka 13/8/40, Iklé, *op. cit.*, p. 168. Stahmer testimony, *IMTFE*/LVIII, pp. 24404, 24530. Halder, *Diary* 23/8/40, IV, p. 169.

[23] Grew to Hull 28/8/40, *FRUS*/Japan/II, p. 168. Matsuoka statement 19/9/40, *IMTFE*/XV, p. 6329. These instructions were laid down at a ministers' conference on September 4. Text in Sommer, *op. cit.*, pp. 509–514. The Appendices 1–4 are of special relevance.

[24] There is some evidence that Ribbentrop had originally thought that German victories alone would cause Japan to assume "her useful function" as a counterweight to the U.S.A. Ribbentrop to Tokyo 9/9/39, *DGFP*/D/VIII, p. 37.

The decisive document setting out the German position was sent to Tokyo in September.[25] This consisted of Ribbentrop's ideas "covering the cooperation of Germany, Italy and Japan for the purpose of neutralizing America" as well as the necessity for a quick decision in the matter. This document contained some fifteen points, the most relevant of which may be summarized as follows:

1. Germany had no desire for a world war and was especially interested in the exclusion of the United States.
2. Germany sought no Japanese military assistance against England.
3. The proper role of Japan was "restraining and preventing the United States from entering the war by all means."
4. There was little chance of a German-American war in the near future, but that a Japanese-American war "cannot ultimately be avoided."[26]
5. A strong and determined Axis attitude would be "a powerful and effective deterrent on the United States."

For Germany, then, as for Japan, America was manifestly the object of the Pact. The only thing that Germany seemed to demand of Japan in exchange for recognition of her Far Eastern hegemony was not, as the Japanese must have feared, a military commitment in Europe, but rather a stiff line toward America. And firmness in policy, as the Japanese well knew, was a matter of interpretation.

The negotiations of the following days revealed Japanese pressure for more general and consultative measures, while the Germans strove for specific, military clauses. Ribbentrop was especially anxious to exempt an attack by the U.S.S.R. from the operation of the Pact in order to leave no doubt whatever that it was aimed at the United States. He also (unsuccessfully) sought

[25] This document has not been found. However, Stahmer recapitulated the contents as he had given them to Matsuoka in a conference of September 9 and 10, at which they were reported to have been "well received." Stahmer and Ott to Foreign Ministry 10/9/40, *DGFP*/D/XI, p. 57.

[26] Ott had been taking this line in Tokyo right along. Ott to Foreign Ministry 21/5/40, 12/6/40, *DGFP*/D/IX, pp. 654, 551.

to include a pledge to go to war at once in order to convince the Americans that if she entered the conflict "she would find herself at war with three great powers."[27] These efforts seemed the more justified by German reports of vigorous American efforts to prevent the Japanese from signing any pact at all. Furthermore, Matsuoka was under very considerable pressure from naval, business and court circles for a moderate policy toward America and freedom of action in military matters.[28] It is evident from these negotiations that the unity on the object of the Pact (the U.S.A.) did not extend to the method to be employed. The now familiar divergence of purpose persisted.

The Pact was signed on September 27 in Berlin.[29] It consisted of a preamble in which cooperation was pledged to maintain a new order in Asia and Europe, followed by six articles. The first two of these recognized the leadership of Germany and Italy in Europe and that of Japan in the Far East. The third article pledged cooperation and assistance "with all political, economic and military means when one of the three contracting parties is attacked by a power not at present involved in the European war or in the Sino-Japanese conflict." The fourth article established a joint technical commission, while the fifth left the present "political standing" of the parties with the U.S.S.R. unaltered. The final article provided a ten-year duration for the arrangement.

The operational clause (article 3) was clearly a compromise between the German demand for a war pledge and the Japanese desire to limit the obligation to consultation. Furthermore, there was no specific mention of the object of the Pact: the United

---

[27] Many of the documents during the negotiations may be found in the so-called Matsumoto Compendium, *IMTFE*/LXIV, pp. 27987–28018. Also, Foreign Ministry to Tokyo Embassy 20/9/40, *DGFP*/D/XI, p. 133.

[28] Ott to Foreign Ministry 23/9/40, *DGFP*/D/XI, p. 156. IMTFE/LXIV, p. 27987. Cabinet sitting and protocol, 16/9/40, *ibid.*, XV, pp. 6345–6378.

[29] For description of the ceremony see Shirer, *Berlin Diary*, p. 536. For text, see *DGFP*/D/XI, p. 204.

States. However, the exception of the U.S.S.R from the operation of the Pact made the target self-evident. As we have seen, the German instructions for negotiating the agreement indicated beyond doubt that intimidation of America was the objective. Moreover, both Hitler and Ribbentrop made the point repeatedly to the Italians during the negotiations that the Pact would be "the best way either to keep America entirely out or render her entry into the war ineffective." The Foreign Minister admitted to Ciano that the Pact might also be useful sometime against Russia, but it was clearly aimed "before all else to cripple America" and cause her to hesitate "one hundred times" before entering the European war.[30]

Ribbentrop at the signature ceremony did not mention America specifically (perhaps at a Japanese suggestion), confining himself to a general warning that any state attacking a Pact member would "have to contend with the combined power of three nations of two hundred and fifty million people."[31] Two days earlier, however, he had been more specific in a letter to Count Schulenberg, the German envoy in Moscow.

> This alliance is exclusively directed against the American warmongers. Its exclusive purpose is to bring the element pressing for America's entry into the war to their senses. This is not to be expressly mentioned in the treaty, but it is unmistakably to be deduced from the context.[32]

At least three Japanese statesmen agreed with this judgment, although one reversed himself after the war.[33] Grew, Hull and Roosevelt accepted the view that their country was the object of

[30] Hitler to Mussolini 17/9/40, 4/10/40, *DGFP*/D/XI, pp. 104, 248. Ciano, *Diary* 19/9/40, p. 291.
[31] Oshima testimony, *IMTFE*/XIII, p. 6054. Quoted in Sommer, *op. cit.*, p. 428.
[32] Ribbentrop to Schulenberg 25/9/40, *NSR*, pp. 195–196.
[33] For Oshima's statement, Grew to Hull 2/10/41, *FRUS*/Japan/II, pp. 171–173. For Konoye's statement 4/10/41, *StS*/Japan/V/60672. For Matsuoka's statement, Grew to Hull 5/10/40, *FRUS*/Japan/II, pp. 171–173. Oshima's denial, *IMTFE*, LXXVI, p. 34012.

the Pact, and post-war German testimony has also generally confirmed this, although stressing the defensive nature of the arrangement.[34]

That the Pact was, by its own terms, defensive and preventative was perfectly true. It was not aimed at the United States in the sense of seeking to provoke that country into the war, but rather the opposite. This cannot, however, alter the fact that the United States was to be rendered inactive so that aggression could proceed unchecked. The specific and repeated mention of the new order in the text make it unmistakably clear that it was an arrangement which sanctioned the ruthless expansion which was the hallmark of that new order. Moreover, as we shall see in the next chapters, the defensive tone of the Pact was no obstacle to its use by Germany in urging a course on her partner which ran the gravest risk of war with the United States. Japan was to put it to similar use in the weeks immediately prior to Pearl Harbor. Finally, it cannot be doubted that the "defensive" Pact might easily have become offensive in the hands of a victorious Axis bloc.

The text was not all there was to the triangle arrangement. There was in addition an exchange of notes between Ott and Matsuoka which revealed the shaky nature of the Japanese contribution. In a letter from Ott to Matsuoka of September 27, following the usual effusive generalities ("a new and decisive phase of world history"), the German Ambassador gave a specific assurance that if Japan were attacked, Germany would consider it a matter of course to give Japan "full support and assist it with all military and economic means." If the Germans expected that the Japanese would thereby be forced into a similar commitment, they were disappointed. Matsuoka merely replied that he had received the German message "with joy."[35]

---

[34] Grew to Hull 29/9/40, *FRUS*/Japan/II, p. 170. Hull, *op. cit.*, p. 429. Roosevelt speech 12/10/40, *PPA*/IX, p. 466. Ribbentrop testimony, *IMT*/X, p. 188. At his trial, Weizsaeker termed the Pact "a warning poster for the United States. Weizsaeker testimony, *Case 11*/XVI, pp. 7898–7995.

[35] Ott to Matsuoka 27/9/40, *DGFP*/D/XI, p. 205. Sommer has an excellent discussion of these exchanges (which were apparently Ott's own initiatives) based partly on personal interviews with Ott. Sommer, *op. cit.*, pp. 436–440.

Even more significant were the substantial mental reservations which the Japanese entertained and which may be found in the proceedings of cabinet meetings on September 16 and 26 during which the right to determine timing of Pact obligations was "strictly reserved." "In this respect, our empire will of course proceed independently."[36] There were then three levels of reality to the Pact: the text known to all, the exchange of notes known to the governments and the Japanese mental reservations known to the Japanese alone. These three levels left the Japanese with ample room for what one scholar called their "diplomatic-exegetic juggler's tricks" in accordance with their changing needs.[37]

In fact, even while the Pact was being negotiated, Grew cabled information that the Japanese were beginning to recognize that Germany might never defeat Great Britain because of American aid. After the news of the destroyer deal, the German victories, according to the American, no longer went to their head "like strong wine." Not only that, but the Japanese were even "beginning to wonder whether a German victory might not ultimately pose a new hazard to their expansionist program."[38] That Ribbentrop, who could have had few illusions about the Japanese, did not at first attempt to press the Japanese for a clear expression of their obligation is yet another proof that, for Berlin, the Pact was a propaganda ploy decked out as a military alliance. If it had the desired effect on America, Japanese reservations in the event of an actual war would have become irrelevant, a view Hitler had expressed in July.[39] But this was not to be. The ineffectiveness of the triangle relationship was being amply demonstrated even before the beginning of the final year.

*

[36] Cabinet meeting 16/9/40, 26/9/40, *IMTFE*/LXIV, p. 27987; XV, p. 6376.
[37] Sommer, *op. cit.*, p. 444. Sommer compares these three levels to Oriental boxes, one inside the other. *Ibid.*, p. 445.
[38] This was reported in the so-called "green light" telegram of 12/9/40, Grew, *Turbulent Years*, II, p. 1225. See also Grew to Hull 29/9/40, *FRUS*/Japan/II, p. 169.
[39] Fuehrer conference, 12/7/40, *FCNA*/1940, p. 62.

The Pact, essentially political and not military, was a gamble and a bluff. The gamble was on a quick German victory over Britain and the bluff was directed against the United States. The gamble did not pay off and the United States was singularly un-bluffed. The tripartite stroke which was to be the definitive intimidation of the American government actually played into Roosevelt's hands by giving substance to the President's thesis of a world conspiracy. Aroused to a sense of danger by the Pact and rumors of more far-reaching secret arrangements, American reaction could not have been more contrary to German expectations and Japanese hopes. Grew had already, during the negotiations, sent his "green light" telegram from Tokyo advocating a more "positive" policy toward Japan even at the risk of war.[40] This was quickly followed by the total embargo on steel and scrap, a new loan to China, Anglo-American staff talks, the strengthening of the American fleet in the Philippines and the evacuation of American citizens from Japanese-controlled areas of Asia. Nor did Roosevelt's vigorous and defiant Columbus Day speech in October give the impression of an intimidated man.[41]

Truculent statements by Japanese officials spelling out the war warning to the United States implicit in the Pact only seemed to strengthen American determination, and Berlin was told that the German connection with the Japanese had caused American anger to turn against them as well.[42] Hitler might say in October that the Americans "had understood the warning" and that the isolationists had been strengthened, but this did not receive much support from Roosevelt's decisive re-election in November.[43] The plain fact was that neither Hitler's desire to see America dis-

---

[40] Grew, *Turbulent Years*, II, pp. 1224–1229; *Ten Years*, pp. 289–298.

[41] The embargo in press report 30/9/40, *FRUS*/Japan/II, p. 222. The other measures in Langer and Gleason, *The Undeclared War*, chap. 2. Roosevelt speech 12/10/40, *PPA*/1940, p. 466.

[42] Statement by Ohashi, Grew to Hull 2/10/40, *FRUS*/ Japan/II, p. 171. Statement by Matsuoka, Grew to Hull 5/10/40, *FRUS*/Japan/II, pp. 171–173. Memo (Woermann), 21/10/40, *DGFP*/D/XI, p. 352.

[43] Halder, *Diary* 15/10/40, IV, p. 232. These sentiments were also expressed at Hendaye to Franco. Serrano-Suñer, *op. cit.*, pp. 253–257. Hitler comment to Count Teleki 20/11/40, *DGFP*/D/XI, p. 362.

tracted from the Atlantic nor Matsuoka's plan to force America to agree to the status quo in the Pacific showed much sign of realization.

The Germans could fall back to some extent upon secondary consolations: American aid to England would be too late due to German air attacks, German power prevented any American military intervention, the German submarine wall rendered an American entry "entirely immaterial."[44] For the Japanese, however, all of this was cold comfort. In the first place, the United States was a genuine and more immediately threatening reality to them, and Japanese anxieties at American policy grew noticeably in October.[45] In the second place, the Japanese had also hoped that the Pact would provide other benefits to the southern expansion drive, especially assistance in the solution of the Chinese question and an agreement with the U.S.S.R. The Pact was quite as fruitless in obtaining these goals as it was in influencing America. In spite of German pressure on him at Japanese request, Chiang Kai-shek was no more intimidated than Roosevelt, and the Chinese "incident" continued with increased Anglo-American and Soviet aid.[46]

No less disappointing to Tokyo was the failure to reach an agreement with the Soviet Union. This was needed by the Japanese to isolate China and clear the northern front for the drive south. The Japanese expected a German initiative here.[47] The initiative was forthcoming because the Japanese requests happened to coincide with a revival of Ribbentrop's grand quadrangle stratagem, in which Russia was to be invited to participate with the tripartite powers in "the great liquidation of the British empire" and the "creation of a world combination of interests." These bombastic notions were presented to Molotov during the

[44] Halder, *Diary* 4/11/40, V, p. 5. Ciano, *Diplomatic Papers* 28/10/40, p. 399. Ribbentrop to Molotov 12/11/40, *DGFP/D/XI*, p. 533.

[45] Grew to Hull 9/10/40, *FRUS*/Japan/II, p. 114. Oshima affidavit, *IMTFE/LXXV*, p. 34021.

[46] Ott to Foreign Ministry 7/11/40, *DGFP/D/XI*, p. 491. Ribbentrop to Chinese Ambassador 11/11/40, *DGFP/D/XI*, p. 515. Ott to Foreign Ministry 21/11/40, *DGFP/D/XI*, p. 533.

[47] Ott to Foreign ministry 11/11/40, 21/11/40, *DGFP/D/XI*, pp. 512, 644.

famous meetings in Berlin in November. The Japanese might well have been less pleased with this overture had they known of the way in which Russian spoils in Asia were being discussed without undue regard for Japanese interest.[48] Molotov's demand for specifics and his general skepticism (no doubt heightened by the necessity of conducting part of the discussions in an air raid shelter) brought the talks to a halt. The vision of a four-power world combination evaporated with the directive for Operation Barbarossa on December 18 (planning for which had in fact begun over three months earlier) and with it all possibility for the Japanese to use the alliance as a vehicle for improved relations with the Soviet Union. The lack of inner substance of the Pact or mutual consideration between the partners was again demonstrated in the German failure to disclose this crucial decision to Japan. Hitler, of course, would in 1941 have his own uses for the Japanese connection when it came to the Russian question.

Meanwhile, to complete the picture, Berlin was made aware of growing Italian doubts about the effectiveness of the Pact and the reliability of the Japanese.[49] Finally, German-Japanese relations became snarled in argument over the implementation of the commission called for in Article Four of the Treaty and in a series of economic disputes over raw materials for Germany from the Dutch East Indies, German negotiations with Vichy over Indo-China and a much postponed trade agreement.[50]

Thus the events of the weeks since the conclusion of the Pact could not have been encouraging, and there is evidence that the lesson had not been lost upon the Fuehrer. Ribbentrop recalled after the war that, by the end of the year, Hitler was very clear that the United States had not been intimidated and not at all

---

[48] Ribbentrop to Stalin 13/10/40, *DGFP/D/XI*, p. 291. Ribbentrop-Molotov conference 12/11/40, *DGFP/D/XI*, p. 533. Schmidt, *op. cit.*, chap. 21. Halder, *Diary* 1/11/40, V, p. 2. Hitler comments to Molotov 12/11/40, *DGFP/D/XI*, p. 543.

[49] Rome to Foreign Ministry 4/20/40, *DGFP/D/XI*, p. 261. Heydrich to Ribbentrop 5/10/40, *DGFP/D/XI*, p. 265. Ciano never had much faith in the Pact as an anti-American device. *Diary* 19/9/40, p. 291.

[50] Ott to Foreign Ministry 5/10/40, *DGFP/D/XI*, p. 262. Memo (Weizsaecker) 13/10/40, *DGFP/D/XI*, p. 316. Foreign Ministry to Rome 1/11/40,

clear about Japanese intentions ("We cannot know what position she will adopt"). Hitler told Admiral Raeder that he doubted in fact that the Japanese would "do anything decisive." Thus if it is true, as Admiral Assmann has stated, that "for Adolf Hitler the development of German-American relations was narrowly coupled with the Japanese disposition to the Tripartite Pact,"[51] then it is clear that at the beginning of the final year this foundation already must have appeared in Berlin to be very uncertain.

It would have appeared even more uncertain if the Germans had known that pro-American forces in Japan had already started initiatives which would culminate in the Hull-Nomura conversations at Washington in February 1941. Prince Konoye had in fact gone so far as to say informally that his government might, under certain circumstances, be willing to nullify the tripartite arrangement *de facto* and even conclude a similar treaty with the United States directed against Germany.[52] It was from the American point of view of the greatest importance to try to cut through the fog of generalities and equivocation and discover the precise reality of Japanese intentions under the Pact.[53] American pressure on the Japanese to reveal these in turn forced the Germans, lest the intimidating edge of the Pact be dulled, to press the Japanese from the other side. This would become doubly important in 1941 as Barbarossa loomed. German pressure took the form of encouraging the Japanese in a course of action which vastly increased the danger of precisely what the Pact was supposed to prevent: the entry of the United States into the war.

DGFP/D/XI, p. 446. Memo (Wiehl) 15/11/40, *DGFP*/D/XI, p. 383.

[51] Ribbentrop testimony, *IMT*/X, p. 333. Fuehrer conference 27/12/40, *FCNA*/ 1940, p. 137. See also Ott testimony in *Case 11*/XXI, p. 10069, and Weizsaeker testimony, *Case 11*/XVII, pp. 8071–8081. Assmann, *Deutsche Schicksalsjahre*, p. 394.

[52] These remarks were made informally to two American church leaders. See *FRUS*/1940/IV, pp. 14-16. Trade, a Philippine guarantee and a China settlement were also mentioned. Hull's reply pressing for more general principles in Hull, *op. cit.*, p. 994.

[53] Thomsen was already cabling by the end of the year that Roosevelt would now concentrate on splitting the Pact. Thomsen to Foreign Ministry 6/10/40, 19/12/40, *StS/USA*/III/62264; 22951.

CHAPTER 14

Germany, the United States and Japanese Expansion

IN THE FATEFUL YEAR 1941, the two leading neutral powers entered the war following a sudden attack by a member of the Tripartite Pact. The European war thereby became World War Two. In neither case were the other partners informed of these momentous plans which would change the whole nature of the conflict, and it can be said that both the Soviet Union and the United States entered the war over the dead body of the alliance. The first step in this escalation to world war, the German assault on Russia, was not without implications for German-American relations. Indeed, Hitler's Barbarossa obsession contributed strongly to the kind of policy he pressed the Japanese to pursue. The ebb and flow of the Eastern campaign powerfully molded German attitudes toward Japanese expansion. Moreover, with the obviously greater relevance of the Pacific, compared with the Atlantic, for his Russian operation, the Fuehrer was prepared to take greater risks (or at least urge the Japanese to do so) regarding the intimidation of America. But the attack at Pearl Harbor is the central event. The role of Germany in the events leading up to "the day of infamy" is part of the more general question of the impact of the United States on the Japanese policy of the Reich during this final year. To understand this we must in turn know about two things specifically: on the one hand, the German image of Japanese foreign policy and the implications of that policy for America; on the other hand, the advice and pressure exerted by Germany on Japan in the light of this knowledge. For Germany in 1941, relations with Japan could not be separated from the problem of America.

The framework of German-Japanese relations in 1941 remained the Tripartite Pact. But it should be borne in mind that in spite of American statements throughout the year that the alliance represented a tightly coordinated conspiracy,[1] in fact the disintegration of trust between Germany and Japan already observed in 1940 continued to run its course. During the year, to be sure, the Pact was dusted off and manipulated in the interests of one or the other partner: the Germans invoking triangle solidarity to urge the Japanese to strike at Britain in the Far East, at Russia in Vladivostok and always to take a firm line with America; the Japanese trying to avoid these commitments until they were ready and then pressing the Germans to stand by them in the forthcoming Japanese-American war. As a functioning military alliance, however, the Pact was moribund.

There was, of course, no lack of loyalty pledges and protestations of solidarity from both sides. The Japanese let it be known that the Pact was "unalterable fact," that it constituted the inevitable basis of Japanese foreign policy, that Japan "trusted the Fuehrer completely" and was prepared to "share Germany's happiness and sorrow." Matsuoka even detected a "divine command" to join with Germany in the dissolution of the British empire.[2] These assurances apparently made some impression on Hitler and Mussolini, and the Germans were equally effusive. "We are in the same boat," Ribbentrop told the Japanese. The Pact had "united the fate of both countries for centuries to come." There was much talk of "historically unique moments" for joint action and "iron determination" on the part of Germany to aid Japan in the building of the new order in Asia as well as of a world-wide division of the spoils flowing from unshakable tripartite cooperation.[3]

The reality of German-Japanese relations, however, lay not in

[1] Hull, *op. cit.*, p. 982. Roosevelt comment 14/3/41, *FRUS*/Japan/II, p. 396. Welles Memo, *ibid.*, p. 183.

[2] Ott to Foreign Ministry 22/11/41, *StS/Japan/V*/60894. Ott to Foreign Ministry 31/5/41, *UStS/Japan-Amerika*/24932. Ott to Foreign Ministry 21/1/41, *StS/Japan/II*/36513. Ribbentrop-Matsuoka meeting 31/3/41, *DGFP/D/XII*, p. 405.

[3] Hitler-Mussolini conference 3/6/41, *DGFP/D/XII*, p. 941. Ott was also somewhat impressed. Ott to foreign ministry 31/5/41, *UStS/Japan-Amerika/*

these clarion calls but rather in less harmonious features such as
strained economic relations and the development of "a certain
distrust," as Ott expressed it, of the Japanese especially regarding
their sense of obligation under the treaty. This distrust was
recognized by Japanese Ambassador Oshima himself, who told
Foreign Minister Toyoda frankly in October that "the Foreign
Ministry staff from Weizsaeker downwards and also everyone in
general are thoroughly disgusted with Japan."[4] This lack of real
confidence was evident, as we shall see, in the constant German
pressure on the Japanese regarding expansion at British expense
and especially in the matter of the proper line to be taken with
the United States. But it also came to the surface in the German
alarm at statements made from time to time by various Japanese
figures which seemed to reveal some slackening in tripartite enthusiasm or even on one occasion an alleged Japanese overture
to mediate in the European war.[5]

For their part, the German failure to inform the Japanese of
the plan to attack Soviet Russia could not have inspired Tokyo
with confidence in the alliance. The basic order of March 5 had
directed that the Japanese not be given any intimation of the
Barbarossa operation.[6] Ribbentrop did tell Matsuoka in March
that German relations with the Soviet Union were "not very
friendly," that a conflict with Russia was "always within the
realm of possibility" and that Germany would crush Stalin if he

---

24932. Ribbentrop-Oshima meeting 23/2/41, *DGFP*/D/XII, p. 146. Hitler-
Matsuoka conference 1/4/41, *DGFP*/D/XII, p. 386. Ribbentrop to Ott 9/5/41,
DGFP/D/XII, p. 745.

[4] Wiehl to Ott 22/1/41, *DGFP*/D/XI, p. 1161. Ott to Foreign Ministry
7/8/41, *StS*/*Japan*/IV/60442. "Memorandum Regarding German-Japanese Economic Questions" (Wiehl) 18/3/41, in *Matsuoka-Besuch, StS*/*Japan*/II/135668–
136734. Ott to Foreign Ministry 22/7/41, *StS*/*Japan*/IV/60398.

[5] Ott 21/8/41, *StS*/*Japan*/IV/60492. Woermann to Tokyo Embassy 3/5/41,
DGFP/D/XII, p. 700. The mediation gesture was supposedly made by the
Japanese Ambassador in London to Eden in February. Ribbentrop to Tokyo
21/2/41, *StS*/*Japan*/II/136567.

[6] Basic order 5/3/41, *IMT*/XXIV, p. 305. Weizsaeker, *op. cit.*, p. 249. Weizsaeker favored telling the Japanese about Barbarossa. Memo (Weizsaeker)
24/3/41, *DGFP*/D/XII, p. 348.

should be foolish enough to adopt policies which were "not in accord with what the Fuehrer considered to be right."[7] These were broad enough general hints of a future eventuality but they hardly constituted the detailed briefing which an ally might reasonably have expected on an event of such significance a mere three months away. Thus it is not surprising that the news of the attack was heard with a certain dismay, although the invasion did relieve Japanese anxieties about a Soviet attack on them. The assault on the Soviet Union jeopardized one of the specific purposes of the Pact in Japanese eyes as well as clouding the whole relationship over with even deeper distrust. Ott reported that the German action had contributed to a growing feeling of isolationism in Tokyo and a strengthened tendency to interpret the Pact strictly according to Japanese lights.[8] Whether Hitler did not realize this or just did not care about Japanese reactions is difficult to say.[9] The astonishing thing is that he apparently expected that in spite of it all, Japan would display full frankness and loyalty toward Germany in regard to her relations with America.

With the steady erosion of the Tripartite Pact by distrust it might easily be supposed that Germany was without influence at all on the Japanese. This has been the line taken in post-war testimony. Weizsaeker has pronounced German influence in the final year "exaggerated," and Erich Kordt, who served in Tokyo, testified that he did not share the opinion that Germany had any influence, practically, on Japanese policy.[10] It is certainly true

---

[7] "A few months, no more Russia" was Ribbentrop's formula. Ribbentrop-Matsuoka conference 31/3/41, *DGFP*/D/XII, pp. 405, 413. Memo (Weizsaeker) 27/5/41, *DGFP*/D/XII, p. 891.

[8] Grew, *Turbulent Years*, II, p. 1279. Ott to Foreign Ministry 23/6/41, *StS/Japan*/III/65778. Ott to Foreign Ministry 4/10/41, *StS/USA*/IX/422096. Ott to Foreign Ministry 4/11/41, *StS/Japan*/V/60808.

[9] See *Wahn und Wirklichkeit*, p. 312, where Kordt stresses this as an example of Hitler's view of the Japanese role purely as an adjunct to the European situation. See also Schroeder, *Axis Alliance and Japanese-American Relations*, p. 140.

[10] Weizsaeker, *op. cit.*, p. 325. Kordt testimony, *Case 11*/XV, p. 7431. Kordt specifically cited the Hull-Nomura conversations as the outstanding example of Japanese indifference to German pressure.

that there was no regular consultation or coordination of policies, and it became increasingly obvious to both Germany and Japan that each was pursuing an independent course. Yet the fact that both sought to maintain the fiction of an alliance and that each of them at some time demanded reassurances from the other indicates at least that there was a mutual interest in being able to manipulate the relationship. Some feeling of a shared fate in the long run appears to have been present, and this did present the Germans with some scope for influencing their Far Eastern partner.[11]

The question of the effectiveness of that influence will have to be examined in the light of more specific problems. What is beyond question is that the Germans tried consciously and continuously to exert pressure throughout the year and every effort was made to activate and guide Japanese policy, especially regarding the United States. The "world triangle" was substantially reduced to a hollow form, yet German Far Eastern policy required that the form be kept alive as a channel for exerting pressure on the Japanese to combat the lengthening shadow of America.

We must now turn against this background of a deteriorating but still useful alliance, to the German image of Japanese foreign policy and the pressures exerted upon Tokyo in the light of this information, first in a general way and then in regard to three particular problems. The more general picture of Japanese foreign policy in Berlin was summarized in the instructions for the German delegation prepared by the Foreign Ministry for talks with Foreign Minister Matsuoka in March and April.[12] Japan was described as a country committed to an expansionist policy. This

[11] Grew wrote Roosevelt that the Japanese were influenced more by the fate of Germany than German policy. Grew to Roosevelt 3/11/41, *Turbulent Years*, II, p. 1279.

[12] These instructions were a series of memoranda dated 18/3/41, and contained in a special section of *Staatssekretaer* file, Japan/II, entitled *Matsuoka Besuch* (136708). The more general observations on Japanese goals were prepared by Woermann. See also Jones, *op. cit.*, chap. I.

expansion was guided by the vision of a "greater East Asia sphere" consisting of Japan (as the dominating power), Manchuria, China, Indo-China, Thailand, the Dutch East Indies, the Philippines and possibly Malaya, Singapore and Burma. In addition to this, a broader field, "Oceana," which included the island world between the American and Asian continents, except for Australia and New Zealand, would be thrown open for settlement of surplus population, Japanese and other.[13] The motives for this expansion were held to be economic, although political-ideological elements centering around visions of Japanese destiny were important in some circles.

The execution of Japanese plans was contingent on two sets of factors: the actions and policies of other powers concerned with the area on the one hand and the flux of Japanese domestic politics on the other.[14] Happily the countries Japan had to cross did not include Germany, at least politically or territorially, and Germany had thus far supported Japanese policy.[15] However, it was necessary, according to the instructions, for Japan to liquidate the Chinese question, to free her back from any Soviet threat and prepare herself for conflict with Britain in case of a "military undertaking which could have as its goal a thrust south in the direction of Hong Kong, the Philippines and Singapore."[16]

The relationship to the United States, the report continued, was a special one because of the American Pacific fleet, the threat from Hawaii and the Philippines to the greater East Asia sphere and the fact of Japanese economic dependence on that country. Since the United States had proceeded with rearmament in the

[13] The Oceana concept had been mentioned by Matsuoka on February 24. Woermann memorandum in *Matsuoka Besuch*.

[14] Jones emphasizes this latter feature in his analyses. He is convinced that there was in fact no master plan of conquest from 1937 to 1941 and describes Japanese foreign policy as "the shuttlecock of domestic politics." Jones, *op. cit.*, p. 450.

[15] Hitler repeated this fact yet again to Kurusu 3/2/41, *DGFP/D/XII*, p. 9. Possible German-Japanese colonial conflict is dismissed in "Memo Regarding Former German Colonies" 18/3/41, *Matsuoka Besuch StS*/Japan/II/136713.

[16] "Memorandum Regarding Japanese Foreign Policy" 18/3/41, *ibid.*/136704.

Pacific and a policy of economic pressure as well as support of independent states in Southeast Asia, the Imperial Government was faced with a difficult problem: how to obtain alternative sources of raw materials without in the process provoking the United States into war.[17]

There were, the instructions concluded, a number of possibilities open to Japan in her policies toward these countries by which she might attempt to achieve the conditions required for expansion. The choice of tactics was largely a function of the second set of factors: the rise and fall of cabinets and especially the fate of Foreign Minister Matsuoka. All of this gave Japanese policy "a certain indecisiveness" (*Ratlosigkeit*) in the German view and led to that "fundamental incoherence of policy which caused Japan to be distrusted and condemned everywhere."[18]

This fluidity of Japanese policy, frustrating as it was to her partners, did however at least allow room for maneuver and pressure on Tokyo. The problem was that Berlin had really very little to offer the Japanese except European victories as a reward for acquiescing in German demands. Nevertheless, German pressure on Japan was persistent. Against this general picture of Japanese policy, the line which Germany urged on Japan throughout 1941 was clear and consistent. In brief, the Japanese were encouraged to expand. Pressure on the Indies and Indo-China, an attack on Singapore and later, as Barbarossa bogged down, on Vladivostok as well, a general drive to the south, seizure of raw material sources and naval activity, particularly that which would tie up the American fleet, were all welcomed. Moreover, the Japanese were urged to be firm and unyielding toward the United States. Japanese-American agreements were discouraged.

[17] *Ibid.*, subsection: Japan-USA. See also memorandum of Ott 22/1/41, *StS/Japan*/II/136526, which detailed the threat of the United States to Japan. On United States support of Indo-China see Memorandum (Weizsaecker) 18/1/41, *DGFP/D/XI*, p. 1125. Also Memo (Dooman) 14/2/41, *FRUS*/Japan/II, p. 137.

[18] Ott to Foreign Ministry 13/10/41, *StS/Japan*/V/60703. The Germans followed Japanese domestic politics with the greatest interest. Ribbentrop-Mussolini conference 14/5/41, *DGFP/D/XII*, p. 797. Comment on cabinet change in Ott to Foreign Ministry 17/7/41, 20/7/41, *StS/Japan*/IV/60348, 60380.

Ambassador William E. Dodd in his Berlin Embassy, 1933.
Wide World Photos

Ambassador Dieckhoff (left) leaves the White House with Chief
of Protocol Richard Southgate after presenting his credentials
to President Roosevelt, 1937. *Wide World Photos*

Picketing crowds outside a Bund meeting in San Francisco, 1938.
Wide World Photos

Bund members saluting at a meeting in Madison Square Garden, 1939.
Wide World Photos

Ambassador Wilson leaves the Chancellory in Berlin after
presenting his credentials to Hitler, 1938.
Wide World Photos

Herbert Hoover in Berlin on his exploratory mission, 1938.
Ambassador Wilson is at the extreme left, and between him and
Mr. Hoover is Dr. Schacht, President of the Reichsbank.
Wide World Photos

Sumner Welles, Winston Churchill and Ambassador Kennedy in London
during Welles' 1940 "fact-finding mission."
Wide World Photos

Hans Dieckhoff returns to Berlin to be greeted by his Washington
Chargé d'Affaires, Hans Thomsen.
Wide World Photos

Japanese anxieties regarding American reaction to all of this were allayed by assurances that Germany also sought to block American entry into the war, that American policy was largely bluff, that even if she should come in it would not alter the course of the struggle due to American military weakness and tripartite strength. Tokyo was given to understand that although direct provocation of America was to be avoided, if war did come with the United States, Germany would immediately recognize her Pact obligations. As the year progressed, the tone of German advice showed that Hitler's desire to keep America out was becoming outweighed by the need for an Asian stroke to relieve the pressure in Europe. If he did not seek a Japanese-American war by his Far Eastern policy, he did urge a course of action on his allies which, in the light of what was well known about Japanese intentions, ran the most serious risk of this occurring.

In addition to these general considerations which guided German policy toward Japan in 1941, the Germans took a special interest in three more specific aspects of Japanese policy: relations with the U.S.S.R., expansionist plans to the south and relations with America. In the first two of these problems the American factor was present though less centrally than in the third. In all three areas Germany exerted great pressure on the Japanese to take courses of action which were bound to affect the position of the United States.

We already know that prior to the German attack on the Soviet Union, the Japanese had strong reasons for seeking improved relations with that country. The Germans were told in February that Japan did not feel bound to join a German-Soviet conflict and the Japanese even signed a Neutrality Pact with the Russians in April.[19] This agreement did not in fact result in a transfer of Soviet military forces from the Far East to the European theater as the Germans, now deep in preparations for

[19] Memorandum (Weizsaeker) 15/2/31, *DGFP*/D/XII, p. 107. Discussion of Neutrality Pact in Jones, *op. cit.*, p. 214.

Barbarossa, must have feared it would do. After the German on-slaught in June the Japanese, as anticipated, proclaimed the neu-trality to which they would adhere until the U.S.S.R. declared war upon them in 1945.[20]

Notwithstanding Hitler's evident desire to avoid Far Eastern complications while Barbarossa was going well, Ribbentrop sought to weaken the Japanese stand. He instructed Ott to in-form Tokyo that Russia was finished and to urge Japanese coop-eration "in the final military solution of the Russian question in its totality and for all time." The Japanese were to be told that it would be inexcusable and impossible if Japan did not seize this opportunity to gain security on her Northern flank and meet Germany halfway across Russia. The "dictate of the hour" was clear: attack Vladivostok at once. This would not only be a death blow to Russia but would more quickly promote the final attack on England. As for America, Ribbentrop was certain that Japanese acts against Russia would paralyze any tendency in that country to mix in the war.[21] The Japanese merely responded to this that while they were preparing for all eventualities regarding the U.S.S.R., they felt that their activities to the south which tied up the Anglo-Saxons were of greater value.[22]

Ribbentrop kept up the pressure. He invited Oshima to the Eastern front to see for himself the inevitable German triumph and instructed Ott to press again for an attack on the Soviet Union in the east, "the sooner the better."[23] Increasingly (per-haps to disguise the real reason for German anxieties: the slowing of the Eastern offensive), the Reich Foreign Minister emphasized

[20] Imperial conference 2/7/41, *IMTFE/XV*, pp. 6567–6569. Kretschmar testi-mony, *ibid.*, LIX, 24618–24619. Ott to Foreign Ministry 26/6/41, 28/6/41, *StS/Japan/III/65780, 65789.

[21] Ribbentrop to Tokyo 1/7/41, *StS/Japan/IV/60234*. Ribbentrop Memo-randum 10/7/41, *NCA/V*, p. 565. Matsuoka told Ott that he had the impression that Hitler did not expect nor really want Japan to act against Russia, in these earlier days. Ott to Foreign Ministry 23/6/41, *StS/Japan/III/65788*.

[22] Ott to Foreign Ministry 3/7/41, *StS/Japan/IV/60244*.

[23] Ribbentrop to Ott 5/7/41, 9/7/41, 10/7/41, *StS/Japan/IV/60256, 60284, 60285*. Ott to Foreign Ministry 14/7/41, *StS/Japan/IV/60316*.

the effect of this attack on Britain and America. He feared that this unique opportunity to free her back and place herself in an entirely new position vis-à-vis the Anglo-Saxons would be passed up. Later, he warned, Japan would be in a less advantageous position to withstand an attack by "a militarily strengthened United States." Neither this nor Ott's presentation of the opportunity of "participation in the final battle against bolshevism in Siberia" moved the Japanese.[24] Not only would Japan not go to war at the German request, she would not even run the risk of antagonizing the Americans by stopping shipment of supplies from that country to Vladivostok. Although Matsuoka had given assurances in this matter in June, Ott had to remind the Japanese in August of the disloyalty implicit in allowing aid to go to an enemy of the German Reich. He also told the Foreign Minister that an impression of weakness would be created in Washington if Japan allowed ships to pass unmolested.[25]

Ribbentrop felt called upon later in August to express this point even more forcefully. If the Japanese let so much as one American ship through to Vladivostok, a difficult precedent would be created. It would start, he pointed out, with harmless shipments but this would be followed by "fuel, guns, airplanes, armament of every sort." Was this in the spirit of the Pact? Were the Japanese really so "childish" as to believe any assurances from Roosevelt in this matter? He suggested that the Japanese might declare a Far Eastern security zone and thereby "beat the Americans at their own game." Nor was Ribbentrop greatly concerned about possible incidents. We already know of the restraint Ribbentrop was demanding of the German admirals in the Atlantic at this time. Did he offer similar cautions to the

---

[24] Ribbentrop to Ott 25/8/41, *StS/Japan*/IV/60520. Ott to Foreign Ministry 11/10/41, *StS/Japan*/V/60693. Mackensen in Rome urged the same line on Japanese Ambassador there. Rome to Foreign Ministry 16/10/41, *StS/Japan*/V/60736.

[25] Ott to Foreign Ministry 25/6/41, *StS/Japan*/III/65780. Ott to Foreign Ministry 16/8/41, 22/8/41, *StS/Japan*/IV/60477, 60495. Matsuoka begged for German "understanding" in the matter.

Japanese? Nothing of the sort. He told Tokyo that while it would probably be better merely to unload the ships and let them go, they should not hesitate to sink them if need be since "the Americans would not dare bring things to a head." In spite of vague promises to do something about the matter, the first American ship arrived in Vladivostok without hindrance early in September. The report from Washington on the occasion ("satisfaction over the successful intimidation of the Japanese") bore out Ribbentrop's worst fears.[26]

The Germans had their own obvious strategic reasons for urging a Japanese attack on Russian Asia, especially after Barbarossa faltered in the autumn, and America was not therefore initially central in their policy in this regard. Yet they were compelled even here to take America into account, and one of the principle reasons for their failure to persuade the Japanese to take action was a difference of opinion about the effect this would have on the United States.

The second aspect of Japanese policy which interested the Germans during this fateful year was the expansion to the south, a project with more direct implications for the United States.[27] By March the Japanese had gone far toward gaining the influence they sought in Indo-China, and Thailand, although the Dutch Indies still eluded them due partially to pressure from Great Britain and the United States.[28] Regarding Singapore, the Germans were told that although "the will to attack" was present, worries about the Anglo-American military reaction as well as the need to liquidate the Chinese "incident" all tended to restrain

[26] Ribbentrop to Tokyo 25/8/41, *StS/Japan*/IV/60520. Thomsen to Foreign Ministry 4/9/41, *StS/Japan*/IV/60570.
[27] For general discussion of this aspect of Japanese policy, Jones, *op. cit.*, chap. VIII. American observations on various phases of this are found in *FRUS*/1941/VI, chap. 1–4.
[28] The general picture in Jones, *op. cit.*, p. 238. For Anglo-American influence see Ott to Foreign Ministry 20/1/41, 21/1/41, *StS/Japan*/II/136511, 136513.

this operation.[29] By late June and July, the Japanese were reportedly attempting to re-establish their expansionist momentum, and Matsuoka told Ott that the tension in the Dutch East Indies was "unbearable" and that Singapore would be occupied in the not too distant future.[30] During the autumn, Ott reported that a drive south was possible "anytime." Faced with the inevitability of a clash with the Anglo-Saxon powers and seriously concerned about oil supplies, the armed forces, Ott reported, were now ready for acts which would involve blockade of Singapore, occupation of Thailand and the Philippines and an attack on Borneo and Sumatra. From the Washington Embassy, Berlin was also informed that the raw material problem was pushing the Japanese southward "and the Philippines must be included in this."[31] In November, Japanese naval movements in a southwestern direction were reported by the German consulate in Saigon, and Ambassador Oshima told Ribbentrop that while a full operation against Singapore was out until the following spring, a move to the south was now "unavoidable" and that the Japanese must prepare even to attack the Philippines. On November 21, Ott cabled Berlin that the time of decision was at hand on these projects, possibly including "a surprise attack on the Philippines."[32]

In all of this, the Germans were left in no doubt at all that the largest factor in Japanese calculations was the United States and that Japanese actions were bound inevitably to involve the United

[29] Memo (Ott) 25/3/41, *DGFP/D/XXI*, p. 361. Ott to Foreign Ministry 6/6/41, *DGFP/D/XII*, p. 967. Memo (Weizsaeker) 23/1/41, *StS/Japan/II/* 136524. Matsuoka told American Ambassador Steinhardt that "under no circumstances would Japan attack Singapore." Moscow Embassy to Washington 24/3/41, *FRUS/*Japan/II, p. 143.

[30] Ott to Foreign Ministry 21/6/41, 4/7/41, *IMTFE/XIX*, p. 7009, 7030. In fact an imperial conference of July 2 had decided to move against Indo-China and Thailand even at the risk of war with the Anglo-Saxons. *IMTFE/XV*, pp. 6557–6559.

[31] Ott to Foreign Ministry 4/10/41, *StS/Japan/V/60672*. Ott to Foreign Ministry 11/10/41, *StS/Japan/V/60693*. Thomsen to Foreign Ministry 31/10/41, *StS/Japan/V/60802*.

[32] Saigon Consulate to Foreign Ministry 13/11/41, *StS/Japan/V/60838*. Memo (Ribbentrop) 17/11/41, *StS/Japan/V/60868*. Ott to Foreign Ministry 21/11/41, 23/11/41, *StS/Japan/V/60885, 60897*.

States, possibly militarily. In January, Ott wrote that Japanese plans were entirely in the German interest except for "the nearly certain entry of the U.S.A." The Americans were pictured as seeking to "sabotage" the new order in Asia and American concern about Japanese imperialism had been made very clear in Tokyo.[33] Matsuoka explained this state of affairs personally to Hitler and predicted a five-year guerrilla war with America as a distinct possibility.[34]

Berlin was warned repeatedly throughout the summer of the imminent risks of American Far Eastern intervention in response to Japanese expansionist moves.[35] The German Naval Attaché in Tokyo pointed specifically to the danger of an American military reply to any operation against the Philippines, while Thomsen came forward with the flat prediction that any such move would lead "beyond doubt to an American declaration of war against Japan."[36] From Washington and Rome came further reports in September and October about American resolution to defend Singapore as well.[37] Ott, commenting on Japanese plans, warned that in the long run Japan might not be able to hold out against continuous American pressure, and might need armaments from Germany to use against the United States.[38] In November, Ott reported that military preparations for an expedition to the south had now been taken up by the armed forces "with all seriousness" and a peaceful solution no longer regarded as possible. The Am-

[33] Ott to Foreign Ministry 31/1/41, *DGFP*/D/XI, p. 1231. Ott to Foreign Ministry 4/2/41, *StS*/*Japan*/II/136550.

[34] Hitler-Matsuoka conference 4/4/41, *DGFP*/D/XII, p. 453.

[35] Memorandum (Weizsaeker) 10/7/41, *StS*/*Japan*/IV/60285. Informationsstelle III 12/7/41, 2/9/41, *ibid.*, 60389, 60553. Ott to Foreign Ministry 15/7/41, 22/7/41, *ibid.*, 60325, 60395. Bangkok Embassy to Foreign Ministry 18/7/41, *ibid.*, 66369.

[36] Tokyo (Naval Attaché) to OKM 22/8/41, *ibid.*, 60518. Thomsen to Foreign Ministry 27/8/41, *ibid.*, 60529. Thomsen added that the United States might not object to a more cautious Japanese expansion in certain areas, however.

[37] Rome Embassy to Foreign Ministry 16/10/41, *StS*/*Japan*/V/60736. Thomsen to Foreign Ministry 26/9/41, *StS*/*Japan*/IV/60654. Ott had cabled the same warning about Singapore earlier. Ott to Foreign Ministry 6/6/41, *DGFP*/D/XII, p. 967.

[38] Ott to Foreign Ministry 11/10/41, *StS*/*Japan*/V/60713.

bassador was entirely convinced that the forthcoming Japanese military moves would draw the United States in since the Japanese could not avoid attacking the Philippines "on military grounds." Germany must take this fact into account and be prepared to sign a pledge of support. Ominously, Ott warned that there was now talk not only of attacking Thailand and Singapore but also of eliminating the threat posed to Japanese plans from American military forces at Guam, the Philippines *and Hawaii.*[39]

Well informed, then, of Japanese expansionist tendencies and of the inherent risk of American involvement, what advice did the German leaders tender to their allies in this matter? The essence of the line Germany was to take throughout 1941 was given on January 8 by Adolf Hitler. He told his admirals that Japan should be encouraged to expand "even if the U.S.A. is then forced to take drastic steps." Ten days later, he added in this regard that he "did not see a great danger from America even if she did come in."[40] At the *Wilhelmstrasse*, as we know, this indifference to an American entry was not fully shared although there is no record of objections from this quarter to the risky policy urged on Japan.[41]

In February Ribbentrop began to exert pressure to attack Singapore, a continuous theme of German policy toward Japan notwithstanding the equally continuous warnings that such an event might well evoke an American military response. A stroke against Singapore by Japan would, according to Ribbentrop, serve three purposes: it would be the final blow against England, it would enable Japan to secure now what she wanted after the war and it would keep America out (providing Japan did not

---

[39] Ott to Foreign Ministry 18/11/41, 20/11/41, *ibid.,* 60875, 60883. (Emphasis mine.)

[40] *FCNA*/1941, 8–9/1/41, p. 13. Raeder testimony, *IMT*/XIV, p. 117. Ribbentrop testimony, *IMT*/X, p. 297. Hitler-Mussolini conversation 20/1/41, *IMT*/XXXIV, p. 462.

[41] Weizsaeker testimony, *Case 11*/XVI, pp. 7907, 8066. Ott's concern in Memorandum (Ott) 31/1/41, *DGFP*/D/XI, pp. 1232–1233.

directly attack an American position and thereby give Roosevelt a pretext). Even if the United States entered, Ribbentrop went on, it could have no effect since the Japanese fleet could easily handle a weak and divided American navy.[42]

In any event the Japanese ought to talk plainly to the Americans and give them to understand that if America should interfere in the construction of the new order in Asia they faced "an iron front."[43] Ten days later the Foreign Minister pursued these topics with Oshima with even greater urgency. It would be "a crime against the spirit of the future" for Japan to evade her responsibilities at this time. American strategic disadvantages were quite overwhelming, he emphasized, and this fact should preclude Japanese anxieties on this score. The quality and quantity of the German armament would take care of the American threat in Europe, but the Japanese ought to make a lightning attack on Singapore to present the United States with a *fait accompli* in the Pacific as well. Oshima assured the Foreign Minister that Japan was preparing to attack Singapore and the Philippines as well if need be. Ribbentrop sounded a note of caution on the latter point. Would it not, he asked, be better tactics for the Japanese to concentrate on Singapore, thus depriving Roosevelt of the excuse of provocation for coming in? If America then entered anyway, it would only prove that she intended to do so all along. In any case, whatever the Japanese decided to do they need not worry about the Americans, for if they were so foolish as to send their fleet beyond Hawaii, the Japanese navy would, Ribbentrop was sure, "do a complete job," and thus bring the war to a rapid conclusion.[44]

More comprehensive general directives for activating Japanese policy in the Far East were contained in basic order number 24 of

---

[42] However, naval circles were less optimistic about the outcome of a Japanese-American naval conflict. See memorandum, "Considerations on the Question of Japan in the Tripartite Pact." *OKM-KTB*/C/VII — Memo 11/2/41.

[43] Ribbentrop-Oshima conference 13/2/41, *NCA*/IV, pp. 471–475. German pressure on the Japanese was noted by Hull, *op. cit.*, p. 1034.

[44] Oshima-Ribbentrop conference 23/2/41, *DGFP*/D/XII, p. 143. See also Memo (Weizsaeker) 22/2/41, *StS/Japan*/II/136576.

March 5. "The aim of the cooperation initiated by the Tripartite Pact must be to bring Japan into active operations in the Far East as soon as possible." The purpose of this was to harass the English and thereby "precisely to keep America out of the war" since that country was in no position to fight Japan. Hitler three weeks later told his admirals that Japan should attack Singapore "as soon as possible" and should do so without fear since the Americans could not possibly cope with Japanese naval power.[45]

The arrival in Berlin of Matsuoka in March gave the Germans an opportunity to press their views in person. At the first meeting on March 29, Ribbentrop spent most of the time explaining American weaknesses to his Japanese colleague. American submarines, for example, were described as so bad "that Japan need not bother at all about them."[46] In meetings on the following two days, Matsuoka expressed Japanese anxieties regarding America and drew a picture of the dangers of a five- or ten-year guerrilla war with the United States. Ribbentrop would have none of it. America, he assured his visitor, undermining a caution he expressed on other occasions, would not fight, even for the Philippines. The Americans would never venture beyond Hawaii and therefore the Japanese should go right ahead and not squander "this unique moment of history."[47] (History for Ribbentrop was filled with "unique moments.")

On April 1, Hitler himself reiterated these points to the Foreign Minister. "Never in human imagination could there be better conditions for a joint effort of the Tripartite Pact countries . . . seldom has a risk been smaller." With England preoccupied, the United States unarmed, the U.S.S.R. facing one hundred and eighty divisions and German disinterest in the Far East, what more could Japan desire? Turning to America, there were, he explained, three courses of action open to that country: to arm

---

[45] Basic order 24, 5/3/41, *NCA*/VI, pp. 906, 967. Fuehrer conference 18/3/41, *FCNA*/1941, p. 37. See also Ribbentrop to Tokyo Embassy 27/3/41, *DGFP*/D/XII, p. 183.

[46] Ribbentrop-Matsuoka conference 29/3/41, *NCA*/IV, p. 521.

[47] Ribbentrop-Matsuoka conference 31/3/41, 1/4/41, *DGFP*/D/XII, pp. 381, 389.

herself, to aid England or to face a two-front war. The first two were long-range propositions and in any event mutually exclusive, while the third was strategically unthinkable. Therefore, America was no factor at all. Matsuoka agreed with everything, but unfortunately he had to admit that not everyone in Japan was of this persuasion. "Certain circles" in Tokyo made life very difficult for him, he explained, and thus he could not really make any pledge at this time regarding Singapore. All he could say was that a Japanese attack would occur "someday." Hitler's disappointment at this letdown may have been visible, for Matsuoka hastened to add that the whole problem was that the Japanese "had not yet found their Fuehrer."[48]

On April 4, there was another meeting between Hitler and Matsuoka which is of the greatest interest. Matsuoka raised again the likelihood of an American military reaction to an attack on Singapore. Hitler admitted that this was undesirable but assured the Foreign Minister that provision had already been made for this contingency. Adding now a significant new inducement to the arguments already employed, Hitler explained that "Germany on her part would immediately take the consequences if Japan should get involved with the United States." The exact circumstances and origins of the involvement were not important. "It does not matter with whom the United States first gets involved, Germany or Japan. Germany would strike without delay." Matsuoka then informed Hitler that Japan was in fact already preparing for war with America and, since the conflict was inevitable anyway, was considering the wisdom of striking the first blow. Hitler entirely subscribed to these comments.[49] In spite of a post-war denial that at this meeting Hitler had presented Japan with a blank check to attack the United States,[50] it is obvious at the very least that Hitler was perfectly aware of the risk that

[48] Hitler-Matsuoka conference 1/4/41, *DGFP*/D/XII, p. 386.
[49] Hitler-Matsuoka conference 4/4/41, *DGFP*/D/XII, p. 453.
[50] Meissner testimony, *Case 11*/X, p. 4545. This view does receive some support from the comment Matsuoka made to U.S. Ambassador Steinhardt in Moscow on his return voyage. Matsuoka had the impression, or so he told the

Japanese expansion would involve American intervention and that he was at this point quite prepared to take this risk and underwrite the Japanese effort to the point of going to war with America.

Nor were German military authorities inactive in pressing the Japanese to the attack at this time. When Admiral Nomura told Raeder in April that the Japanese could not take on Britain and the United States until the solution of East Asian problems, Raeder considered this attitude "a great strategic mistake." Japan should certainly take advantage of "this uniquely favorable opportunity" to attack Singapore. In Washington, as we know, Boetticher was busy convincing the Japanese Military Attaché there of American weakness and bluff.[51]

During the summer, Ribbentrop sought to revive the flagging Japanese interest in Singapore and in October tried specifically to counteract American intimidation of Japan. It was, he assured Tokyo, all a "mask." America was strained to the breaking point already and could be no threat at all. So long as the Philippines were not affected Japan should make "decisive strokes" in the Far East quite without fear of American retaliation.[52] In November, as Barbarossa became increasingly mired, the Germans went to great lengths to emphasize American incapacity to check Japan no matter where she struck in the Far East. The Boetticher reports of American military weakness were now given special play.[53] Ribbentrop was concerned that the Japanese would not

American, that Hitler and Mussolini wanted to avoid war with America. Steinhardt to Hull 11/4/41, *FRUS*/Japan/II, p. 184.

[51] *OKM-KTB*/A/XX — 22/4/41, *OKM-KTB*/C/VIII/ — 20/11/41. Boetticher 21/9/41, *StS*/*USA*/VIII/375844. Although obviously more concerned with the Atlantic, there was in general considerable comment in naval circles on the course of Japanese-American relations (*OKM-KTB*/A/XXII — 13/6/41). "Considerations Regarding the Question of Japan in the Pact" (11/2/41 — *OKM-KTB*/C/VII).

[52] Ribbentrop to Tokyo Embassy 28/6/41, *StS*/Japan/III/65788. Ribbentrop to Tokyo (undated but probably late October), *StS*/*USA*/IX.

[53] Ribbentrop Memo 4/11/41, *StS*/Japan/V/60809. Woermann testimony, *Case 11*/XXIII, p. 11253. Ribbentrop to Ott 7/11/41, *StS*/Japan/V/60815.

perceive "the weak side of the American situation." Referring to Boetticher's appraisals of American productive capacity, he instructed Ott to make clear to the Japanese that they might strike at any moment without fear of American involvement.[54]

In this second aspect of Japanese policy, America became a central factor in German calculations and the German line was clear. In the face of abundant evidence that a Japanese expansion to the south would, in all likelihood, provoke an American military reaction, the Germans pressed their allies toward aggression. The occasional note of caution regarding the Philippines is not impressive as evidence of German restraint. Berlin had been informed that the Philippines were regarded as an intolerable threat to the new order and would have to be incorporated into the greater East Asian sphere. Not only that, but the feeling in Japan, as the Germans knew well, was that the United States could not remain aloof militarily even from an attack on Singapore alone. Hitler and Ribbentrop were no doubt influenced by the Boetticher reports, but if they were really so convinced that American military weakness rendered intervention from that source out of the question, why the caution regarding the Philippines at all? It is probable that the blitzkrieg mentality played a decisive role here, in spite of Japanese warnings of an extended guerrilla war. Also, things were moving very rapidly and the ebb and flow of Barbarossa altered perspectives. The Germans had indicated their hope that rapid strokes in Europe would be matched by those in the Far East, and America would thereby be deprived of any basis on which to intervene. In any case, German willingness to run the risk of American entry is apparent in her reaction to Japanese ambitions.

[54] Ribbentrop again suggested that there be no direct attack on the Philippines. Ribbentrop to Ott 9/11/41, *StS/Japan*/V/60829.

CHAPTER 15

Germany and Pearl Harbor

GERMAN REACTION to Japanese policy toward the U.S.S.R. and expansion southward clearly involved the United States. There remains now a third aspect of Japanese foreign policy: Japanese-American relations as such and German efforts to influence them. These relations were a source of the greatest concern to Berlin.[1] The picture of Japanese overtures to the Americans was not a comforting one. With the opening of conversations between Secretary Hull and Ambassador Nomura in February, which were to last with interruptions down to the final days before Pearl Harbor, German anxieties were sharply aroused. The Nazi leaders were especially worried that the talks would weaken the image of the Pact in American eyes.[2] The Japanese sought continuously to allay these fears. They hastened to assure the Germans that the purpose of the talks was to prevent an American entry and that the Admiral had been instructed to dwell most emphatically on Japan's loyalty to the alliance. In May, Matsuoka gave further assurances on this point to Ott. He had, he reported, made "unequivocally plain" to the American and British ambassadors that further unneutral acts by the United

[1] Oshima testified after the war that Ribbentrop continuously asked about the state of Japanese-American relations, the negotiations in Washington and public and official opinion in Tokyo regarding the United States. Oshima affidavit, *IMTFE*/LXXVI, p. 34028.

[2] Opening of the Hull-Nomura talks, Memo (Hull) 8/3/41, *FRUS*/Japan/II, p. 389. Kordt testified after the war that the German Embassy in Tokyo tried to heighten German anxieties on the subject in order to make Berlin more aware of the dangers of an American intervention. Kordt testimony, *Case 11*/XV, p. 7426. See also Ott testimony, *Case 11*/XXI, pp. 10175, 10176. The Pact issue was in fact raised by Hull early in the proceedings. Memo (Hull) 14/3/41, *FRUS*/Japan/II, p. 396. Hull, *op. cit.*, p. 1061.

States in the Atlantic might "at any time" be declared a *casus foederis*.[3]

In spite of this Ott found the Japanese toying with new American proposals which, if accepted, would result in rendering the Pact ineffective and neutralizing Japan for the duration of the war. He added that the proposals were finding a ready reception in naval and commercial circles.[4] Furthermore, the German envoy passed on an alleged comment of Roosevelt following a meeting with Nomura that the Japanese "would be likely to withdraw gradually from the Pact."[5] Ott was instructed to convey to the Japanese German "surprise" that the Americans were not being told more specifically of Japanese obligations to the Axis, and Ribbentrop told Matsuoka personally that he regarded the conversations as "not a good thing."[6] The Japanese again responded with a flurry of reassurances. The Germans would be kept informed and the Japanese had no illusions about American intentions. Roosevelt was determined on war but the Japanese insisted that they were doing everything possible to prevent American entry through the negotiations and by tying up the American fleet in the Pacific.[7] However, Ott termed it "questionable" that

[3] Ott to Foreign Minister 10/2/41, *IMTFE*/XV, p. 6464. Ott to Foreign Ministry 10/5/41, *StS/USA*/VI/245087. Ott to Foreign Ministry 15/5/41, *DGFP*/D/XII, p. 818. Grew had raised the matter and told Matsuoka that this stand might have "grave and far-reaching implications," *FRUS*/1941/IV, p. 189.

[4] Ott to Foreign Ministry 5/5/41, *DGFP*/D/XII, p. 714. The American proposals as Ott understood them had involved a joint American-Japanese declaration renouncing participation in the European War, American pressure on Chiang Kai-shek to come to an agreement with Japan, resumption of normal trade, American recognition of Manchukuo and a joint guarantee of the Philippines.

[5] Ott to Foreign Ministry 31/5/41, *DGFP*/D/XII, p. 931. See *FRUS*/1941/IV, pp. 973–974. Hull, *op. cit.*, pp. 1001, 1002. Nomura had told Hull on May 28 that a German-American war would not necessarily involve Japan and that any decision regarding Japanese Pact obligations remained strictly Japanese. Memorandum (Hull) 28/5/41, *FRUS*/Japan/II, p. 440.

[6] Ott to Foreign Ministry 11/5/41, *StS/USA*/VI/24511. Ribbentrop to Matsuoka 14/5/41, *DGFP*/D/XII, p. 804. Kordt testimony, *Case 11*/XV, p. 7742. Weizsaeker to Ribbentrop 15/5/41, *StS/USA*/VII/245148. See also Weizsaeker testimony, *Case 11*/XIX, p. 19179.

[7] Ott to Foreign Ministry 18/5/41, *DGFP*/D/XII, p. 848. Ott to Foreign Ministry 4/6/41, *StS/USA*/VI/245336. Memo (Weizsaeker) 3/7/41, *StS/Japan*/VI/373609.

in a German-American war arising from American aid to England Japan would recognize any Pact obligation at all.[8]

During the summer, reports of increasing American pressure and public statements by the Japanese extolling Japanese-American friendship and disclaiming any participation in "a German plan for world conquest" alternated with Matsuoka's constant protests of tripartite loyalty.[9] These unsettling inconsistencies set off a barrage of inquiries from Berlin. Was it possible, Ribbentrop asked, that the Japanese were giving the Americans verbal guarantees of one kind or another? What was the Japanese reaction to American provocations of Germany? Could the "impudence" (*Unverfrorenheit*) with which the Americans seized Iceland have been a result of their having received Japanese assurances? Why were the Japanese not more informative?[10] The summer brought little relief from these anxieties.

In August, as reports from Washington pictured a more blatant policy of American economic intimidation and rumors abounded about new Japanese-American arrangements, Berlin was jolted by the anti-German statement made in America by a member of the Japanese Diet who declared the Pact to have been "a great blunder." He had publicly assured Americans that although certain countries wished for a Japanese-American war, the Japanese fleet "would not let itself be abused as the passive tool of a third party to fight the United States." Thomsen added that as a result of this "unexampled" outburst, the United States was now "on its high horse" and would be deaf to Japanese peace overtures so long as the intimidation policy brought such results.[11] To make matters worse, the Japanese announced plans for the reopening of the Washington conversations (which had been suspended on

[8] Ott to Foreign Ministry 6/6/41, *DGFP*/D/XII, p. 967.

[9] On American pressure, Ott to Foreign Ministry 12/7/41, *StS*/Japan/IV/60301. Konoye statement to the United Press, Thomsen to Foreign Ministry 30/6/41, *StS*/Japan/III/65795. Matsuoka's assurances to Ott in Ott to Foreign Ministry 14/7/41, *StS*/USA/VII/373673 and 20/7/41, *StS*/Japan/IV/60380.

[10] Memo (Ribbentrop) 11/6/41, *StS*/USA/VI/245388. Ribbentrop to Tokyo Embassy 9/7/41, *StS*/Japan/IV/60284.

[11] Thomsen to Foreign Ministry 12/8/41, *StS*/Japan/IV/60458. Thomsen to Foreign Ministry 30/8/41, *ibid.*, 60543.

July 31) in order "to clear the atmosphere." The Japanese blandly explained that they had until then actually been tougher with the Americans than the Germans had been. This had not produced satisfactory results and now Tokyo considered it tactically right to try the softer "German" approach. If this explanation was designed to disarm the Germans, it failed.[12]

It is not clear how much the Germans knew of the proposal later in August by Prime Minister Prince Konoye for a conference with President Roosevelt for the settlement of outstanding problems.[13] Ribbentrop would have found the details of the project truly alarming, for in pressing the Americans to agree to such a meeting, the Japanese started from the premise that German-Japanese relations could be "adjusted in many ways" while the Anglo-Saxon danger was a constant regardless of Germany's fate.[14] The Japanese went very far in their advocacy of the meeting toward reducing the Pact, at least verbally, to what Ambassador Grew described as a "dead letter." The American was told that while the Japanese could not give a prior undertaking to disregard any act by the United States against Germany, an understanding had in fact been reached "which would enable Prince Konoye to give orally and directly to the President an assurance with regard to the attitudes of Japan which would be entirely satisfactory to the President."[15] By October, however, Ott could describe the growth of pro-Axis sentiment in Tokyo, and in the final month of peace the Tokyo dispatches accurately

[12] Ott to Foreign Ministry 29/8/41, *ibid.*, 60541. See also Ott testimony, *Case 11/XXI/*, p. 10610. Ott to Foreign Ministry 5/9/41, StS/Japan/IV/60581. Ott to Foreign Ministry 4/9/41, *UStS/Japan-Amerika/*24993.

[13] Ott made inquiries about rumors of such a project, but these had been dismissed as groundless. Ott to Foreign Ministry 17/9/41, StS/Japan/V/60739. For general discussion of this see Langer and Gleason, *The Undeclared War*, pp. 698–709.

[14] Japanese tactics on this are discussed in Jones, *op. cit.*, pp. 281–282. Grew to Roosevelt 29/9/41, *FRUS*/Japan/II, p. 645.

[15] Memo (Dooman) 18/9/41, *ibid.*, pp. 626–629. Toyoda pressed Grew on the matter and Grew declared himself to be "convinced that he [Konoye] now means business." Grew to Roosevelt 22/9/41, *ibid.*, p. 631. Hull's opposition probably sealed the fate of the proposal. Memo (Hull) 2/10/41, *ibid.*, p. 656; Hull, *op. cit.*, 1021–1027.

reflected the deterioration of Japanese-American relations.[16]

From early November until December 7 events moved very rapidly and eventually outpaced diplomacy. Before examining these fateful weeks and the German role in the attack on Pearl Harbor, we should bear clearly in mind what the Germans had been pressing Tokyo to do regarding America down to that time.

This advice to the Japanese took two general lines: first, that they should display the greatest firmness and avoid all agreements; second, as we have already seen in the German encouragement to the Japanese regarding expansion southward, every effort was made to convince Tokyo that there was nothing whatever to fear from the United States, since American threats were bluff used to conceal military weakness. Oshima testified after the war that "Germany expressed her approval of Japanese-American negotiations in so far as they would induce the United States to observe neutrality."[17] This contention is not borne out by the documents. Ribbentrop, as we know, not only expressed his view to Oshima that the talks were "not a good idea" but even suggested the possibility of breaking off not only the negotiations but diplomatic relations as well "to awaken the American people."[18]

Weizsaeker shared Ribbentrop's distrust of the talks. In a memorandum prepared in May, the State Secretary declared that "political agreements of any sort between Japan and the United States are undesirable at the present time . . ." since they would "leave the field of conflict with England and the United States to us alone and the Pact would be discredited."[19] As the talks between Hull and Nomura got underway, both Hitler and Ribbentrop urged that if the Japanese really had to go on with them, they should at least use them as an instrument of tripartite soli-

---

16 Ott to Foreign Ministry 2/10/41, 4/10/41, *StS/Japan*/V/60669, 60672. Ott to Foreign Ministry 17/10/41, 20/10/41, *ibid.*, 60741, 60768. The secretary of the Japanese Embassy at Berlin told Woermann that the new cabinet would tolerate "no half measures" regarding America. Memo (Woermann) 7/11/41, *ibid.*, 60825.

17 Oshima testimony, *IMTFE*/IXXX, pp. 34029–34030.

18 Ribbentrop-Oshima conference 14/5/41, *DGFP*/D/XII, p. 804. Ribbentrop-Oshima conference 13/2/41, *NCA*/IV, p. 471.

19 Memo (Weizsaeker) 15/5/41, *DGFP*/D/XII, p. 819.

darity by taking a stiff line with the Roosevelt administration.[20] "The United States," Ribbentrop informed Oshima, "had to understand that any aggressive ambitions would find themselves up against an iron wall of determined nations, one which comprised virtually the whole world."[21]

This initial hope that Japan would use the negotiations to intimidate America received a rude shock with the report of an interview Nomura had given American journalists in Washington. In this, he had characterized the issue of whether an American war with Germany meant one with Japan as well as "a question of treaty interpretation which I do not want to go into."[22] Ribbentrop immediately fired off an angry cable to Ott demanding explanations. The issue was, Ott was to tell the Japanese, "unequivocally clarified by the text of the Pact." It would have been more expedient if Nomura had simply referred to that text.[23]

The Matsuoka visit to Berlin late in March provided renewed opportunities for pressure to be firm with the Americans, as well as, as we have seen, encouragement to expand regardless of the United States. The Foreign Minister reminded his Japanese colleague that the goal of the Pact was "to frighten America into abandoning the course she has chosen." In accomplishing this purpose, the Japanese had their vital role to play by being unyielding and by refusing to sign any agreement with the United States.[24] Hitler made the same point to the Japanese diplomat on March 4. In the latter meeting, he assured Japan that regardless

[20] Hitler-Kurusu meeting 3/2/41, *DGFP*/D/XII, p. 9. Ribbentrop-Oshima conference 23/2/41, *ibid.*, p. 139. Wakamatsu affidavit, *IMTFE*/LXXV, p. 33702.

[21] Ribbentrop-Oshima conference 23/2/41, *DGFP*/D/XII, p. 139. The text of this conference was sent to Ott with instructions to continue pressure along these lines in Tokyo. Foreign Ministry to Tokyo Embassy 28/2/41, *StS/Japan*/II/136587.

[22] Thomsen to Foreign Ministry 21/2/41, *ibid.*, 136573.

[23] Ribbentrop to Tokyo 24/2/41, *DGFP*/D/XII, p. 154. Ott to Foreign Ministry 25/2/41, 27/2/41, *StS/Japan*/II/13653, 136585. Ott to Foreign Ministry 6/3/41, *ibid.*, 136615.

[24] Ribbentrop-Matsuoka conference 31/3/41, *DGFP*/D/XII, p. 376.

of which country became involved first in war against America, Germany or Japan, Germany would "take the necessary steps at once." He warned that the Americans "would always be interested in disposing of one country first, not with the idea of coming to an agreement with the other, but with the idea of disposing of it next." Therefore, a bold and united front must be shown or the Pact partners might be defeated separately.[25]

On May 11, Ribbentrop instructed Ott to tell the Japanese that the war in which the Axis was now engaged was in fact "a death struggle" for Japan as well. The defeat of Germany and Italy would leave the Japanese to face an overpowering Anglo-Saxon coalition which might also include the Soviet Union. It was essential to make Roosevelt's decisions as difficult as possible. Japan simply could not allow the President to inject an element of uncertainty into this proposition through Japanese equivocation. Ribbentrop then got more specific. The Japanese, he wrote, must surely be aware that Roosevelt was waging a *de facto* war against Germany through a continuous series of unneutral acts. Under these circumstances, the Japanese ought to tell the Americans flatly that in their view American policy had been unneutral and that a continuation of this policy by such means as patrol activity or convoys would "be considered as a deliberate step toward war" and consequently would unfailingly compel Japan also to enter the war immediately. Finally, Ribbentrop ordered Ott to request to see a text of any reply Japan should make to American proposals.[26]

However in spite of "vigorous initiatives on my part," Ott was not able to prevent the dispatch of instructions to Nomura prior to German inspection.[27] When he did see them, after the fact, he was appalled. "This instruction," he informed Matsuoka,

---

[25] Hitler-Matsuoka conference 1/4/41, 4/4/41, *DGFP*/D/XII, pp. 386, 453.

[26] Ribbentrop to Ott 11/5/41, *ibid.*, p. 777. Ott to Foreign Ministry 11/5/41, *ibid.*, p. 753. Langer and Gleason believe that mid-May offered the best hope for a Japanese-American settlement and that German pressure was paramount in preventing it. *The Undeclared War*, p. 477.

[27] Ott to Foreign Ministry 13/5/41, *DGFP*/D/XIII, p. 794.

"breathes an atmosphere from which even the mildest criticism of America's unneutral conduct is excluded." It amounted in Ott's view in fact to "a legitimation of America's intimidation policy," since it suggested a renunciation of the new order envisioned by the Triangle Pact and in addition went "very far in relieving America in the Pacific." Matsuoka's only response was to dismiss the contents of the message as "figures of speech" and to ask the Germans to have confidence in him. Ott was not impressed by these explanations, although considering the bellicose tone Matsuoka adopted that same day with U.S. Ambassador Grew, the plea for confidence was not entirely unjustified. To Ribbentrop the Japanese action was "inexplicable" and Tokyo, he feared, was already "on the downward path."[28]

During the summer Ribbentrop kept up a steady stream of reminders to Tokyo. The Japanese, if they thought for a moment of coming to an agreement with the Anglo-Saxons, were pursuing "an extraordinarily short-sighted policy" and ought to be told this.[29] The problem, as he saw it, was that the Japanese were not aware of their own strength and of the weakness of the United States and Great Britain. Ott was requested to make the following points absolutely clear to the Japanese: Germany had triumphed in Russia ("the core of the red army has been destroyed"); the failure of the United States to carry through reprisals against the Japanese for the occupation of Indo-China, coupled with the verbal emptiness which resulted from the Atlantic conference, gave the real picture of the American situation. It was now clear that American threats to Japan were an "obvious

28 Ott to Foreign Ministry 14/5/41, *ibid.*, p. 806. The text of the instructions is found in *FRUS*/Japan/II, pp. 420–425. Matsuoka was not entirely unjustified in requesting German confidence. He had told Grew that Hitler had shown "patience and generosity" toward American provocation and that an American attack on German submarines would be regarded by Japan as "an act of American aggression." Grew to Roosevelt 14/5/41, *ibid.*, p. 145. Ribbentrop to Tokyo Embassy 15/5/41, *DGFP*/D/XII, pp. 820–821.

29 Ribbentrop to Tokyo Embassy 10/7/41, *StS*/Japan/IV/60285. Ribbentrop to Tokyo Embassy 19/7/41, *ibid.*, 60372. Ott to Foreign Ministry 21/7/41, *ibid.*, 60395.

sign of weakness and proof that America does not dare militarily to undertake anything serious against Japan." It was equally well known that the American people opposed war, except for "articles in Jewish newspapers." Thus there was every reason for the Japanese to call this bluff without delay.[30]

Roosevelt's "shoot at sight" speech in September, which had so alarmed German naval circles, offered a new opportunity of reminding the Japanese of their proper role regarding the United States. Ribbentrop described the speech as an attempt by Roosevelt to picture Germany as the aggressor, thus relieving Japan of her obligations in the event of a German-American war. The President wanted to "explode the triangle" and remove the prospect of a two-front war, than which "there is nothing the American people fear so much." Germany would not yield to these provocations in the Atlantic, Ribbentrop went on, but the Japanese must certainly recognize by now that under the circumstances negotiations with America were "hopeless." The Japanese had now at long last to make clear to the Americans by "an unmistakable declaration" that a further step by Roosevelt on the road to aggression against the Axis would lead necessarily to war "against the triumphant alliance." Foreign Minister Toyoda could only ask once again that Germany "trust Japan that the negotiations with America are being conducted in the spirit of the alliance."[31]

In October, Japanese diplomats in Washington and Tokyo complained to their American counterparts that German representations to be firm with America had become "exceedingly powerful"; that the Germans were "insatiably pressing" the Japa-

[30] Ribbentrop to Tokyo Embassy 25/8/41, *ibid.* Ott got the usual vague reply to this polemic. Ott to Foreign Ministry 29/8/41, *UStS/Japan-Amerika/*24984. See also Ott to Foreign Ministry 5/9/41, 12/9/41, *StS/Japan/*IV/60581, 60602, in which Ott demanded "something authoritative" about the Japanese responses to America.

[31] Ribbentrop to Tokyo Embassy 13/9/41, *StS/Japan/*IV/60606. Ott to Foreign Ministry 13/9/41, *ibid.* Toyoda replied in general terms but again refused to let the German Ambassador see the texts of the Japanese replies to Washington.

nese for a flat statement that Japan would declare war on America in the event of a German-American conflict.[32] The Germans seemed especially anxious during this month to counteract any tendency of American policy moves to intimidate the Japanese or weaken their resolve. Repeal of the Neutrality Acts and the arming of merchant ships simply made it all the more urgent to adopt, in the triangle spirit, a firm line for, as Ribbentrop put it early in November, the weaker the Japanese appeared, "the stronger the threat of Mr. Roosevelt."[33]

The final hectic weeks were now at hand. The pressures within the triangle dramatically shifted their direction and German Far Eastern policy was overtaken by the preparation and execution of the attack on Pearl Harbor. This basic train of events was set in motion at a cabinet meeting in Tokyo on November 5. At this meeting the Japanese government decided to continue negotiations until November 25 while proceeding with war preparations in case the talks should break down. Meanwhile, if the outlook for the discussions grew dim, the Japanese were to sound out their triangle partners on support in the event of a Japanese-American war, the decision for which, however, was to be taken independently and regardless of Axis support.[34]

Carrying forward these directives, proposals were submitted to Washington "as a last possible bargain."[35] This was followed a week later by the dispatch of the former Japanese Ambassador at Berlin, Kurusu, to assist Admiral Nomura in these efforts. The Germans did not know of the specific cabinet decisions but Ott's dispatches during this time warned repeatedly that government and public opinion alike were being steeled for conflict, that pro-American sentiment had dried up and that military preparations

---

[32] Welles-Wakasugi conference 13/10/41, *FRUS*/Japan/II, p. 680. Memo (Grew) 15/10/41, *ibid.*, p. 686.

[33] Ott to Foreign Ministry 28/10/41, 31/10/41, StS/Japan/V/60796, 60798. Ribbentrop to Tokyo Embassy 9/11/41, *ibid.*, 60829.

[34] Cabinet meeting 5/11/41, *IMTFE*/XXX, pp. 10333–10338.

[35] These were the so-called "A" and "B" proposals. *FRUS*/Japan/II, pp. 709, 755. Grew had warned that Japanese military action might come with "dramatic and dangerous suddenness." Grew to Roosevelt 3/11/41, *ibid.*, p. 704.

were being accelerated.[36] Foreign Minister Togo personally assured Ott that Kurusu would negotiate only "within the firm boundaries of the Pact which cannot now be overstepped" while Ambassador Oshima in Berlin confirmed that the Kurusu mission would be an almost certain failure, after which foreign policy with America would have to be "activated."[37] A public speech by Prime Minister Tojo, which was sent on to Germany, seemed to confirm all of this: the Pact was eulogized, the Anglo-Saxons termed "a vital threat" and Japanese-American relations pictured as so bad that "catastrophe" threatened.[38]

Still more ominous in the days following the November 5 meeting was the noticeable reversal of the flow of diplomatic pressure between Berlin and Tokyo. The *Japanese* now began to press the *Germans* regarding Pact obligations in the event of a Japanese-American war. The soundings were begun by diplomatic and military representatives to try and ensure triangle solidarity in the forthcoming conflict.[39] On November 21, Ribbentrop replied to these overtures unequivocally. He instructed Ott to tell the Japanese that in the event of a war with the United States, Germany's involvement was "*selbstverstaendlich*" (automatic), that there could be no separate peace "in the event of a war between Germany or Japan and the United States for any reason whatsoever" and that Germany would be quite prepared to lay down a specific agreement in writing to this effect.[40] The Japanese War Minister expressed gratification to Ott that in the event of such a war Japan "would not be left in the lurch." However, he wanted to be quite certain on one point: did the Japanese understand it correctly that Germany would stand by Japan

---

[36] Ott to Foreign Ministry 5/11/41, StS/Japan/V/60810.

[37] Ott to Foreign Ministry 6/11/41, *ibid.*, 60819. Memorandum (Erdmannsdorf) 13/11/41, *ibid.*, 60846. Thomsen to Foreign Ministry 15/11/41, *ibid.*, 60856.

[38] Ott to Foreign Ministry 17/11/41, *ibid.*, 60859.

[39] Ott to Foreign Ministry 5/11/41, 6/11/41, *ibid.*, 60810, 60819. Memorandum (Weizsaeker) 7/11/41, StS/USA/IX/422316. Ott to Foreign Ministry 18/11/41, StS/Japan/V/60873. Kretschmar testimony, *IMTFE*/LIX, p. 24643.

[40] Ribbentrop to Tokyo Embassy 21/11/41, StS/Japan/V/60879.

"even in the event of Japan opening the war against the U.S.A.?"
(my italics). Ott's reply was definite: "I referred him to the
[Ribbentrop] statement and to our readiness to sign a mutual
agreement on the subject."[41]

This was the situation two weeks before Pearl Harbor. The
final decision to fight was taken by the Japanese on November
27. Again, the German diplomats did not know of this specifically but the reports reaching Berlin in these final two weeks
were somber in the extreme regarding a Japanese-American conflict. The struggle within the Tokyo government had now
reached "the decisive stage," Berlin was told. If the United States
did not yield now, "the most extreme consequences for which
America alone carries the responsibility are unavoidable." The
Japanese reaction to the American "comprehensive settlement"
(which had proposed, *inter alia*, a virtual nullification of Japan's
role in the Triangle Pact) had been met by a mood of "grim resistance," and intensified military preparations, according to
Ott.[42]

The only question in the Ambassador's mind was whether at
this late stage the Americans could still think that the Japanese
were bluffing.[43] On November 30, the Japanese Ambassador at
Berlin was instructed by Foreign Minister Togo to transmit the
news officially to Hitler and Ribbentrop that the Washington
talks had collapsed, that Japan would have to resort to military
measures to curtail the American threat and that there was "an
extreme danger of war" between the two countries which "may
come quicker than anyone dreams."[44] On December 3, Ott
cabled Berlin that "the critical point is at hand," that the rudeness
(*Schoffheit*) of the American ultimatum had extinguished all

---

[41] Ott to Foreign Ministry 23/11/41, *ibid.*, 60897.

[42] Ott to Foreign Ministry 20/11/41, 21/11/41, *ibid.*, 60883, 60885. The American proposals of 26/11/41, in *FRUS*/Japan/II, pp. 768–770. Japanese reaction in
Ott to Foreign Ministry, *StS*/Japan/V/60901.

[43] Liaison conference 27/11/41, *IMTFE*/LXXX, p. 35706. Ott to Foreign
Ministry 29/11/41, *StS*/Japan/V/60995. Thomsen to Foreign Ministry 29/11/41,
3/12/41, *ibid.*, 60099, 60920.

[44] Tokyo to Embassy in Berlin 30/11/41, *NCA*/VI, p. 308.

hope of peace and that military operations could now be expected "in the nearest future."[45] On December 5, in the final notes before Pearl Harbor, Ott spoke of the destruction of "the last rays of hope" and "the unavoidable conflict with the United States."[46]

Meanwhile, with full knowledge of the extremely perilous state of Japanese-American relations, including a cable from Ott the previous week specifically mentioning Hawaii as a possible target, Ribbentrop continued to give the Japanese all the assurances they could wish at a crucial interview with Ambassador Oshima at the *Wilhelmstrasse* on November 29. He summoned the Ambassador to tell him that it was "essential for Japan to effect the new order in East Asia without losing this opportunity." Oshima first reminded the Foreign Minister that there was no hope of peace between America and Japan and then sought to pin him down by asking him point blank if war between Japan and America under any circumstances would mean an automatic German-American war as well. Ribbentrop seemed to draw back for the moment and merely replied that "Roosevelt is a fanatic and it is impossible to tell what he would do." However, later in the conference, Ribbentrop asserted that "Germany would of course join the war immediately." And once having joined it, she would sign no separate peace. "The Fuehrer," he added, "is determined on that point."[47]

Ribbentrop after the war accused Oshima of misinterpreting his words and Oshima himself at the Tokyo trial disclaimed any recollection of Ribbentrop's assurances, adding that even if he

[45] Ott to Foreign Ministry 3/12/41, *StS/Japan/*V/80924. On the same day, the Japanese Ambassador at Rome told Mussolini that "the outlook for a conflict between Japan and the United States . . . must now be regarded as possible and due to start immediately." Ciano, *Diary* 3/12/41, p. 461.

[46] Ott to Foreign Ministry 5/12/41, *UStS/Japan-Amerika/*25043. Ott to Foreign Ministry 5/12/41, *StS/USA/*X/44731. The German Naval Attaché at Tokyo cabled on December 6 that the Japanese armed forces had decided on war with the United States three weeks previously. An attack was expected before Christmas. *NCA*, sup. A, pp. 991, 992. However it is doubtful if this reached the Foreign Ministry prior to the news of Pearl Harbor.

[47] Ribbentrop-Oshima conference 29/11/41, *NCA/*VII, pp. 160–162. Ott to Foreign Ministry 20/11/41, 21/11/41, *StS/Japan/*V/60883, 60885.

(Ribbentrop) had said such things, "it was just for effect."[48] If true, it is difficult to see what "effect" the Reich Foreign Minister could have been seeking in this case. In addition, we have Ribbentrop's earlier statement on the matter given by Ott in Tokyo and Oshima's own cable on the conversation in which he expressed the conviction that on the basis of what Ribbentrop had said, "Germany would not refuse to fight."[49] To make the position even clearer, when Ott was summoned to the Japanese Foreign Ministry on November 30 and told that "the Japanese did not fear the rupture of relations and hoped that for their part Germany and Italy would stand by Japan in accordance with the Pact," Ott replied that of Germany's position in the event of a Japanese-American war "there could be no doubt." When Togo asked if he could assume that Germany in this case "viewed its relationship to Japan as a complete community of fate," Ott replied affirmatively and reiterated German willingness to sign an agreement in the matter.[50]

This is precisely what the Japanese now set about to arrange. Instructions were sent from Tokyo on December 2 to start negotiations on a "no separate peace" pact. Although it will be recalled that the Germans had by this time been warned of "an extreme danger of war" which might come "quicker than anyone dreams," Berlin encouraged the project.[51] Ribbentrop accepted in principle on December 5 an agreement providing for complete mutuality of obligation covering all aspects of a war between the United States and any tripartite member, including full military support.[52] On the same day Ott cabled the news that war with

[48] Ribbentrop testimony, *IMT*/X, p. 38. Oshima affidavit, *IMTFE*/LXXVI, pp. 34030–34033.
[49] Oshima to Tokyo 29/11/41, *NCA*/VII, p. 160.
[50] Ott to Foreign Ministry 30/11/41, *StS*/*Japan*/V/60917.
[51] Togo to Oshima 2/12/41, *IMTFE*/LVIII, p. 24031. Tokyo to Oshima 30/11/41, *NCA*/VI, p. 308. Oshima to Tokyo 2/12/41, *IMTFE*/LXXVI, p. 34031.
[52] Oshima to Tokyo 5/12/41, in Jones, *op. cit.*, p. 327. Mussolini had assured the Japanese on December 3 on the same point. Ciano quotes the Duce as follows: "Thus we arrive at a war between continents, which I have foreseen since 1939." Ciano, *Diary* 3/12/41, pp. 405–406.

America was now "unavoidable" and that Japan assumed that its outbreak under any circumstances would be a *casus foederis.* Events had now overtaken diplomacy (there had been some delay in contacting Hitler at the front) and before the pact could be signed a cable from Tokyo dated December 7 explained why this formality was no longer needed.[53]

The German leaders were genuinely surprised by the assault on Pearl Harbor. Otto Dietrich, Hitler's Press Chief, who first told the Fuehrer of the attack, described him as "utterly surprised" at the news and Weizsaeker testified that the Fuehrer at first refused to believe it. General Jodl recalled that Hitler seemed "stunned" by the news in the map room that evening. Ribbentrop testified that it took the whole Foreign Ministry "completely by surprise" and that he himself thought it an Allied hoax.[54] Weizsaeker also thought the report some kind of "newspaper trick" and insisted at his trial that "nobody envisioned that [Pearl Harbor] as a possibility." To Thomsen in Washington and Ott in Tokyo it was "a bolt of lightning." Doenitz, Raeder and Jodl all testified to their astonishment at the Japanese stroke, while the naval war diary registered "total surprise" although the admiralty evidently found it painful that it was the Japanese and not the German navy which had struck the first blow.[55]

The attack on Pearl Harbor was unilateral in the sense that the Germans had not been informed of the specific target. Thus, the surprise in Berlin was undoubtedly genuine. Yet this surprise did not occasion any hesitation about going to war with America al-

---

[53] Ott to Foreign Ministry 5/12/41, *UStS/Japan-Amerika/25043.* Tokyo to Oshima 7/12/41, in Jones, *op. cit.,* p. 328.

[54] Dietrich, *op. cit.,* 85. Weizsaeker testimony, *Case 11/XVI,* p. 7908. Jodl testimony, *IMT/XV,* p. 397. Ribbentrop testimony, *IMT/X,* p. 201. See also pre-trial examination of Ribbentrop in *NCA,* sup. B, p. 1201. Also Ribbentrop, *op. cit.,* p. 211.

[55] Ribbentrop testimony, *IMT/X,* pp. 296, 297. Weizsaeker, *op. cit.,* p. 328. Weizsaeker testimony, *Case 11/XVI,* p. 7908. Thomsen to Foreign Ministry 7/12/41, *StS/USA/X/44738.* Ott testimony, *Case 11/XXI,* p. 10164. Doenitz testimony, *IMT/XIII,* p. 477. Raeder testimony, *IMT/XIV,* p. 120. Jodl testimony, *IMT/XV,* p. 397. *OKM-KTB/XXVIII/A—7/12/41.*

though, since Japan was the aggressor, there was no legal obligation to do so.[56] Hitler's reasons for declaring war so quickly and before America had done so are not entirely clear. According to Ribbentrop, Hitler by December had decided that the American policy in the Atlantic had "practically created a state of war" and that, therefore, the declaration was merely a formality. In addition, Ribbentrop quoted Hitler as saying that the Japanese would "never forget if we do not take the consequences."[57] Moreover, national and personal prestige probably entered in. Erich Kordt quotes Hitler as remarking that "a great power like Germany declares war itself and does not wait for war to be declared on it," while the interpreter, Dr. Schmidt, had the impression that Hitler wanted to precede Roosevelt with the war declaration for reasons of personal prestige.[58]

We must above all remember Hitler's state of mind in those early December days. Slowed by rain in October and encountering unexpected Russian resistance, Barbarossa had not been going well as the winter set in. On November 24, General von Kleist's armored group had been defeated, and during the first week in December the German drive ground to a halt and was even thrown into reverse in the snows around Moscow. For the first time Hitler was experiencing defeat — and that in a theater where victory was to have brought all other successes in its train. The frosty recollection of Napoleon's Grand Army was no doubt present as Hitler mused upon this situation. In these circumstances, the sudden attack at Pearl Harbor must have seemed to the destiny-conscious mind of the Fuehrer one of those fateful strokes to which a "world historical figure" must respond.[59]

In any event there is testimony that surprise in Berlin soon turned to "an ecstasy of rejoicing" and the entry of the Japanese

[56] Weizsaeker described the German declaration as "a judicial error and a political mistake." Weizsaeker, *op. cit.*, p. 328. Ribbentrop agreed on the legal point, *IMT/X*, p. 297.

[57] *Ibid.*, p. 298. Ribbentrop, *op. cit.*, p. 170. See reference to Hitler statement in *NYT* 2/11/41.

[58] *Wahn und Wirklichkeit*, p. 325. Schmidt, *op. cit.*, p. 554.

[59] This was quite ironic, for precisely at the moment of Hitler's exultant war declaration on the United States, the Russians, informed in advance (possibly by the German comintern agent Richard Sorge) that the Japanese did not intend

into the war was viewed then as "a deliverance" and "a new lease on life." Hitler's speech to the Reichstag on December 11 consisted, as we have seen in an earlier chapter, largely of violent personal abuse of Roosevelt coupled with distinct expressions of relief that German-American relations had finally come to a head. The declaration was duly dispatched to Washington,[60] and Hitler evidently came to feel a certain pride in the Pearl Harbor attack as a proper method of conducting international relations. "You gave the right declaration of war," he told Oshima. This was the way Germany handled things. In Washington, there was some inclination to grant Hitler his pride in the fateful event of December 7. Describing the scene at the White House that Sunday afternoon, Harry Hopkins wrote: "The conference met in not too tense an atmosphere because I think that all of us believed that in the last analysis, the enemy was Hitler."[61]

When Ribbentrop gave his opinion that "the alliance thus brought about what we had wanted to avoid at all costs: a war between Germany and America,"[62] he attributed far too much substance to the Tripartite Pact. All of the weaknesses so glaringly apparent in German-Japanese relations from the signing of the Anti-Comintern Pact down to the establishment of the "world

---

to strike northwards, had been able to throw against the Germans crucial reinforcements withdrawn from the Far East. From this moment, Barbarossa was probably doomed. J. Erickson, *The Soviet High Command*, pp. 599, 631, 662. For Hitler's mood see also General Warlimont's statement that Hitler was "literally mesmerized by his concept of the political situation" and unable to grasp its ultimate implications. Warlimont, *op. cit.*, p. 50.

[60] *Wahn und Wirklichkeit*, pp. 311, 325. Papan, *op. cit.*, p. 484. Ribbentrop sounded "joyful" to Ciano on the telephone. "He was so happy in fact that I congratulated him even though I am not so sure of the advantages." *Diary* 8/12/41, p. 407. Hitler's Reichstag speech of December 11, in Prange, *Hitler's Words*, pp. 367–377. Warlimont, *op. cit.*, p. 207. Ribbentrop to Washington Embassy 11/12/41, *FRUS/1941/I*, p. 588. Japan requested Germany to declare war at once. Tokyo to Foreign Ministry 8/12/41, *StS/USA/44742*. Louis Lochner has recorded his impression that most Berliners thought Hitler too clever to declare war on America after Pearl Harbor. Lochner, *op. cit.*, pp. 199–200.

[61] Hitler-Oshima conference 14/12/41, *NCA/V*, p. 603. Quoted in Langer and Gleason, *The Undeclared War*, p. 977.

[62] Ribbentrop, *op. cit.*, p. 159.

triangle" were manifest during 1941. There had still been no agreement on a proper picture for the frame. Even the common goal of intimidating America was viewed from quite different perspectives. There was no real community of interest, for the Japanese were receptive to German suggestions according to the needs of national policy and the state of balance between pro- and anti-Axis elements in the government. Yet the evidence does not support the view that German pressure was without weight in Japanese decisions or that the fate of Germany was irrelevant. In the question of how the Germans used such influence as they had, the matter of intention as well as tendency naturally arises.

According to the Nuremberg prosecutor, "Japan was given every encouragement to adopt a policy which would almost certainly bring the United States into the war."[63] Not surprisingly, this allegation was disputed at the trial and in other post-war testimony. Ribbentrop told the tribunal that Germany had done everything right down to Pearl Harbor to keep America out, and several of the diplomats, expressing rare agreement with their former chief, upheld this view. Weizsaeker added that Germany had been anxious for Japan to enter the war against Great Britain and the Soviet Union but not against America.[64] General Jodl declared that "we should have much preferred a new and powerful ally without a new and powerful enemy" in speaking of the circumstances of the Japanese entry into the war. The only dissenting post-war testimony on the German side comes from Captain Reinecke, formerly of the operations staff of the *Oberkommando der Marine*. Testifying at the diplomats' trial, he recalled hearing plans for pushing the Japanese into the war against "the enemies and potential enemies of Germany, including the United States."[65]

The evidence generally supports the view that Germany would

[63] *IMT*/XXII, p. 458.
[64] Ribbentrop testimony, *IMT*/X, p. 379. Kordt testimony, *Case 11*/XV, p. 7430. Woermann testimony, *ibid.*, XXIII, pp. 11251, 11257. Weizsaeker, *op. cit.*, p. 325.
[65] Jodl testimony, *IMT*/XV, p. 398. Reinecke testimony, *Case 11*/IV, p. 1904.

have preferred a Japanese attack elsewhere. The immediate intention was not to goad Tokyo into a direct attack on the United States.[66] In urging triangle unity the Germans may well have believed sincerely that America could have been sidetracked. Moreover, a certain indifference to American involvement based on belief in her military weakness as well as the denial of any real basis for entry through rapid Japanese action undoubtedly played a role. However, this does not undermine the assertion of the Nuremberg prosecutor as to the tendency of German pressure nor acquit the Berlin regime of the knowledge that what they were urging the Japanese to do ran at least the gravest risk of provoking America into the war. That risk was plainly there, as it had been in the Atlantic. But in the Pacific Hitler was prepared to take it, especially as his dream of Eastern *Lebensraum* began to go sour.

By pressing upon Tokyo the virtual inevitability of a Japanese-American war, by stressing American military weakness and bluff, by urging an attack on Russia and on American supplies to that country, by encouraging a southward expansion in the full knowledge that this must involve vital American interests, by advocating that the Japanese adopt a completely uncompromising attitude in their relations with America and finally in the face of continuous and dire warnings of imminent hostilities by promising the Japanese full military and political support even if Japan were the aggressor, Berlin made itself a party to the course of events which culminated in the attack of December 7. The German surprise at Pearl Harbor was genuine, but this is merely a sad reflection on the inability of the German leadership to grasp the implications of their own deliberate and increasingly reckless policy in the Far East. This policy, in spite of disclaimers of the intention of doing so, in fact played a substantial role in converting the European conflict into the Second World War.

[66] As late as December 5, Ott requested that the Japanese avoid a direct attack on American territory. Ott to Foreign Ministry 5/12/41, *UStS/Japan-Amerika/* 25043.

PART IV

*The Swastika
and the Eagle*

CHAPTER 16

German Aggression Toward the United States

WE HAVE OBSERVED in Part III that down to 1941 the impact of America on German foreign and military policy on the continent of Europe was negligible but that it did appear significantly in the Atlantic and the Pacific. The American factor in German calculations has thus far been dealt with in reference to policies which Germany actually pursued. It remains now to consider a final problem of somewhat different nature: aggression against America itself. Germany did not, of course, actually attack the United States, but it would seem worthwhile to examine any consideration which the Nazi leadership may have given to such a project and, more theoretically, to look at the possibility that Hitler might have launched an American operation had he won the war in Europe.

In discussing the possibility of German aggression against the United States, three aspects of the evidence merit special attention: the tendency of Hitler's general political and strategic orientation regarding such an adventure; Hitler's expressed views on the subject; and the existence of any plans for fulfilling such a project. On the first point the evidence is largely negative. Hitler's continentalism and his disinterest in overseas matters and naval affairs (one recalls especially his hesitations over Sea Lion), all militate against extensive involvement in the Western hemisphere. His prejudices against the United States, his reliance on American isolationism and seeming indifference to the prospect of an American intervention do not suggest much interest in undertaking so formidable a military task as an invasion of the

United States. All of this could, of course, ultimately have been overridden if an insatiable will to power was in Hitler's case decisive and rendered his ambitions limitless. This cannot be excluded and will be considered further in connection with America and a Nazi Europe. It suffices to say here that down to 1941, Hitler was preoccupied with Europe and clearly disinterested in areas and military problems which would have concerned him in mounting an American operation.

Second, in regard to statements, we have, needless to say, repeated denials of intention to attack the United States. In addition to the usual sentiments of German-American friendship which he expressed on any encounter with an American diplomat or journalist, Hitler explained in his Reichstag speech of January 1939 that an attack on the United States could be "disposed of with a mere laugh."[1] In his scornful reply to Roosevelt in April of that year he "solemnly" declared that

> all assertions which have been circulated in any way concerning an intended German attack or invasion on or in America are rank frauds and gross untruths, quite apart from the fact that such assertions as far as military possibilities are concerned could have their origins only in a stupid imagination.[2]

He told Karl von Wiegand, the American journalist, in June 1940 that a German invasion of America was "childish and grotesque."[3] The Fuehrer informed the former American diplomat Cudahy in May 1941 that rumors of a German invasion of America were absolutely absurd and the warmongers knew it. When told that many Americans nevertheless believed this, Hitler dismissed it as "ridiculous chatter" which would be considered laughable by American generals and admirals.[4] Ribbentrop had the same message for Sumner Welles and for the Japanese who, as we have

---

[1] Speech 31/1/39, Prange, *op. cit.*, p. 348.
[2] Speech 28/4/39, Baynes, *op. cit.*, p. 1649.
[3] Interview of 9/6/40, *Monatshefte fuer Auswaertige Politik*, July 1940.
[4] Hitler-Cudahy conference 23/5/41, *DGFP/D/XII*, pp. 855–857.

seen, were uneasy on this issue. "We have not," he told Matsuoka, "the faintest interest in war with the U.S.A."[5]

Post-war German testimony has also denied any inclination to attack the United States. Ribbentrop claimed that Hitler absolutely opposed war with America, and Weizsaeker at his trial insisted that nothing "was more removed from Hitler's thought." He also said that there was no Foreign Ministry plan for war with the United States. Woermann of the Political Department had the impression that "Hitler's and Ribbentrop's policy was absolutely directed toward avoiding war between Germany and the United States."[6] Goering held that "there was never any question of a threat against the American continent," while Admiral Ruge wrote that a German attack on the U.S.A. was "never planned and in view of the strength of the American navy utterly impossible."[7] Hess told his interrogators that "Germany had no designs on America. The so-called German peril was a ludicrous figure of the imagination. Hitler's interests were European."[8]

The evidence of Hitler's personal tendencies and statements is not all one-sided, however. The aforementioned possibility that Hitler's goals were inherently unlimited must be kept in mind. Moreover, his extreme subjectivity, reliance on intuition and inclination to believe the worst about American national life and weakness might have overridden the appalling military problems attendant on an attack in the Western hemisphere and the objective advice he might have received about it.

Regarding Hitler's own words, there were of course no public statements advocating a military attack on America. Reference to the subject was, however, made privately on several occasions.

---

[5] Welles-Ribbentrop conference 1/3/40, *FRUS*/1940/I, p. 33. Ribbentrop-Matsuoka conference 31/3/41, *DGFP*/D/XII, p. 405. Ott to Foreign Ministry 10/9/40, *DGFP*/D/XI, p. 57. Japanese discussion of this in joint cabinet conference of 12/7/40. *IMTFE*/XIV, p. 6199.

[6] Ribbentrop examination, *NCA*, sup. B, p. 1197. Weizsaeker testimony, *Case 11*/XVI, pp. 7903, 7904; XVII, pp. 8062, 8085. Woermann testimony, *Case 11*/XXIII, p. 11252. Von Strempel testimony, *NCA*/sup. A, p. 561.

[7] Goering testimony, *IMT*/IX, p. 402; Ruge, *Der Seekrieg*, p. 178.

[8] Hess examination, *NCA*/VII, p. 614.

We have seen that in several of the Fuehrer conferences on naval affairs in 1940 and 1941, Hitler told his admirals that he was interested in the Azores in connection with America. "They are the only facility for attacking the United States" in the event of a German-American war, he explained in November 1940. In May 1941 he held the occupation of the Azores desirable "in order to be able to operate long-range bombers from there against the U.S.A." "The occasion for this," he had said, "may arrive in the autumn."[9] On several occasions he expressed, as we have seen in an earlier chapter, the wish to postpone hostilities (but not necessarily to prevent them permanently). After the liquidation of Russia, he explained on July 25, he "reserved the right to take severe action against the United States as well."[10]

He assured Matsuoka in April 1941 that Germany would "conduct a most energetic fight with her U-boats and her *Luftwaffe* against America." Moreover, due to American military inexperience, Germany "would be vastly superior and that quite apart from the fact that the German soldier naturally ranks high above the Americans."[11] Japanese Ambassador Kurusu was told by Hitler that Germany and America would be enemies for one or two centuries at least and Ribbentrop added that a struggle against America was inevitable since there was "a fundamental difference in the very right to exist between the Axis and the United States."[12]

The context of these assertions is important here. The statements to his admirals were at least in part an attempt to deflect their urgent requests for unleashing German naval power in the Atlantic until after Barbarossa; to fob them off, in other words, with promises of full support for naval action at some future date.

[9] Fuehrer conference of 14/11/40, *FCNA*/1940, p. 123. Fuehrer conference of 22/5/41, *FCNA*/1941, p. 52.

[10] Fuehrer conferences of 10/7/41, 8–9/1/41, 25/7/41, *FCNA*/1941, pp. 91, 13, 94. Fuehrer conference 25/7/41, *FCNA*/1941, p. 93.

[11] Hitler-Matsuoka conference 4/4/41, *DGFP/D/XII*, p. 524.

[12] Hitler-Kurusu conference 3/2/41, *DGFP/D/XII*, p. 9. Ott to Foreign Ministry 10/9/40, *DGFP/D/XI*, p. 57. Ribbentrop-Oshima conversation 29/11/41, *NCA/VII*, p. 160.

The statements to the Japanese were part of the assurances which the Germans continuously gave to bolster the faltering Tripartite Pact. The time element is also important. William Shirer has concluded from the evidence that "it was not a question, then, of whether Hitler intended to go to war with the United States but of the date he would choose to embark on it."[13] But Hitler, as we have seen, was by 1941 neither anxious for war with America nor greatly disturbed by the prospect of it. All had to wait on the final outcome of the Russian campaign, a matter of weeks or a few months at most, as he thought at the time. Were Hitler's references to hostilities with America, then, the merest speculation on vague eventualities for a far distant time? Was he simply trying to influence his listeners? Or was it, as Shirer understands it, a matter of months before an aggressive attack against the United States would be set in motion? There is another statement by the Fuehrer which throws some light on this. In his conversation with Molotov in November 1940, Hitler reverted to a notion which had come up in the *Zweites Buch* and which was examined in the second chapter. This was the vision of a continental confrontation across the Atlantic between Europe and the United States. He expressed it this way to the Soviet Foreign Minister:

> In the distant future it would be a question of establishing a great solidarity among those countries which might be involved in case of an extension of the sphere of this Anglo-Saxon power [the U.S.A.] which has a more solid foundation by far than England.

However, he went on, it was

not a question for the immediate future. Not in 1945 but in 1970 or 1980 at the earliest would the freedom of other nations be seriously endangered by this Anglo-Saxon power. In any event the continent of Europe had to adjust now to this develop-

[13] Shirer, *Third Reich*, p. 879.

ment and had to act jointly against the Anglo-Saxons and against any attempt to acquire dangerous bases.[14]

Again, the context should be borne in mind. Hitler was trying (although he had little faith that he would succeed) to persuade the stubborn Molotov of a quadruple arrangement which would concede German supremacy in Europe. The American "threat" was one of several arguments employed. This danger was not presented urgently; thirty to forty years at the earliest is not evidence of a pressing political or military consideration. What these various comments do show is that there was nothing incredible, unthinkable or, to use his own word, "grotesque" about a German-American war. For Hitler in these years it was a prospect which, under certain circumstances, was not at all excluded from consideration and execution by any inherent limitations in Hitler's outlook.

Finally an important source of evidence must inevitably lie in the existence of an actual military plan for an attack on the United States or of systematic consideration of the possibility in high military circles. Of a plan down to December 1941, the author can find no trace at all, either for the wartime or post-war period.[15] Of consideration of the possibility by military leaders, there is some evidence. Goebbels told Cudahy in May 1941 that the general staff had in fact examined the possibility of an invasion of America but had found the whole idea to be "impossible."[16] A Fuehrer directive of July 14, 1941, contained reference to the well-worn theme of concentration on the navy and air force after the Russian defeat and directed these services to plan for the final battle against Great Britain and "against America should the case arise."[17] But there is no evidence that this

[14] Hitler-Molotov conference 12/11/41, *DGFP*/D/XI, p. 546.
[15] See for example "Thoughts of the SKL regarding the build-up of the fleet after the war," in which there is talk of a German Europe, a German central Africa, but not a word regarding the United States, *OKM-KTB*/C/VII, p. 163.
[16] Thomsen to Foreign Ministry 2/5/41, *StS/USA*/VI/245044.
[17] Directive 14/7/41, *NCA*/V, pp. 905, 906.

resulted in preparations in the following months for combat with the United States.

The document used at Nuremberg and most frequently cited subsequently as proof of the existence of military consideration of an attack on the United States is the memorandum of Major Freiherr von Falkenstein, dated October 29, 1940.[18] This report, entitled "A brief résumé of the military questions current here for your personal information," was sent to General von Waldau of the operations staff of the *Luftwaffe*. After a broad survey of the main theaters of operation, Falkenstein added this comment:

> The Fuehrer is at present occupied with the question of the Atlantic Islands with a view to the prosecution of a war against America at a later date. Deliberations on this subject are being embarked upon here. Essential conditions are at present: no other operational commitment, Portuguese neutrality, the support of Spain and France.

At Nuremberg Goering dismissed this as "a general staff note . . . of no consequence." Jodl put the note into an entirely precautionary context. The Atlantic islands were considered to be "an outpost in case of American intervention and so we had to take the idea into consideration. We had to consider these matters in theory at least and this is what he [Falkenstein] tells General von Waldau in this letter."[19]

It seems clear that war against America was certainly considered but evidently not as a sufficiently serious or immediate possibility to warrant detailed planning for it. We recall in this connection General Warlimont's rather pathetic admission that German military planning regarding the United States began with a telephone call the day after Pearl Harbor. The Nuremberg judgment that "the possibility of a direct attack on the United States was considered and discussed as a matter for the future" is a reasonable summary of the evidence. But as the prose-

[18] Falkenstein memorandum 29/10/41, *IMT*/III, p. 389.
[19] Goering testimony, *IMT*/IX, p. 347. Jodl testimony, *IMT*/XV, p. 397.

cutor admitted, "their intentions against the United States must be viewed in the focus of both their overall plan and their immediate commitment elsewhere."[20] The overall plan, if there was one, was directed at the conquest of Europe, and Hitler was never able to free himself from commitment elsewhere. Thus it was also in accordance with the evidence that the charge of planning and conspiring to attack the United States was held to be "unproved."[21]

There were of course indirect and non-military techniques which might have been used to secure a German penetration of the United States. Ideological subversion would have appealed to Hitler's notion of working from within to undermine the "will to self-preservation" of a people. As we have seen earlier Hitler did specifically toy with the idea of a national socialist revolution in America in the early days. According to an American source, Goebbels, when asked in 1939 about the next target after France and England, allegedly replied, "You know what is next: the United States. It will come from the inside."[22] We recall the various projects undertaken and suggestions made by party groups for stirring up the German-Americans and carrying on propaganda and espionage activities. However, as the diplomats perceived, these efforts were for the most part spasmodic, clumsy and self-defeating. They do not suggest any concerted or urgent plan of action for destroying the United States from within. Nor is there any evidence of a drive for economic penetration. On the contrary, as described in earlier chapters, German-American economic relations were continuously snarled in a series of disputes which remained unresolved down to the American entry into the war.

Another indirect approach which might have been used was the securing of an ideological, economic and perhaps ultimately military base in Latin America for later action against the United States. The Roosevelt administration was convinced that this was

---

[20] *IMT*/I, p. 215. *IMT*/III, p. 388.

[21] This fact was used at later trials. *Case 11*/LVII, p. 27705.

[22] Roosevelt repeated this alleged conversation between Goebbels and a friend to Ickes. Ickes, *op. cit.*, p. 720, entry for 9/9/49.

precisely what was happening. Most notably there was the famous map which the President referred to in a speech of October 27, 1941, which purportedly showed actual and planned German penetration of Latin America. Although much doubt has been cast on the authenticity of this particular item, the President and his colleagues were genuinely convinced of the German danger to the south. The administration reacted sharply to disturbances and violence in these countries which were often felt to be inspired from Berlin.[23] Hull found German propaganda against the United States "fierce and ceaseless." He became convinced that South America was "the psychological and economic springboard" for Nazism in the Western hemisphere. Had Britain fallen, Hull wrote after the war, Germany would have pursued this program of penetration and control with all of the implications for the United States to the letter.[24] These fears were, as we have seen, transmitted by Thomsen to Berlin, along with considerable commentary on the subject in the American press.[25]

Was there any substance to such apprehensions? Post-war testimony once again is negative. Ribbentrop described charges of Nazi plans to operate in South America as "grotesque . . . tommyrot . . . absolute nonsense"; he denied the slightest thought of any such idea. Goering insisted that German economic efforts were hopeless from the start because of Anglo-American domination ("Not the mark but the dollar ruled there"). The former German Ambassador in Chile denied German fifth-column activity in that country and termed German economic influence no more than perfectly normal.[26] Moreover

[23] Langer and Gleason refer to the map as "an item of clumsy propaganda, wholly unworthy of the notice he gave it." *The Undeclared War*, p. 595. Watson feels that the President exaggerated the extent of German activity to scare Congress into supporting his foreign policy. Watson, *op. cit.*, p. 96.

[24] Hull, *op. cit.*, pp. 601, 813, 814.

[25] Thomsen to Foreign Ministry 12/8/38, *DGFP*/D/I, p. 731. Thomsen to Foreign Ministry 5/6/40, *StS*/*USA*/II/12200. See for example press items in *NYT* 13/2/33, 19/6/40.

[26] Ribbentrop, *op. cit.*, p. 80. Ribbentrop examination, *NCA*, sup. B, p. 1198. Goering testimony, *IMT*/IX, p. 402. Statement of former Ambassador in Chile, *Case 11*/VII, pp. 3204, 3206, 3216, 3219.

the concern felt in North America and by some South American publicists was evidently not shared by some of the political leaders of the area. The President of Mexico, for example, assured the American Ambassador that he had no fear of German influence or German penetration.[27] It is also true that Germany exhibited no interest in the American possessions of the European powers.

Yet German activity in Latin America was in point of fact on a very considerable scale. There were continuous efforts to counteract American influence and to discredit the United States in Latin eyes. Neutralist sentiment was cultivated actively and Embassy propaganda activities were very extensive.[28] Notwithstanding post-war disclaimers, the mark was giving the dollar persistent competition on a broad front. From 1933 to 1936 German exports to Brazil trebled and the Reich moved from fourth to first place. German interest and investment in industrialization projects in South America came in many cases to exceed that of the United States. In communication, transportation, power and the extractive industries German interests were especially important in Brazil, Chile, Peru, Uruguay and Ecuador while the strategic value of Brazil as an Atlantic base, of a foothold in Central America adjacent to the canal and of a harbor in Peru did not go unnoticed at this time. Extensive post-war plans of economic penetration were envisaged.[29]

Certain statements by German officials also suggest a more than perfunctory interest in expanding German economic activ-

[27] Daniels to State Department 23/9/39, *FRUS*/1939/V, p. 56. A more alarming view of the whole situation was given in Fernandez-Artucio, *The Nazi Octopus in Latin America*.

[28] Weizsaeker to Embassies at Santiago, Rio de Janeiro, Mexico City 16/5/40, *DGFP/D/IX*, p. 358. Political Department to Embassy in Santiago 21/5/40, *ibid.*, p. 397.

[29] These facts were contained in a report *Deutsche Wirtschaftsoffensive*, Juedischer Weltkongress (1937), paper 2, pp. 2–12. For German documentation of economic activity see for example: Economic department to Embassies in Argentina, Brazil, Uruguay, Colombia, Ecuador 23/6/34, *DGFP/C/III*, p. 74. Head of Trade Delegation in South America to State Secretary 14/2/35, *DGFP/C/III*, p. 930. Memoranda (Economic Department) 3/10/38, 9/1/39, *DGFP/D/V*, pp. 874, 889. There was extensive correspondence regarding post-war

ity. Ribbentrop assured the Japanese that due to German policy South America was now turning increasingly to Europe for economic support.[30] The director of the Economic Department at the *Wilhelmstrasse* informed the principal German Embassies in South America of the German desire "to participate extensively" in a rearmament of these countries by extending to them unlimited deliveries as soon as the war was over. Meanwhile, captured arms would be available for "special political reasons."[31]

There was also considerable national socialist activity among the 300,000 *Reichsdeutsche* and 1,750,000 *Volksdeutsche* in Latin America. Cultural, party and para-military groups and agitation abounded; schools and journals were established; and the alleged successes of this work were trumpeted continuously in the German press, in spite of the considerable anxieties expressed by the resident German diplomats. In fact this ideological work revealed many of the inadequacies of similar efforts in North America and in any event appeared to be less prominent after 1939. Nevertheless, the German diplomats in South America evidently suspected greater objectives lurking behind these various economic political and propaganda activities. Meeting in Rio de Janeiro in in the summer of 1938, the envoys requested from Berlin a clarification of Germany's goals. "Does she want," they asked, "to confine herself to economic and cultural problems? Or does she wish to go further and pursue aims of power or combat North American policies from South America?"[32]

The Japanese were as convinced as Hull that expanding German interests in the Western hemisphere were bound to conflict

---

plans in the summer of 1940. See for example: Embassy in Rio de Janeiro to Foreign Ministry 18/6/40, *DGFP/D/IX*, p. 598. Ribbentrop Circular Telegram 3/7/40, *DGFP/D/X*, p. 102. Economic Department to Rio Embassy 10/7/40, *DGFP/D/X*, p. 177.

30 *DIA/1939-1945*. *Hitler's Europe*, p. 170. Memorandum, Ribbentrop-Sato conference 9/7/40, *DGFP/D/X*, p. 166.

31 Economic Department to Embassies in Argentina, Brazil, Chile and Uruguay 23/8/40, *DGFP/D/X*, p. 530.

32 See paper *Die kuenstlerische Schaffung deutscher Minderheiten in Suedamerika;* Juedischer Weltkongress, paper 3, pp. 2-15. Also Langer and Gleason,

with the Monroe Doctrine and lead to a German-American war.[33]
Certainly the Germans could have been in no doubt of the extreme sensitivity of the United States regarding South America.
Even Boetticher had urged the greatest caution there since German activity acceptable elsewhere would inevitably provoke
Washington if carried out in the Western hemisphere. There
was no specific plan prior to American entry into the war to use
South America as a base for attacking the United States, but there
is no reason to dismiss as insignificant the considerable German
interest and activity in this area.

In summary, the conclusion must be that down to December
1941 there was no German plan for a military attack on the
United States. Such a possibility was discussed but not in any
urgent sense. No strategic directives were drawn up, there was
no commitment of resources and no operational policy in the
matter was evolved prior to Pearl Harbor. Indirectly, the Germans were not inactive in economic, propaganda and subversive
undertakings in North and South America. What this might have
meant if Hitler's continental hands had become free remains to
be considered. Prior to that time he lacked the opportunity, the
basis and, no doubt, the inclination to develop any real political
or military program for the Western hemisphere.

There remains a final point to be considered. Even assuming
that there were no plans for attacking the United States prior to
the declaration of war, would Hitler have eventually come into
collision with America if he had succeeded in fulfilling his continental ambition? Would a Nazi Europe have satisfied him or

---

The Challenge to Isolation, pp. 607–613. For German press comment, *Deutsche
Allgemeine Zeitung* 9/10/33; *Voelkischer Beobachter* 15/2/35, 21/2/36, 20/1/38,
7/3/39; *Frankfurter Zeitung* 21/3/37, 2/4/37. The diplomatic complaints were
very similar to those raised by Thomsen and Dieckhoff in North America.
Examples in: Embassy in Argentina to Foreign Ministry 18/5/38; Memo (Weizsaeker) 18/5/38; Memo (meeting of German diplomats in South America)
2/8/38; all in *DGFP/D/V*, pp. 851, 847, 863.

[33] Joint conference 12/7/40, 16/7/40, *IMTFE/XIV*, p. 6201, 6226.

would he then have turned his wrath and power on the United States? In other words, would Hitler have moved from the second level described in Chapter 2 as the application of his central ideas in Europe to level three, in which these ideas, now based on a conquered continent, would be expanded by force to cover non-European areas such as the United States? Many of the points raised above regarding possible aggression against the United States prior to 1941 must be kept in mind when considering this more theoretical question. But it must of course remain largely a matter of speculation in spite of the considerable body of evidence we now have regarding Hitler and America.

Neither Roosevelt nor his Secretary of State had any doubt about the scope of German ambition and they were not shy about expressing their views of the matter publicly and privately. The President told Nomura that Hitler aimed at nothing less than "the complete domination of the world."[34] Hull told French Ambassador Henry-Haye that Hitler was "the most devastating and all-pervading conquerer and destroyer in the last thousand years and we believe there is no geographical limit whatsoever to his infamous plans." He spoke to the Senate of the vast proportions of the Fuehrer's program and "the savagery of his unlimited objectives." Two weeks before Pearl Harbor he pictured the Fuehrer initiating "a march of invasion across the earth with ten million soldiers and thirty thousand airplanes." Notwithstanding a certain use of hyperbole for effect, there is no question that this was substantially the view of the Washington administration, and that it was, by 1941, shared in general by American public opinion.[35]

---

[34] Roosevelt press conference 14/6/40, *PPA*/1940, pp. 634–638. Memo (Welles) 24/7/41, *FRUS*/Japan/II, p. 527. See also Roosevelt letter to Hull 29/1/38, *Roosevelt Letters*, III, p. 230.

[35] Hull, *op. cit.*, pp. 824, 847, 924, 1048. Memorandum (Hull) 17/11/41, *FRUS*/Japan/II, p. 740. See Hull's certainty regarding public opinion in memorandum, *FRUS*/Japan/II, p. 754. Also Grew to Hull 21/1/41, Grew, *Turbulent Years*, II, p. 1259. Grew-Oshima conversation 16/7/41, *FRUS*/Japan/II, p. 510.

But was it accurate? Was Hitler a man of universal ambition or were his perspectives limited? If the will to dominate was an objective in itself, if power was the end rather than the means of achieving a program, then we may agree with Alan Bullock that Hitler was embarked upon a "policy of expansion that in the end admitted no limit."[36] If Hitler was to be taken literally that "war is eternal, war is life," then the struggle for racial survival would have to go on indefinitely and no actual or imaginable status quo could have satisfied Hitler's insatiable ambitions.

Can this be reconciled with the mass of evidence which attests to Hitler's European orientation and to his notable disinterest in overseas matters as reflected in countless statements and in the actual conduct of German foreign policy? The answer here lies not in the denial of his European disposition but in the use to which he would have put his conquered Europe. Would he really have been content to build ever longer autobahns and to harvest wheat in the Ukraine, or would the dictates, as he saw them, of racial and political survival have required an expansion of ever wider scope? Hitler himself once told a party gathering in Munich that "world empires arise on a national basis but quickly leave it far behind."[37] We have seen that from time to time world perspectives did appear in the Fuehrer's conversations, notably in the conference with Molotov in the autumn of 1940, while Ribbentrop's effusions about "world power constellations" more than suggest an elasticity in future German demands. Certainly the Japanese were quite unimpressed that these aspirations were formulated in terms of a quadruple division of the world rather than a direct German conquest.[38]

Even the colonial question to which Hitler seemed so impervious was receiving renewed attention in some circles in 1940 and

---

[36] Bullock, *op. cit.*, p. 327.

[37] Rauschning, *op. cit.*, p. 50.

[38] Hitler-Molotov conference 13/11/40, *DGFP*/D/XI, p. 559. Hitler spoke here of world division rather than conquest. However, the scope of his conception is clear enough. See also Ribbentrop's specific proposals in Ribbentrop-Molotov conference 13/11/40, *DGFP*/D/XI, pp. 564, 565. Ribbentrop-Oshima conference 23/2/31, *DGFP*/D/XII, p. 146. Arita to Sato 13/7/40, *IMTFE*/XIV, p. 6186.

1941, an interest evoked no doubt by the imminent prospect of German continental fulfillment. In various books and articles on the subject the call went out for a reconsideration of overseas possibilities. Colonies were now nothing less than "the necessary living space for a vital racial community," a source of raw materials lacking in the Reich and a "hallmark of the new Europe."[39] The navy at this time drew up post-war plans based on "a giant middle African colonial empire from the Atlantic to the Indian Ocean."[40]

There was an extended exposition of colonial plans drawn up by the Foreign Ministry in November 1940. This called for the return of all old German colonies then being held by England, France, Belgium, Australia, New Zealand and South Africa. Special arrangements were to be made for those held by Japan, and Germany was to acquire control over vast new areas in Africa along with naval bases along the West African coast. The purpose of all this was to supply the new Europe and coordinate the European economies. The report was considered important enough to be placed in the "Fuehrer file."[41] There was nothing entirely new in all of this, except perhaps in scope and detail, since as we know from Hitler's statements he had never closed the door to the acquisition of African colonies as an adjunct to the new order in Europe. It is also true that in this material there is no mention of colonies in America. But it does weaken the claim that Hitler would never have strayed beyond Europe. A spate of such material in the context of a controlled press does at least suggest that wider perspectives were being canvassed. The possibility that Hitler might have become, in the course of things, more receptive to colonial adventures cannot certainly be discounted.

Within Europe itself, Hitler had shown himself capable of

---

[39] J. Krumbach, *Kolonialpolitik Heute*, p. 15. *Jahrbuch der Auslandsorganisation*, 1940, p. 24. O. Weisse, "Dakar," *Monatshefte fuer Auswaertige Politik*, Oct. 1941.

[40] *OKM-KTB*/C/VII/1940, p. 163. See also Halder, *Diary* 13/7/40, III, p. 117. Memorandum (department X) 6/11/40, *DGFP*/D/XI, pp. 483-491.

[41] Memorandum (department X) 6/11/40, *DGFP*/D/XI, pp. 483-491.

expanding and changing the direction of his goals. We know, for example, that in spite of his preference for a localized war against Poland, he was prepared to run the risk of Western intervention and, armed with the Soviet Pact, the success of the *Blitzkrieg* and lack of Western resistance, the scope of the war was deliberately extended to "the destruction of our Western enemies."[42] In short, success and lack of resistance led to expansion of objectives. Would Hitler's continentalism have prevented a similar escalation from European to world objectives? He admitted to Molotov in November 1940 that "factors have arisen which had not been anticipated." In order, he said, to oppose England Germany "had to penetrate into territories remote from her and in which she was not basically interested politically or economically."[43] Thus the lack of actual specific planning for the Western hemisphere prior to a European victory need not unduly detain us. Although the question must necessarily remain open, it is entirely possible that the "eternal struggle for maintenance" might have come to embrace the Western hemisphere. The author is convinced that inflated by success and drawn along by a certain momentum of conquest, Hitler would not have indefinitely confined himself to Europe.

Even if he had wished to confine himself territorially, however, the economic and political effects of his conquests on America to say nothing of the ideological tension would have virtually nullified any hope of avoiding a collision between the United States and a Nazi Europe. Franklin Roosevelt was in no doubt on this point. He was convinced that a German conquest of Europe would provide Hitler with a base of operations which would, regardless of an actual attack, have made life almost impossible for the United States. The President told Harold Ickes before the war that Hitler need not even conquer all of Europe "to make it difficult for us economically." Cudahy told Hitler personally of American anxiety over the economic consequences of German

[42] Directive 6, 9/10/39, *IMT*/XXXIV, p. 266.
[43] Hitler-Molotov conference 12/11/40, *DGFP*/D/XI, p. 543.

domination. Thomsen reported Roosevelt's view that a German victory over England would mean "humiliation and ignominy" for the United States and recalled the President's comment that "if Germany wins, the world is lost."[44]

Roosevelt announced publicly in 1940 his view that the resources of the Western hemisphere would be irresistible to Hitler and that the collapse of England would place the country at the mercy of the German and Italian fleets.[45] In his address of May 1941, declaring the unlimited national emergency, Roosevelt predicted flatly that if England fell "Germany would close in relentlessly on this hemisphere." At the time in a private letter Roosevelt expressed his general anxieties. "Even if our continental limits remained intact," he wrote, "I, personally, should hate to live the rest of my days in a world dominated by the Hitler philosophy."[46]

Adolf Hitler, on December 11, 1941, provided support for the President's fears. As he stood before the Reichstag, declaring with relief that the struggle had now spread to the Western hemisphere and shouting abuse at the hated Roosevelt, he called his people to renewed dedication in "this historic struggle which for the next five hundred to a thousand years will be described as decisive not only for the history of Germany but for the whole of Europe and indeed for the world."[47]

[44] Ickes, *op. cit.*, II, p. 568. Entry for 29/1/38. Hitler-Cudahy conference 23/5/41, *DGFP*/D/XII, p. 859.

[45] Roosevelt press conference 14/6/40, *PPA*/1940, p. 634. The idea that the resources of the Western Hemisphere might prove an irresistible magnet for Hitler is contained in a report from Ambassador Wilson 16/7/40, Wilson, *Career Diplomat*, p. 105.

[46] Speech of 27/5/41, *PPA*/1941, p. 181. Grew told Ohashi that the United States "would not sit idly by and see Germany control the seas." Grew-Ohashi conference 16/7/41, *FRUS*/Japan/II, p. 510. Letter of 26/5/41, quoted in W. Range, *Franklin D. Roosevelt's World Order*, p. 79.

[47] Prange, *op. cit.*, p. 370.

CHAPTER 17

Conclusions

IN ONE STROKE the Pearl Harbor attack converted the European conflict into a war of universal dimensions. With the German declaration of war upon the United States four days later German-American tensions became part of the wider military struggles of the Second World War. Roosevelt and Hitler at last stood opposed to one another on the battlefield. This belligerency was ironic, for Hitler had not intended it and never fully realized its implications, yet he contributed enormously to it. In the pattern of events preceding the outbreak of hostilities, which may now be usefully recapitulated, we see clearly revealed some of the general defects, limitations and paradoxes of his politics and strategy.

The Fuehrer, we recall, was prepared to reject America out of hand because of his requirements for national greatness, his proposed solution of the German question and the limitations of his strategic world. National power, based upon blood, individual genius and the will to survive, required the authoritarian state and not liberal democracy which was always fraudulent and anti-racial. Germany's problems could not be met through colonial or economic solutions but only through the acquisition of contiguous *Lebensraum* in the East. Finally, Hitler's world was, at least as he described it, primarily Central European and did not seem to involve non-European areas in any immediate way, although intensive conquest might well have become extensive had he secured his European base.

We found that Hitler's spoken and written comments on

America were, as expected, vague and ill-informed. He relied here on random unofficial and party sources whose information was then passed through a clutter of prejudices, emerging for the most part as invective to be used on suitable occasions. He listened to Ludecke, Hanfstaengl, Ross and others with obvious impatience, selecting what was useful to him. Little about this country could have been appetizing. Capitalist materialism, the large Jewish element, the free press, the democratic idealism of Franklin Roosevelt to say nothing of the distance from Europe and the maritime factors involved violated almost every rule of national greatness and most of the criteria for admission to Hitler's world. He scarcely bothered to conceal his contempt. The country was decadent, Roosevelt the enemy of civilization. Unwilling to face the importance of the American role in the first war and using Wilson as a scapegoat for the German defeat, he convinced himself that the internal condition and external position of the United States rendered an American role in Europe out of the question. A picture of isolation, military weakness, social division, economic distress and racial decay now allowed Hitler to tend to more congenial continental problems. Toward American aid to Germany's enemies and even a possible entry into the war, he professed the most complete indifference.

For his diplomats, whom he distrusted but could not dispense with, America had always been an important factor and they accorded that country a considerable role in their reports and recommendations. Those concerned with American affairs in Berlin as well as the chiefs of the Washington mission were in general balanced and realistic in their approach. Without illusions concerning American hostility to German domestic and foreign policy, they presented a picture in Berlin quite at variance with what Hitler chose to believe. Economic power, potential military strength, national unity and a determined and popular leadership were the features of American life which most impressed the diplomats. As these features could by definition not be those of a capitalist democracy and racial melting pot, they were not entertained at the Reichschancellory.

In foreign policy, the isolationism upon which Hitler relied as
the only possible stance for a country so lacking in national virtue
was waved aside (perhaps too lightly) in the dispatches as a temporary thing already seriously weakened by the vigorous reaction to German aggression. Berlin was repeatedly warned that
America would not sit idly by and see England defeated; that
economic aid would be forthcoming and military assistance not
impossible; that Americans were convinced of a world conspiracy
of aggression which was bound to affect their hemisphere; that
in 1940 and 1941 American policy was moving boldly from neutrality to a *de facto* participation in the war. Above all, there
were warnings against complacency regarding the effect on
German destiny of American intervention and strong recommendations that caution and restraint be used to keep America
out. Exceptional were the reactions of General von Boetticher,
whose cheerful political commentary on American weakness,
pessimism about Britain and the influence of an isolationist and
pro-German "General Staff" were received with pleasure by
Hitler. This was what he wished to hear and not the sobering
reports of the experts with their tiresome doubts about his intuition.

Early in the war, busy with his initial conquests, Hitler felt no
need to take note of America, and as one surveys the concepts
and plans of the political leadership of the Reich, the notes of
meetings, the diaries, the speeches and comments of the time;
when one views the diplomatic and military arrangements and
activities which brought Hitler victory after victory in Europe,
the influence of the United States seems modest indeed. This may
have been reasonable so long as the war was confined to the continent of Europe. But in 1940, Hitler suffered his first reverse:
Britain, with whom he had hoped to make an arrangement, refused to surrender. And this resistance brought into play the
American influence which Hitler could not merely wave aside.
With American support playing an ever-increasing role in the
British refusal to capitulate, the vision of an Anglo-Saxon bloc

assumed increasing clarity. This was an unanticipated and unwelcome development, and he resisted its implications. Hitler's
attention was forced outward and that extraordinary combination
of fanatic attachment to goals and opportunistic sense of tactical
expedience which had served him so well in Europe began to
come unstuck.

He clung on the one hand to his own instincts, so well reflected in Boetticher's image of a weak and divided America
whose unlikely intervention could in any event be disregarded in
the face of German superiority, while on the other hand the
reality of the American commitment, substantiating the reports
of the Washington Embassy, imposed upon him the need to take
America into account. His solution to the dilemma was altogether
typical. He retreated from the whole prospect of naval warfare
against the Anglo-Saxons into the comfortable certainties of
Operation Barbarossa. Here Roosevelt's appeals could be dismissed with contempt, for even the diplomats were dubious about
the possibility of a continental invasion by American military
forces. Here the Fuehrer was on home ground, safe in *Festung
Europa*, untroubled by maritime and other baffling considerations. Still, some policy had to be carried out vis-à-vis the United
States pending the final solution of the Russian question. This
task he handed over to his navy (whose problems he could not
understand) and to the Japanese (whose situation he could not
appreciate).

In the Atlantic, the burden of dealing with America fell upon
the navy. Against the background of a confused naval tradition
and Hitler's relative indifference to naval affairs, which had
rendered the navy at once unprepared for the war and subordinate to the other services, the Fuehrer refused to allow his
admirals to engage in operations which might provoke the Americans and thereby distract him from his maps of the Ukraine.
To his admirals' pleas to challenge the flow of American aid on
the high seas, Hitler turned a deaf ear. Requests to apply prize
law and open operations within the American security zone were

rebuffed. Adopting this unusual posture of restraint, he revealed some inconsistency with his own expressed contempt for American power and he demonstrated even more clearly the dangers implicit in his single-minded fixation with Barbarossa. For the battle of the Atlantic, which he continued to view as a holding operation having little connection with the immediate business at hand, had in fact become a crucially important aspect of the German war effort.

In the Pacific his instrument for dealing with the Americans was Japan. He had long proclaimed a lack of interest in the Far East, and there was little solid foundation on which to build German-Japanese relations. The Anti-Comintern Pact and the German pressure prior to the war for an alliance were based on the usefulness such arrangements might have for German continental ambitions. As the Anglo-German war continued and American aid increased, he invoked the Far East once again, for even the Washington Embassy had reported on American fear of a two-ocean war. Hitler moved toward the Tripartite Pact in an attempt to intimidate Roosevelt. Once again, however, the instinct regarding foreign peoples which had served him so well in Europe, but so badly in America, failed him in dealing with an unfamiliar area. For Japan the problem of the United States was of immediate economic and strategic significance. For Hitler it was a nuisance to be held at bay. Japan needed a firm commitment, but also had to move cautiously regarding the Americans. Hitler wanted no Far Eastern commitment for Germany but a threatening stance by the Japanese to subdue the already weak and divided Americans. Hence Japan was encouraged to block American shipping to Russia and expand rapidly to the south in the full knowledge that this would almost certainly provoke an American military response. The Japanese were told of American weakness and encouraged to adopt an unyielding line in their dealings with the United States or preferably to break off the dealings altogether. Finally, the Japanese were given a blank check regarding a Japanese-American war and assured of the fullest German support even in the event of a Japanese attack.

The contradiction between Atlantic caution and Pacific recklessness is notable. There was probably an irreducible element
of inconsistency in Hitler's response, doubtless a natural result
of the intrusion of an unexpected factor into a mind filled with
idées fixes. But there was also a kind of logic in what Hitler did.
British resistance had invoked the American factor, but if the defeat of Russia would, as Hitler believed, have settled the whole
question in short order, then it was reasonable for him to measure
any response to the secondary American challenge by the effect
it would have upon Barbarossa.

The United States could be checked in the Atlantic or in the
Pacific. The former, however, had little connection, as far as
Hitler could see, with the Eastern campaign. Therefore, it was
just not worth provoking the Americans in order to win a subsidiary fight. In the Pacific, however, in areas involving Soviet
security interests in the Far East, Hitler could see greater prizes
at stake. Here was a chance simultaneously to weaken British
interests, to keep the Americans distracted and, especially as
Barbarossa slowed, to divert Russian military strength from the
German lines. Moreover, in the Pacific someone else's armed
forces would have to do the fighting. All of this made the risk of
an American entry more worth taking.

Although these considerations would have been a reasonable
basis on which to formulate a comprehensive policy toward the
United States, there is no evidence that such an overall strategy
was actually worked out. It is doubtful that Hitler would have
given that much of his time to the study of a situation which
every instinct and selected bit of information told him ought not
to have developed at all. It cannot be surprising, then, that there
was, as we learned in the previous chapter, also no plan for attacking the United States nor for dealing with that country as a military target had Hitler achieved continental fulfillment.

Thus the contradiction between Atlantic hesitation and Pacific
provocation as well as the failure adequately to plan for a confron-

tation with America either before the entry of that country or after history had awarded him his European prize are symptomatic of Hitler's political and military limitations; of his inability to grasp the war as a strategic whole, East and West, on land and sea, in Europe and beyond; of his failure to bridge the gap between immediate military problems and that wider conflict which was looming and which was so much the product of his own policies; of his inadequacy in not rising above his prejudices and fixations when faced with realities which offended him.

It is really doubtful if these problems occurred to him. He remained hunched over his map tables before and after Pearl Harbor, pursuing the final solution to the Russian problem, which would, he knew, either shut out the rash and absurd intrusion of the Americans into German affairs or leave him free to attend to these impossible people as he saw fit. But the Russian question proved insoluble. The shadow of America fell more deeply across *Festung Europa*, because Hitler had first ignored the United States and then, when this became no longer possible, because he did not know how to cope with the implications of American Power.

During the final days in the Berlin bunker, Hitler declared that "The war with America is a tragedy; illogical, devoid of fundamental reality."[1] This is an ironic statement of the matter. For Hitler, the American entry was indeed a tragedy. But American involvement was not illogical, given the circumstances and the use Hitler made of them and it was in fact his own outlook toward that country which had, in the years down through 1941, been "devoid of fundamental reality."

[1] *Testament*, p. 57.

Source Abbreviations

Bibliography

Source Abbreviations

UNPUBLISHED SOURCES

NOTE: Serial numbers are given in the bibliography. Frame numbers of the individual documents are given in the citations from the State Secretary, Under-State Secretary, Pol VIII, Pol IX, and RAM files. However, no frame numbers were available on the documents from the former German Embassy in Washington.

AHAl/Pol Bez: Archives of former German embassy, Politische Beziehungen, USA-Deutschland.

AHAl/AAP: Archives of former German embassy Allgemeine Auswaertige Politik der USA.

StS/USA: Buero des Staatssekretaers, Akten betreffend USA.

StS/Krieg: Buero des Staatssekretaers, Akten betreffend Krieg.

StS/Japan: Buero des Staatssekretaers, Akten betreffend Japan.

UStS/USA: Buero des Unterstaatssekretaers, Akten betreffend USA.

UStS/Seekrieg: Buero des Unterstaatssekretaers, Seekrieg.

UStS/Jap-Am: Buero des Unterstaatssekretaers, Japan-Amerika.

AAP: Politische Abteilung (Pol IX), Allgemeine Auswaertige Politik der USA.

Pol Bez: Politische Abteilung (Pol IX), Politische Beziehungen der V. St. von Amerika zu Deutschland.

RAM: Buero des Reichsaussenministers, USA.

OKM-ATT: Oberkommando der Marine, Anfragen, Berichte Deutscher Attaches.

OKM-KTB: Oberkommando der Marine (SKL), Kriegstagebuch.

FCNA: Fuehrer Conference on Naval Affairs.

PUBLISHED SOURCES

Case 11: Nuremberg Military Tribunal, Trial of former German Diplomats.

DGFP: Documents of German Foreign Policy.

DIA: Documents in International Affairs.

DDI: I Documenti Diplomatici Italiani.

FRUS: Foreign Relations of the United States.

IMT: International Military Tribunal, Trial of Major War Criminals.

IMTFE: International Military Tribunal in the Far East.

NCA: Nazi Conspiracy and Aggression.

NSR: Nazi Soviet Relations.

SIA: Survey of International Affairs.

Bibliography

PRIMARY SOURCES

UNPUBLISHED

Official documents and records

Archives of the former German embassy in Washington, selection by
the Committee for the Study of War Documents, American Historical
Association (Series AHAI)

Politische Beziehungen USA-Deutschland (Po2a), vols. III–V, 1933–
1936
Allgemeine Auswaertige Politik der USA (Po2b), vols. IV–V, 1933–
1937
Deutsche Innere Politik (Po3)
Amerika-England (Po3), vol. IV
Amerika-Japan (Po3), vols. V–VII, 1933–1936
Tschechoslovakei (Po3), vols. IV, V, 1938
Amerikanische Marineangelegenheiten, vols. II, 1933–1936

Auswaertiges Amt: Buero des Staatssekretaers

Akten betreffend USA, vols. II–X (1940–1941) serials 19, 35, 84, 589,
593, 1527, 1543, 987, 64
Akten betreffend Krieg, vols. VIII–X (1940–1941) serial 490
Akten betreffend Japan, vols. II–V (1941) serials 82, 100, 174, 597
Schriftwechsel des Herrn Staatssekretaers in politischen Angelegen-
heiten, vols. I–X (1936–1941) serials 381, 417, 440, 439, 1198, 1199,
1200, 2165H

Auswaertiges Amt: Buero des Unterstaatssekretaers

Seekrieg, vols. I, II (1939–1941) serial 51
USA, Mittel-und-Sued Amerika, Unneutrales Verhalten (1939–1941)
serials 57, 264
USA, vols. I, II (1938–1941) serials 38, 2418
Japan-Amerika (1941–1942) serial 32
Roosevelt Telegramm von 15/4/39, serial 57

Auswaertiges Amt: Politische Abteilung (Pol VIII)

Politische Beziehungen Japan-Deutschland, vols. I–V (1936–1939) serials 155, 556, 597
Politische Beziehungen Japan-USA, vols. I, II (1937–1940) serials 158, 597

Auswaertiges Amt: Politische Abteilung (Pol IX)

Akten betreffend Allgemeiner Auswaertiger Politik der Vereinigten Staaten von Amerika, vols. I–VI (1936–1940) serials 2431H, 6333H
Akten betreffend Politischer Beziehungen der Vereinigten Staaten von Amerika zu Deutschland, vols. I–XVI, serials 599, 886, 1038, 1039, 1040, 1041, 1042, 1043, 2422H, 6334H, 7039H
Akten betreffend Politischer und Kultureller Propaganda in den USA, vol. III, serial 896

Auswaertiges Amt: Buero des Chefs der Auslands-organisation, Akten betreffend USA, serials 49, 809

Buero des Reichsaussenministers, USA, vol. I

Oberkommando der Marine: Marinearchiv

Anfragen, Berichte Deutscher Attaches, 1936–1939
Fuehrerweisungen, vols. I, II (1939–1941)
Voelkerrecht
    Material betreffend Aktiven Massnahmen der USA zur Beein-flussung des Kriegsablaufs, 1941
    Handhabung der Neutralen, USA, 1941

Oberkommando der Marine: Marineattache, Amerika, vol. I (1938–1941)

Oberkommando der Marine: Seekriegsleitung: Kriegstagebuch

Teil A: vols. I–XXVIII (1939–1941)
Teil B: vol. VII — Ueberlegungen des Chefs der SKL und Nieder-schriften ueber Besprechungen mit dem Fuehrer; vol. VIII — Voelkerrecht, Propaganda, Politik, 1941

Fuehrer Conferences on Naval Affairs, 1939–1941

Juedischer Weltkongress, Reports, 1936, concerning German economic and cultural penetration in Latin America

Private papers

Halder, F., General. *Diaries,* vols. 1–7
Jodl, A., General. *Diaries,* 1937–1940 (1780–PS, 1809–PS, 1811–PS)

PUBLISHED

Official documents

FRANCE

Le Livre Jaune Français, Documents Diplomatiques, 1938–1939, Paris, 1939

GERMANY

Documents on German Foreign Policy, London, Series C, vols. 1–4, Series D, vols. 1–12
Hitler's Weisungen fuer die Kriegsfuehrung, W. Hubatsch (ed.), Frankfurt, 1962
Nazi Conspiracy and Aggression, Washington, 1946, vols. 1–10
Nazi-Soviet Relations, Washington, 1948
International Military Tribunal, Nuremberg, 1947, Trial of the Major War Criminals, Proceedings, vols. 1–24, Documents in Evidence, vols. 25–47
Nuremberg Military Tribunal, Nuremberg, 1949, Case 11 (German Diplomats), Documents and Proceedings, vols. 4, 7, 9, 10, 15–25, 28, 36, 40–44, 53
Documents in International Affairs, 1933–1941, London

ITALY

I Documenti Diplomatici Italiani, Rome, Series VIII, vols. 12, 13, Series IX, vols. 1–4

JAPAN

International Military Tribunal in the Far East, Documents and Proceedings, vols. 14, 16, 20, 58, 61, 75, 76, 77, 79, 83, 85

USSR

Documents of Soviet Foreign Policy, London, 1953, vol. 3

USA

Foreign Relations of the United States, Washington, 1933–1941, vols. 1–5; Japan, vols. 1, 2

Private papers

AUSTRIA

Schuschnigg, K. *Requiem in Rot-Weiss-Rot*, Zurich, 1946

ENGLAND

 Churchill, W. *The Second World War*, vols. 1–3, London, 1950
 Henderson, N. *Failure of a Mission*, London, 1940

FRANCE

 Coulondre, R. *De Staline à Hitler*, Paris, 1950
 François-Ponçet, A. *Souvenirs d'une Ambassade à Berline*, Paris, 1946

ITALY

 Ciano, G. *Diplomatic Papers*, London, 1948
 Ciano, G. *Diaries, 1937–1938*, London, 1952
 Ciano, G. *Diaries, 1939–1943*, London, 1947

SPAIN

 Serrano-Suñer, R. *Entre Hendaye y Gibraltar*, Mexico, 1947

USA
Diaries

 Dodd, W. *Ambassador Dodd's Diary*, London, 1940
 Grew, J. *Turbulent Years*, London, 1953
 Ickes, H. *Secret Diaries*, New York, 1954
 Morgenthau, J. *From the Morgenthau Diaries*, Boston, 1959
 Shirer, W. *Berlin Diary*, New York, 1941

Correspondence

 Moffatt, J. *The Moffatt Papers*, Cambridge, 1956
 Roosevelt, F. *The Roosevelt Letters*, vol. 3, London, 1952
 Wilson, H. *Career Diplomat*, New York, 1960

Speeches

 Roosevelt, F. *Public Papers and Addresses*, vols. 2–10, Washington,
   1950

Memoirs

 Dodd, M. *Through Embassy Eyes*, New York, 1939
 Hull, C. *Memoirs*, vols. 1, 2, London, 1948
 Phillips, W. *Ventures in Diplomacy*, London, 1955
 Welles, S. *Time for Decision*, London, 1944

GERMANY
Diaries

 Goebbels, P. *Diaries*, London, 1948
 Goebbels, P. *The Early Goebbels Diaries*, London, 1962
 Hassell, U. von. *Diaries*, London, 1948

Rosenberg, A. *Das Politische Tagebuch Alfred Rosenbergs*, Goettingen, 1956

Correspondence

Les Lettres Secrètes Enchangées par Hitler et Mussolini, Paris, 1946

Speeches and Conversations

Hitler's Reden, Munich, 1933
Hitler's Rede (Fifth Anniversary of Nazi Power) (Fichtebund Pamphlet 1062), Hamburg, 1938
Hitler's Speeches, vols. 1, 2 (N. Baynes, ed.), London, 1942
Hitler's Table Talk, London, 1952
Hitler's Words (G. Prange, ed.), Washington, 1944
Rauschning, H. *Hitler Speaks*, London, 1939
Testament of Adolf Hitler (F. Genoud, ed.), London, 1961

Memoirs

Dietrich, O. *Zwoelf Jahre mit Hitler*, Munich, 1935
Dirksen, H. von. *Moskau, London, Tokio*, Stuttgart, 1949
Doenitz, K. *Memoirs*, London, 1959
Hanfstaengl, E. *Hitler, The Missing Years*, London, 1957
Hitler, A. *Mein Kampf*, New York, 1939
Hoffman, H. *Hitler Was My Friend*, London, 1955
Hossbach, F. *Zwischen Wehrmacht und Hitler*, Hanover, 1949
Kordt, E. *Nicht Aus Den Akten*, Stuttgart, 1946
Ludecke, K. *I Knew Hitler*, London, 1938
Papen, F. von. *Memoirs*, London, 1952
Prittwitz und Gaffron, F. *Zwischen Petersburg und Washington*, Munich, 1952
Raeder, E. *My Life*, Annapolis, 1950
Ribbentrop, J. von. *Memoirs*, London, 1956
Schacht, H. *My First Seventy-Six Years*, London, 1955
Schellenberg, W. *Memoirs*, London, 1956
Schmidt, P. *Statist auf diplomatischer Buehne*, Bonn, 1949
Warlimont, W. *Inside Hitler's Headquarters*, London, 1964
Weizsaeker, E. von E. *Erinnerungen*, Munich, 1950

SECONDARY SOURCES

Biographies

ENGLAND

Feiling, K. *Chamberlain*, London, 1946

GERMANY

Bullock, A. *Hitler*, London, 1952
Foerster, H. *Ein General Kaempft Gegen Den Krieg* (Beck), Munich, 1948
Heiden, K. *Der Fuehrer*, London, 1954

Contemporary studies

Berber, F. *Die Amerikanische Neutralitaet im Kriege*, 1939–1941, Essen, 1943
Burlingham, C. *The German Reich and Americans of German Origin*, New York, 1938
Dieckhoff, H. *Zur Vorgeschichte des Rooseveltkriegs*, Berlin, 1943
Donnevert, R. *Wehrmacht und Partei*, Leipzig, 1939
Ehrich, E. *Die Aussenpolitik der NSDAP*, Berlin, 1937
Fernandez-Artucio, H. *The Nazi Octopus in Latin America*, London, 1943
Goering, H. *Aufbau einer Nation*, Berlin, 1934
Hitler, A. *Zweites Buch*, Stuttgart, 1961
Kloss, H. *Deutschtum in Ausland*, Stuttgart, 1938
Kloss, H. *Um die Einigung des Deutschamerikanertums*, Berlin, 1937
Krumbach, J. *Kolonialpolitik Heute*, Berlin, 1941
Lochner, L. P. *What About Germany?* New York, 1942
Maerz, J. *Seeherrschaft*, Leipzig, 1937
Prittwitz und Gaffron, F. *Deutschland und die Vereinigten Staaten*, Leipzig, 1934
Ross, C. *Amerikas Schicksalsstunde*, Leipzig, 1937
Ross, C. *Unser Amerika*, Leipzig, 1936
Schadewaldt, K. *Was Will Roosevelt?* Dusseldorf, 1941
Schmitz, E. *Die Deutsche Leistung in den Vereinigten Staaten von Nordamerika* (Reichsorganisations-leiter der NSDAP-Schulungs-unterlage)
Strausz-Hupé, R. *Axis America*, New York, 1941

Historical studies

Assmann, K. *Deutsche Seestrategie in Zwei Weltkriegen*, Heidelberg, 1957
Assmann, K. *Deutsche Seekriegsfuehrung* (Balanz des Zweiten Weltkriegs), Frankfurt, 1953
Assmann, K. *Deutsche Schicksalsjahre*, Wiesbaden, 1958
Beloff, M. *Soviet Foreign Policy*, London, 1947
Bensel, R. *Die Deutsche Flottenpolitik von 1933 bis 1939* (Beiheft 3, Marinerundschau), Berlin, 1958
Butow, R. J. *Tojo and the Coming of the War*, Princeton, 1961

Carr, E. *German-Soviet Relations Between Two World Wars,* Baltimore, 1951

Carr, E. *Twenty Year Crisis,* London, 1958

Celovsky, B. *Das Muenchener Abkommen,* Bonn, 1958

Cole, W. S. *America First,* Madison, 1953

Craig, G. *The Diplomats,* Princeton, 1953

Craig, G. *Totalitarian Approaches to Diplomatic Negotiation,* in Sarkissian, *Studies in Diplomatic History,* London, 1961

DeJong, L. *German Fifth Column in the Second World War,* London, 1956

Drummond, D. *The Passing of American Neutrality,* Ann Arbor, 1955

Erbe, Rene. *Die Nationalsozialistische Wirtschaftspolitik, 1933–1939,* Zurich, 1958

Erickson, J. *The Soviet High Command,* London, 1962

Feis, H. *The Road to Pearl Harbor,* Princeton, 1950

Friedlander, S. *Hitler et les États Unis,* Geneva, 1964

Gilbert, F. *Hitler Directs His War,* New York, 1950

Goerlitz, W. *The German General Staff,* New York, 1957

Halder, F. *Hitler als Feldherr,* Munich, 1949

Hinsley, F. *Hitler's Strategy,* Cambridge, 1951

Hofer, W. *Der Nationalsozialismus,* Frankfurt, 1959

Hofer, W. *Entfesselung des Zweiten Weltkriegs,* Frankfurt, 1960

Iklé, F. *German-Japanese Relations,* New York, 1956

Johnson, W. *Battle Against Isolation,* New York, 1956

Jones, F. *Japan's New Order in East Asia,* London, 1954

Kordt, E. *Wahn und Wirklichkeit,* Stuttgart, 1948

Langer, W. (and Gleason). *The Challenge to Isolation,* New York, 1952

Langer, W. (and Gleason). *The Undeclared War,* New York, 1953

Leuschner, J. *Volk und Raum zum Stil der Nationalsozialistischen Aussenpolitik,* Goettingen, 1958

Martiensen, A. *Hitler and His Admirals,* London, 1949

Matloff, J. *Strategic Planning for Coalition War,* Washington, 1959

Milward, A. *The German Economy at War,* London, 1965

Mohler, A. *Die Konservative Revolution in Deutschland,* Stuttgart, 1950

Morison, S. *Battle of the Atlantic,* Boston, 1955

Morton, L. *Grand Strategy,* vol. 2, Washington, 1953

Namier, L. *Diplomatic Prelude,* London, 1948

Namier, L. *Europe in Decay,* London, 1950

Namier, L. *In the Nazi Era,* London, 1952

Presseisen, E. *German-Japanese Relations,* The Hague, 1958

Range, W. *Franklin Roosevelt's World Order,* Athens, Georgia, 1959

Rauch, R. *Roosevelt, Munich to Pearl Harbor,* New York, 1950

Robertson, E. *Hitler's Pre-War Plans,* London, 1963
Rogge, O. *Official German Report,* New York, 1961
Rosinski, H. *Sea Power in the Pacific,* Princeton, 1942
Roskill, S. *War at Sea,* vol. I, London, 1954
Rothfels, H. *The German Resistance in Its International Implica-
tions,* in Sarkissian, *Studies in Diplomatic History,* London, 1961
Rothfels, H. *Deutsche Opposition,* Frankfurt, 1956
Ruge, R. *Der Seekrieg,* Stuttgart, 1954
Schlabrendorff, F. *Offiziere Gegen Hitler,* Frankfurt, 1946
Schroeder, P. *Axis Alliance and Japanese-American Relations,* Ithaca,
1958
Seabury, P. *The Wilhelmstrasse,* Berkeley, 1954
Shirer, W. *The Rise and Fall of the Third Reich,* New York, 1959
Sommer, T. *Deutschland und Japan Zwischen den Maechten,* Tue-
bingen, 1962
Tansill, C. *Backdoor to War,* Chicago, 1952
Taylor, A. *The Origins of the Second World War,* London, 1961
Toscano, M. *Le Origini Diplomatiche del Patto d'Acciaio,* Florence,
1956
Trefousse, H. *Germany and American Neutrality,* New York, 1951
Trevor-Roper, H. *The Last Days of Hitler,* London, 1952
Vermeil, E. *The Third Reich,* London, 1955
Walters, P. *A History of the League of Nations,* London, 1952
Watson, M. *Pre-War Plans and Preparations,* Washington, 1950
Weinberg, G. *Germany and the Soviet Union,* Leiden, 1954
Westphall, S. *Heer in Fesseln,* Bonn, 1950
Wheatley, R. *Operation Sea Lion,* London, 1958
Wheeler-Bennett, J. *Munich,* London, 1948
Wheeler-Bennett, J. *Nemesis of Power,* London, 1953
Wiskemann, E. *Rome-Berlin Axis,* London, 1949

Contemporary articles

American Institute of International Law, Oct. 1940, Symposium on
Legal Aspects of American Neutrality

Foreign Affairs, New York

Brinton, C. "Napoleon and Hitler," XX, 2, Jan. 1942
Joesten, J. "Hitler's Frontier in the Ukraine," XXI, 2, Jan. 1941

International Affairs, London

Ensor, R. "Mein Kampf and Europe," XVIII, 4, 1939
Fisher, A. "German Trade Drive in South Eastern Europe," XVIII,
2, 1939
Henlein, K. "German Minority in Czechoslovakia," XV, 4, 1936

Jakh, E. "German Drive in the Balkans," XVIII, 6, 1939
Lothian, Lord. "Germany and the Peace of Europe," XVI, 6, 1937
Toynbee, A. "After Munich," XVIII, I, 1939

Monatschrift fuer Auswaertige Politik, Berlin

Scheunen. "Die Neutralitaetspolitik der USA," VIII, 1941

Monatschefte fuer Auswaertige Politik, Essen

"Die Vereinigten Staaten und der Krieg in Europa," Feb. 1940
"Zum Besuch von Sumner Welles," Mar. 1940
"Der Fuehrer der USA," July 1940
Berber, F. "Der Buendnispakt Berlin-Rom-Tokio," Oct. 1940
Grewe, G. "Das Englandhilfgesetz der USA," Mar. 1941
Silvanus. "Die USA and Japan," Jan./Feb. 1942
Silvanus. "Deutschland und die Vereinigten Staaten," Nov. 1940
Trott, Adam von. "Die Fernostpolitik der Vereinigten Staaten,"
Nov. 1940

Zeitschrift fuer Geopolitik, Berlin

Anderle, O. "Landschaft-Raum-Schicksal," Dec. 1938
Haupt, U. "Eindruecke der USA," June 1939
Haushofer, K. "Bericht aus dem Indopazifischen Raum," Nov. 1937

Historical articles

American Historical Review, Washington

Butow, R. "The Hull-Nomura Conversations," July 1960
Nichols, J. "Roosevelt's Monetary Diplomacy," Jan. 1951

Far Eastern Quarterly, Ann Arbor, Michigan

Trefousse, H. "Germany and Pearl Harbor," Nov. 1951

Foreign Affairs, New York

Assmann, K. "Why U-Boat Warfare Failed," July 1950
Poole, D. "Light on Nazi Foreign Policy," Oct. 1946
Sontag, R. "Last Months of Peace," April 1957

International Affairs, London

Wallace, W. "New Documents on the History of Munich," Oct.
1959
Watt, D. "An Earlier Model for the Pact of Steel," April 1957

Journal of Central European Affairs, Boulder, Colorado

Boeninger, H. "Hitler and the German Generals," April 1954
Ritter, G. "Prussian Army and Politics," Jan. 1956

Watt, D. "German Diplomacy and the Nazi Leaders," July 1955

Journal of Modern History

Fischer, G. "Vlasov and Hitler," Mar. 1951
Remak, J. "The Bund and German-American Relations," Mar. 1957
Simpson, A. "Struggle for Control of the German Economy," Mar. 1959
Watt, D. "The Anglo-German Naval Agreement of 1935," June 1956
Weinberg, G. "May Crisis 1938," Sept. 1957

Journal of Politics, Chicago

Watt, D. "Rome-Berlin Axis," Oct. 1960

Marinerundschau, Berlin

Handel-Mazzetti, P. "Monroedoktrin und Seemacht der Staaten," 1957

Mississippi Valley Historical Review, Lincoln, Nebraska

Trefousse, H. "Failure of German Intelligence in the United States," June 1955

Revue Historique de la Deuxième Guerre Mondiale, Paris

Adler-Bresse, M. "Jugements Allemandes sur la Wehrmacht," April 1956
Anchieri, E. "Les Rapports Italo-Allemandes," April 1957
Bloch, C. "Les Relations Anglo-Allemandes," April/July 1955
Duroselle, J. "L'Evolution des États Unis vers la Guerre," April 1955
L'Huilliert, F. "Joachim Ribbentrop," April 1956
Medlicott, W. "La Marche vers la Guerre," Jan. 1956
Van Velkenhuyzen, J. "Le Plan Allemand pour L'Attaque à l'Ouest," April 1956

United States Naval Institute Proceedings, Annapolis

Assmann, K. "Hitler and the German Officer Corps," May 1956
Assmann, K. "Operation Sea Lion," Jan. 1950
Fagan, G. "Franklin D. Roosevelt and Naval Limitation," April 1953
Kauffman, D. "German Naval Strategy in World War Two," Jan. 1954
Lundeberg, P. "German Naval Literature of World War Two," Jan. 1956
Masland, J. "Japanese-German Naval Collaboration in World War Two," Feb. 1949
Reinecke, H. "German Surface Force Strategy in World War Two," Jan. 1957

Vierteljahresheft fuer Zeitgeschichte, Munich

Bracher, K. "Das Anfangsstadium der Hitlerischen Aussenpolitik," Jan. 1957

Bruegel, J. "Eine Zerstoerte Legende um Hitlers Aussenpolitik," Oct. 1957

Deuerlein. "Hitlers Eintritt in die Politik," April 1959

Faul, E. "Hitlers Uebermachiavellismus," Oct. 1954

Gruchmann, L. "Zur Amerikanischen Neutralitaetspolitik," Oct. 1960

Heiber, H. "Der Generalplan Ost," July 1958

"Hitlers Denkschrift zum Vierteljahresplan," April 1955

Kluke, P. "Hitler und das Volkswagenprojekt," Oct. 1960; "National-sozialistische Europaideologie," July 1955

Krausnick, H. "Legenden ueber Hitlers Aussenpolitik," July 1954

Lutz, H. "Faelschungen zur Hitlers Auslandsfinanzierung," Oct. 1954

Mersey, R. "Hitler als Braunschweiger Regierungsrat," Oct. 1960

Moltmann, G. "Die Fruehe Amerikanische Deutschlandplanung," July 1957

Rothfels, H. "Adam Trott und das State Department," July 1959

Treve, W. "Rede Hitlers vor der Deutschen Presse, 10 November 1938," April 1958

Trevor-Roper, H. "Hitlers Kriegsziele," April 1960

Watt, D. "Die Bayerischen Bemuehungen um Ausweisung Hitlers 1924," July 1958

Weinberg, G. "Deutsch-japanische Verhandlungen ueber das Suedse-emandat," Oct. 1956

Weinberg, G. "Hitlers Entschluss zum Angriff auf die Sowjetunion," Oct. 1953

Weinberg, G. "Die Geheimen Abkommen zum Antikominternpakt," July 1954

Wehrwissenschaftliche Rundschau, Munich

Baum, W. "Vollziehende Gewalt und Kriegsverwaltung im Dritten Reich," Sept. 1956

Jacobsen, H. "Hitlers Gedanken zur Kriegsfuehrung im Westen," Oct. 1955

World Affairs Quarterly, New York

Burdick, C. "German Military Planning and France, 1930–38," Jan. 1960

Remak, J. "Two German Views of the United States," April 1957

World Politics, Princeton

Parker, R. "France and the Rhineland Crisis of 1936," April 1956

Annual publications, yearbooks, etc.

Brassey's *Naval Annual*, London

Rosinski, H. *German Theories of Sea Warfare* (1940)
Rosinski, H. *Strategy and Propaganda in German Naval Thought* (1945)
Ruge, F. *The New German Navy* (1937)

Jahrbuch der Auslandsorganisation, 1940–1941, Berlin

Jahrbuch der Deutschen Kriegsmarine, Leipzig

Alleweldt. *Seemacht USA*, 1940

Nauticus — Jahrbuch fuer Deutschlands Seeinteressen — 1938–1941, Berlin

Periodicals screened

New York Times
Der Angriff (Berlin)
Deutsche Allgemeine Zeitung (Berlin)
Frankfurter Zeitung
Muenchener Neueste Nachrichten
National Zeitung (Essen)
Voelkischer Beobachter (Munich)
Westdeutscher Beobachter (Cologne)
Westdeutsche Zeitung (Krefeld)

Index

Index